THE ESSENTIAL *basics*

A Simple Guide to Living the Wellness Lifestyle

Thank you to the many contributors for their collective Genius in bringing this work together and sharing a vision of how plants and natural remedies bring new levels of wellness to powerfully impact our lives.

5th EDITION

The information contained in this book has not been evaluated or approved by the U.S. Food and Drug Administration or any other regulatory agency. The information is not intended to diagnose, treat, cure, prevent or otherwise reduce the effects of any disease or ailment. The information is not, and nothing contained herein is claimed to be, written, edited, endorsed or researched by a licensed health care provider or medical professional or borne out by any specific medical science. In fact, it is not. The information referenced herein is intended for educational purposes only and is not meant to and should not otherwise be implied to substitute for seeking qualified medical care from a licensed medical doctor or to seek a prescribed treatment in lieu of a treatment prescribed by any licensed medical professional for a specific health condition. Consult a licensed and qualified health care provider for diagnosis, medical care and treatment.

The information contained in this book does not in any way seek to promote or endorse any specific brand of essential oils, nutritional products or other products offered or provided by any specific company. Any mention in this book of a specific brand name is not an endorsement or recommendation of any specific product or company.

The authors of this book have expressed their good faith opinions, which are not established by conventional medical professionals. Total Wellness Publishing, LLC and any contributor to this book expressly disclaim any liability arising from the use of the information contained in this book or for any adverse outcome resulting from the use of the information contained herein for any reason, including but not limited to any misdiagnosis of any condition or any misunderstanding, misapplication or misinterpretation of the information set forth herein. In no event shall the authors of this book or Total Wellness Publishing, LLC be liable for any direct, indirect, consequential, special, exemplary, or other damages related to the use of the infor

TOTAL WELLNE
PUBLISHI

ISBN 9 781532 384080

Table of Contents

Section 1 INTRODUCTION

Section 2 QUICK REFERENCE

Section 3 NATURAL SOLUTIONS

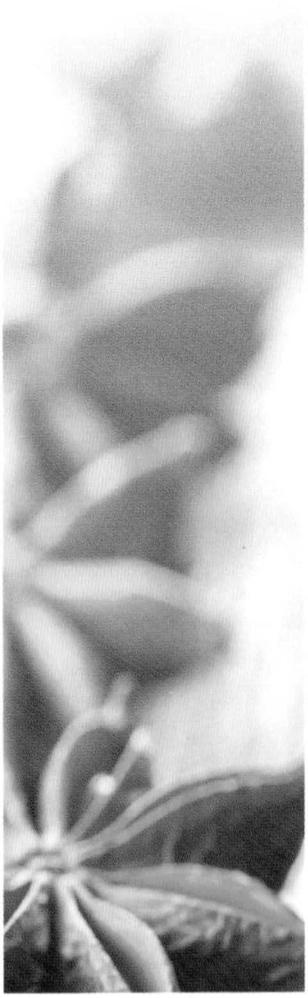

BODY SYSTEMS & FOCUS AREAS — *Section* 4

SUPPLEMENTAL — *Section* 5

INDEX — *Section* 6

Section 1
INTRODUCTION

How to Use this Guide

THE ESSENTIAL BASICS is a composition of everything essential for a vibrant life. For the new and the experienced essential oil user, it provides both simple, quick-reference information and expert-level knowledge. This book brings together the best research and proven solutions to provide you, the user, a trusted, credible and comprehensive guide. *Start by learning how to use each section of this book.*

SECTION 1: Introduction

Establish a foundation of simple knowledge for using essential oils. Learn what oils are, where they come from, and how to use them effectively and safely.

SECTION 2: Quick Reference

Quickly look up any ailment, and link it to commonly used essential oils with this A-Z index of ailments. Learn basic application methods for recommended remedies and easy cross references for more in-depth understanding.

SECTION 3: Natural Solutions

Become familiar with detailed information about individual essential oils and essential oil blends, as well as supplementary products. Discover how oils are distilled, common uses, basic emotional benefits, and tips for each oil.

SECTION 4: Body Systems & Focus Areas

Reference the Body Systems to experience the deepest level of healing knowledge and learn to address wellness in a holistic way. Explore both disease symptoms and body symptoms to better identify root causes and corresponding healing tools.

SECTION 5: Supplemental

Explore other in-depth information about essential oils through charts, index, and other resources.

Reach for your oils and refer to this book often – enjoy *THE ESSENTIAL BASICS!*

SECTION 6: Index

Why the Wellness Lifestyle

What does it mean to be well? Wellness can be characterized by not merely the absence of disease, but by feeling good and enjoying one's life. How you feel – physically, mentally and emotionally – determines the state of your overall health and well being. It might be said that your health is your greatest asset, since it affects how you think, feel, move, interact, prosper, and achieve. When you don't feel well, every other aspect of your life is impacted.

Poor lifestyle habits put people at high risk for virtually every physical and mental illness. The Centers for Disease Control and Prevention (CDC) report that heart disease is the leading cause of death for men and women, accounting for one in every four deaths in the U.S. According to the National Institute of Mental Health, 75 to 90 percent of all doctor office visits in the U.S. are for stress-related ailments and complaints. Sometimes major life events, such as divorce, loss of a loved one, financial problems, or the birth of a child, can combine with genetic or biologic predispositions to prompt a stress-related health crisis. Our culture often encourages a dependence on doctors, drugs, and health care systems to fix and heal these physical and emotional ailments. Yet it is widely known and accepted within the medical community that learned behaviors and lifestyle choices, such as poor stress management, inadequate nutrition, physical inactivity, insufficient sleep, smoking, and excessive alcohol consumption, are major contributors to illness and a diminished quality of life.

Modern medicine tends to fixate on diagnosis and treatment, whereas a wellness lifestyle focuses on education, self-awareness, and prevention. Instead of merely treating disease, the wellness lifestyle addresses its causes – what lies beneath the disease and its symptoms. Our thoughts, feelings, beliefs, habits, and choices are fueling the fires of inflammation, pain, toxicity, and illness in the body. By addressing the root causes of disease rather than merely treating the symptoms we can assist the body in healing itself.

The wave of the future is Integrative Medicine, wherein traditional allopathic treatments work in conjunction with alternative, non-traditional practices to treat the whole person instead of just the disease. In this way, patients and practitioners form a partnership whose goal is to treat the mind, body, and spirit, all at the same time.

Your body is capable of healing itself naturally. Most times, it does not need synthetic medications to take over its job, but simply the right support tools the enable it to do what it was engineered to do. The key to wellness is simply learning what serves the body, then restoring to the body what it needs. This will yield lasting healing and continued wellness.

Plant remedies, known as essential oils, have been used throughout the world for millennia and are one of nature's most powerful support tools available to help your body heal itself. Essential oils can be used in many aspects of our daily lives. Typical uses include cleaning, cooking, skin care, animal care, enhancing the air in a room, and supporting the emotional and physical needs of the body.

The overall quality of essential oils is very important when using them therapeutically. The most important factor when selecting essential oils is that they be tested and certified to be pure, potent, genuine, and authentic.

The bottom line to wellness is that each and every day you make choices that affect your health. Ultimately your health rests in your hands. You have the power to live a life of optimal health. We invite you to join us in living the wellness lifestyle, using this book as your guide. Your journey to health and wellness begins here.

What is an Essential Oil?

Prevalent in cultures for well over a thousand years, essential oils are the extracted volatile, aromatic compounds found in the leaves, flowers, bark, stems, roots, resin, seeds of plants or pith of citrus fruits and are treasured for their enhancement of beauty, flavor, and health.

Scientifically speaking, an essential oil is comprised of hundreds of chemical constituents, the combination of which provides plants with distinctive qualities and healing properties. Their function in nature is as secondary metabolites in their plant of origin. Whereas a primary metabolite is essential to a plant's survival, essential oils provide protection from predators or other threatening influences, and promote healthy reproduction, contributing to attracting pollinators and other vital processes.

HOW THEY ARE EXTRACTED

Essential oils are produced by one of two primary methods of extraction, steam-distillation or cold pressing *(a process unique to citrus peel or rind oils)*. When skillfully carried out, the end product is a therapeutic-grade essential oil that harnesses the maximum potency and health benefits. By contrast, lower grade essential oils are more often extracted through chemical processes or with solvents to increase yield and profit.

HOW THEY WORK

To better appreciate the value of essential oils, it helps to understand how they assist their own plant to flourish in their environment. Consider this example of how they provide protection from predators. Melaleuca alternifolia is a small tree typically growing along streams and in the swampy areas of Australia where weather is consistently hot and humid. Think about the variety of types and numbers of microbes growing in such a warm, moist area and the natural breeding ground this creates for mold, fungus, and bacteria. A plant growing in this terrain must have a strong internal immune system in order to both survive and thrive *(produce and reproduce)*. The magic lies in the primary constituents of the aromatic compounds found in the melaleuca tree, namely a- & y-terpinenes, Terpinen-4-ol and p-cymene, which are naturally antiseptic, antibacterial, antifungal and analgesic in their nature.

Since humans are carbon-based just like plants, extracted essential oils are compatible and beneficial. As demonstrated, melaleuca aromatic compounds protect its tree from dangerous microbes inherent in its immediate environment. We can likewise use the oil to strengthen protection from microbes in our own terrain.

Another unique quality of essential oils is the molecular size of their active compounds. Terrifically small on a molecular level, they easily pass through the dermal layers of the skin, are absorbed directly into the bloodstream, cross the blood-brain barrier, and penetrate the cell membrane. Essentially, they are accessible and transferrable to the body.

CONCLUSION

Recognition of essential oils as powerful promoters of physical, mental and emotional health is rapidly expanding globally. Backed by growing scientific validation, this rediscovery of holistic self-care with oils is demonstrated in the wide range of popular uses from improving mood, rejuvenating the skin and overall health, cooking, and cleaning. They are fast becoming the number one choice as THE natural way to keep oneself and loved ones healthy.

Essential Oil Classifications

Understanding plant classifications helps you come to know essential oils categorically. This gives you a broader knowledge of the general attributes and characteristics, improving your ability to identify oils that best serve in specific circumstances. Keep in mind that while oils within a classification have common characteristics, each individual oil has far more specific and even unique properties. *See Oil Properties and Oils by Property (pgs. 260 & 272) to learn more.*

Citrus trees grow juicy fruit with a pulpy rind in warm climates. Oils are cold-pressed or steam distilled from the rind.

Top Properties:

- Stimulating
- Uplifting
- Antiseptic
- Calming
- Antimicrobial
- Energizing
- Antioxidant

Positive energy and emotions heightened by citrus oils:

- Invigorated, joy, energized, validated, feeling worthy, enlivened, restored, productive, mindful

Negative energy and emotions addressed by citrus oils:

- Discouraged, gloomy, distressed, depleted, drained, oppressed, faint, mindless

Florals are flowers. Oils are distilled from the petals or aerial parts of plants.

Top Properties:

- Anti-inflammatory
- Antispasmodic
- Relaxant
- Antihistamine
- Analgesic
- Regenerative
- Antiviral

Positive energy and emotions heightened by floral oils:

- Better able to express oneself, reassured, mended, purposeful, light-filled, loved, exuberant, expressive

Negative energy and emotions addressed by floral oils:

- Fearful, worried, hurt, unheard, wounded, neglected, frustrated, depressed, isolated, burdened

Spices are aromatic, flavorful plants. Oil is distilled from the bark, roots, seeds, and buds of the plant.

Top Properties:

- Warming
- Digestive stimulant
- Immunostimulant
- Aphrodisiac
- Antiemetic
- Anti-infectious
- Anti-parasitic

Positive energy and emotions heightened by spice oils:

- Honest, charitable, bold, receptive, supported, participating, activated, empowered

Negative energy and emotions addressed by spice oils:

- Repressed, self-centered, uncertain, denied, dominated, apprehensive, apathetic, somber, disinterested, bored

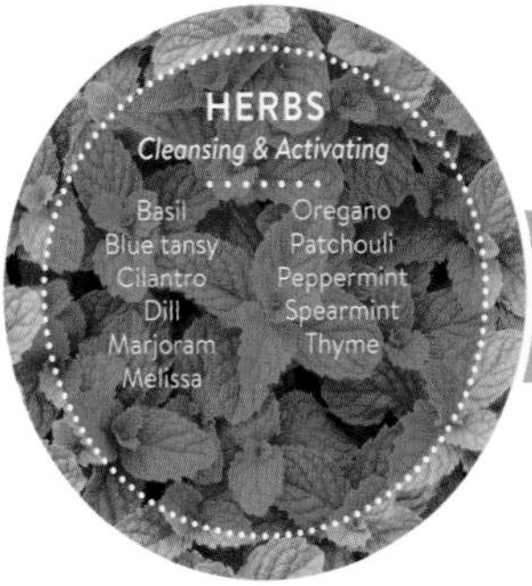

Herbs are seed-bearing, flowering plants that do not have woody tissue in the stem. Oils are distilled from the green leafy part of these low-growing plants.

Top Properties:

- Immunostimulant
- Detoxifier
- Antiviral
- Antifungal
- Carminative
- Antibacterial
- Anti-parasitic

Positive energy and emotions heightened by herb oils:

- Accepting, yielding, open-minded, invigorated, enhanced, unattached, trusting, progressing, enlightened, relieved

Negative energy and emotions addressed by herb oils:

- Stubborn, angry, unyielding, confused, hindered, degraded, obstinate, doubtful, stalled, limited, inundated

Roots are the plant fibers that attach it to the ground and receive water and nourishment for the plant. Oils are distilled from roots.

Top Properties:

- Calming
- Nervine
- Grounding
- Neurotonic
- Sedative
- Restorative
- Neuroprotective

Positive energy and emotions heightened by root oils:

- Rooted, flowing, centered, elevated, aware, peaceful, meditative, prioritized

Negative energy and emotions addressed by root oils:

- Ungrounded, obstructed, discontented, erratic, unattentive, agitative, scattered

Woods typically grow high off the ground and are characterized by a single trunk. Oils are distilled from the leaves, twigs, branches, needles, berries, bark, and wood.

Top Properties:

- Anticatarrhal
- Regenerative
- Relaxant
- Grounding
- Steroidal
- Analgesic
- Astringent

Positive energy and emotions heightened by wood oils:

- Receiving, devoted, collected, stimulated, progressing, alone, courageous, composed

Negative energy and emotions addressed by wood oils:

- Blocked, uninspired, unsure, congested, stalled, connected, cowardly, overzealous, grieving, sad, ashamed

Resins are a natural sticky substance that come from certain trees and are insoluble in water. Oils are distilled from hardened resins.

Top Properties:

- Anti-inflammatory
- Cytophylactic
- Analgesic
- Restorative
- Antidepressant
- Immunostimulant
- Antimutagenic

Positive energy and emotions heightened by resin oils:

- Unified, connected, grounded, nurtured, enlightened, inoculated, bonded, awakened

Negative energy and emotions addressed by resin oils:

- Separated, disconnected, stressed, malnourished, unprotected, abandoned, darkened, weak

Leaves are an outgrowth of the plant stem that manufacture plant nutrients by photosynthesis. Oils are steam distilled from the leaves.

Top Properties:

- Antiseptic
- Invigorating
- Anti-inflammatory
- Insecticide
- Analgesic
- Antibacterial
- Antimicrobial

Positive energy and emotions heightened by leaf oils:

- Accepting, yielding, open-minded, invigorated, enhanced, unattached, trusting, progressing, enlightened, relieved

Negative energy and emotions addressed by leaf oils:

- Stubborn, angry, unyielding, confused, hindered, degraded, obstinate, doubtful, stalled, limited, inundated

Why Quality Matters

SOURCING

When it comes to sourcing essential oils, the terrain and soil of origin matter. If a field is sprayed with toxic chemicals, or these chemicals are added to the soil, it affects the chemistry of the plants. The distillation process, temperature, and the use of toxic solvents and chemicals for extraction also affect the purity and potency of the essential oil.

Variations in the natural chemistry of oils is permitted, as this is a legitimate expression of nature. As one truly studies the art of growing, harvesting, and distilling essential oils, one discovers the grower's craft and the beauty of this expert human art. Today we experience the best of tradition in growers' expertise and wisdom handed down through the generations, combined with advancements in science, farming, and distillation practices.

SUPPLIER

When it comes to healing, choosing a supplier of essential oils who is well known for quality and efficacy is, well, "essential." Every oil has specific constituents, which provide varying levels of therapeutic effects. Therefore, it is necessary to sort through dozens of species of a single plant source, from a myriad of geographical locations, to find the right combination of therapeutic compounds.

This is one of the supplier's greatest tasks: to responsibly search the world for the highest quality compounds that produce the best possible essential oils nature can provide. One of the best ways this is accomplished is by creating trusted alliances with honest growers and distillers.

AUTHENTICITY

Regulation of therapeutic grade essential oils is limited and standards are minimal. This leaves suppliers to self-regulate quality. The term "therapeutic grade" is simply insufficient to identify a level of quality. There exists, therefore, two very distinctly different views. In one, compromised sourcing is permissible and synthetic additives are acceptable components. In the other, true holistic healing requires unprocessed oils that are sourced directly from nature with nothing added. These strict standards allow the oils to remain rich and complex as nature created them. One should expect to pay a higher price for these genuine, authentic, pure, and potent superior-grade essential oils.

QUALITY

To be truly therapeutic and superior grade, an essential oil needs to be tested and certified as pure, potent, genuine, and authentic. Each of these terms is important and meaningful in reference to measurements of quality. It is vital to note that although chemists have successfully recreated multiple constituents of plants, they have never replicated a complete essential oil. Why? They simply have not discovered or identified every compound nature produces.

PROCESS

To protect and maintain the highest quality essential oils, plants must be patiently harvested by those who are knowledgeable, honest, and committed to gathering only the "one" specie, and who allow the plant proper maturation time.

After harvesting, the plant material is ready for distillation. In order to carefully extract the precious constituents, this process must be conducted gently, slowly, and skillfully. Quality distillation requires reduced pressure and temperature, protecting these essences from being oxidized or destroyed by excessive heat.

Once distillation is complete, the essential oils are moved to distribution companies or to middlemen, known as brokers. As a general rule, the farther down the supply chain you go, the less likely you are to get pure product. Most companies that sell essential oils have no ability *(or in many cases no desire)* to verify the quality of the oils they receive from their supplier before they pass it on to their customers. Look for companies that work directly with growers, sourced from all over the world.

There is a growing number of products falsely claiming to be an essential oil or to contain essential oils. Too often, these products use fragrant synthetic chemical substitutes to dilute or replace more expensive essential oil extracts. These claims deceive many consumers who believe they are using natural products.

Essential oils are comprised of only three elements: carbon, hydrogen, and oxygen. The molecules in essential oils are primarily monoterpenes, sesquiterpenes, and their oxygenated derivatives. Essential oils are volatile organic liquids. There are no vitamins, minerals, essential fatty acids, or hormones in essential oils. Any claim of such ingredients simply reveals the impurity of a product.

AROMA

One of the most telling ways to detect pure, high-quality oils is by the aroma. Superb aroma is earned and is the result of quality plant sourcing, quality distillation processes, and the absence of chemical solvents. Generally, the more pure and "sweet" an aroma, the greater the purity and the better the sourcing.

SUPPLIER RESPONSIBILITY

It is the distributing company's responsibility to provide the consumer with carefully extracted, pure *(no fillers or artificial ingredients)* essential oils. Rigorous quality testing, above and beyond the minimum required, helps ensure oils are free of contaminants. Look for companies that verify the quality and purity multiple times prior to making the product available to the consumer. Additionally, the distributor is responsible for labeling products according to FDA GRAS *(Generally Regarded As Safe)* standards.

MEASURING QUALITY

Measurements of quality fall under specific categories of genuine, authentic, pure, and potent.

Authentic

In the world of essential oils, the term "Authenticity" means:

- The composition of an oil is equal to the plant specified on the label.
- The oil is not a mixture of plant species, rather the plant specified.
- The oil is not the product of a mixture of plants or weeds growing alongside the species.
- The oil is comprised of and distilled from only the plant parts clearly identified.
- In total, the oil is characterized precisely so as to clearly identify its healing qualities through consistently occurring compounds.

Genuine

The term "Genuine" is equivalent to the term "Unadulterated," meaning:

- The essential oil is 100 percent natural and contains no addition of any other substances – even other natural substances. It contains NO synthetics, agents, diluents, or additives.
- The essential oil is 100 percent pure and contains NO similar essential oil or hybrid, added to extend supply.
- The essential oil is 100 percent complete and has been fully distilled. Almost all essential oils are distilled in a single process. Ylang ylang is an exception, as it passes through more than one distillation to be complete. Distillation processes that are disrupted can produce I, II, III, and "extra" essential oil classes.

Pure

Purity alone does not necessarily mean an oil is good quality. A pure oil can be distilled incorrectly or may be obtained from a particular variety of inferior plant species. Additionally, oils may contain contaminants, pesticides, herbicides, solvents, inferior and / or unlabeled plant sources, other unlabeled species, and synthetic compounds. The distillation process may magnify the concentration of these undesirable elements.

Potent

Essential oils are the most potent form of plant material. The chemical constituents found in the plant material will either increase or decrease the potency of the essential oil. The climate and soil composition affect the potency of plant matter. This is why sourcing an oil from its native habitat is essential.

PERSONAL RESPONSIBILITY

When it comes to obtaining quality essential oils, the consumer must do his own research, use common sense, exercise prudence, and do what is best for himself and his family. Education is key to becoming a skilled user of these potent plant extracts.

How to Know Which Oils to Use

The greater the number of oils you have at your disposal, the more choices you make and results you can create. Deciding which oil to use in certain circumstance can at times be overwhelming, especially with so many options for use and overlapping qualities and properties. Good news! You can't go wrong!

The skill to develop here is learning to make better choices to create even better results. Remember this: oils, to the best of their ability, move you to a more balanced state of homeostasis. Necessarily then, ask yourself, "What might I experience on my way to greater balance and wholeness *(e.g. temporary discomfort or symptoms due to poor elimination or lack of nutrients)*? Am I providing proper support for my body's needs *(e.g. adequate nutrition & rest, proper diet)* to help get me where I want to be in the most successful way?"

Following are a number of highly beneficial ways to make oil selections. Enjoy the process of getting to know each oil as if it were a friend you've learned to count on in times of need or want. The most important factors in your decision-making are you and your experiences. Interactions with the oils vary from person to person. Even with the same condition, people are drawn to and benefited by different solutions. Keep a log or journal, or simple notations right here in the pages of this book, about what you've learned. Become your own best advocate, knowing greater health and wellness, modeling it for generations to come, and inviting those around you to do the same.

SELECTION TOOLS:

On-Hand – In a moment of need, your go-to choices are what you have on hand. Put each of your oils to work for you by looking them up in this book and learning what they do best. As your interest grows in making essential oils your first line of response, identify health issues *(and desired changes and results)*, research them here in the book, and then increase your personal collection accordingly. It's what you do every day that matters most.

Intuition – Nothing could be more powerful in essential oil use than simply paying attention to what you are attracted to. Trust that feedback and act on it. Again, make notations so you can repeat what you've done before and, with experience, better your results.

Look Things Up in the Book

A-Z Quick Reference (pg. 38) Find the health condition you want to resolve. Pay attention to the five oils listed and considered to be among the top choices for that particular ailment. This immediately narrows your focus to just a few options.

Oil Properties (pg. 260) The last section of this book is designated for the more experienced and committed Power User. Utilize the resources provided. The Oil Properties chart is a superb advanced way to learn about how oils work. Notice as well that on the second page of every Body Systems section you will find oils listed by "Related Properties." In other words, certain essential oil properties excel in their capacity to address unique aspects of each body system.

Body Systems – Look up your condition(s) in *Body Systems & Focus Areas (pg. 194)*. First go to the body system that relates to your concern (*e.g. Respiratory for a cough; Cardiovascular for a heart or circulation issue*), and then look for specific conditions or symptoms you want to relieve. Note both oil suggestions and remedies are provided.

Online – If you need more detailed knowledge about what to address, first look up your condition online so you better understand it. For example, learn about the different facets of whatever ails you and discover what body parts are involved. With these specific areas of focus identified, now utilize the book as described above to pursue your essential oil solutions.

Smell – Like intuition, the value of smelling an oil to discover what you love or are drawn to cannot be overemphasized. This is one of the most wonderful aspects of essential oil use. After all, it is called aromatherapy! Don't limit your thinking to what is taught. Deliberately choose to make selections by aroma. It is both scientific *(every oil has very precise chemistry hence a unique aroma)* and traditional to do so. There is a reason why smelling oils prior to selection is so commonplace and the natural inclination. Even animals and small children quickly identify their favorites and what their body most needs.

Emotions (pg. 236) – Perhaps the idea of matching an oil to an emotional state is new to you. However, it is the number one way to narrow selections. Here's why. Consider two people have arthritis. One is impatient and the other is resigned. In each case, a different emotional profile is found as well as different needs to be met. Learn more about the connection between essential oils and emotions by first reading Emotional Well-Being *(pg. 236)*. The science and chemistry behind this correlation make it well worth your understanding and application. Then at the end of that section, use the charts in the Emotions Index to introduce the connection of what oil for what emotion. Also, see Mood & Behavior *(pg. 220)*. Consider acquiring additional resources on this topic.

Oil Personalities – Learn your oils by their 'personalities' and get a sense for which oils and blends work best for you. Where and how they grow, plant parts used, and chemistry contained, are all significant aspects of the oils, revealing much about the 'energy' profile they provide. Here is an example. Cinnamon, considered a spice oil (*see Emotions Index (pg. 248) to learn more)*, has warming properties *(see pg. 272 for more information)*. This heat both wards off unwanted predators and warms up a cold heart or body, serving as both an Immuno-stimulant and Aphrodisiac (two more properties). Upon use, the user has a sense of feeling more protected, safe, and warm, and is thus more willing to be intimate and sexually / emotionally vulnerable.

Individual Test – Utilize a personal digital scan or applied kinesiology *(also known as muscle response testing)* to quickly identify what resonates as beneficial to your body at the time of evaluation.

How to Use Essential Oils

AROMATIC

The very term **aromatherapy** was derived from the fact that essential oils are, by nature, aromatic. Their aromas can elicit powerful physiologic, mental, and emotional responses. Essential oils are also volatile, meaning they evaporate quickly and are rapidly absorbed into the body. The process of conveying aromas to the brain is called olfaction, or simply, smelling. It happens courtesy of the olfactory system.

As a person inhales an essential oil, the molecules of oil go up into the back of each nostril to the postage-sized epithelium patch. There the molecules attach to receptors on the cilia hairs, which convert to nerves on the other side of the mucous patch. These nerves send the odor information to the olfactory bulb in the brain. This means the essential oil itself is not sent to the brain, but instead a neural translation or "message" of the complex chemistry it contains is delivered. The millions of nerves enter the olfactory bulb, which communicates directly with the amygdala, hippocampus, and other brain structures.

The amygdala, a center for emotions in the limbic system, links our sense of smell to our ability to learn emotionally. Here, aromatic information is connected to the emotions of the situation. This capacity to pair the two, information and emotions, is inextricably connected to our survival ability, making essential oils a powerful partner in creating and maintaining emotional health. Inhalation of essential oils is also received through the alveoli of the lungs and, from there, into the bloodstream.

The easiest way to aromatically use essential oils is to open a bottle and simply breathe in the aroma through the nose. This technique is known as **direct inhalation**. To enhance this method, place a drop of an oil or blend in the hands, rub them together, and then cup around the nose and mouth *(not necessary to make contact with the face)* and breathe in. Additionally, oil drops can be placed on a piece of cloth or tissue, held close to the face, and inhaled.

Diffusing essential oils aromatically is beneficial for affecting mood, killing airborne pathogens, and changing the aroma of a space such as a room, office, or car. Other uses include a targeted approach for relaxing or stimulating the mind. Additionally, one of the most effective ways to impact a respiratory condition is to use a diffuser as an inhalation device, whether being in a room where diffusing is occurring or purposely breathing in the vapor. **Diffusers** are devices that can be used to evaporate an essential oil into a surrounding environment. There are four main types of diffusers: atomizing, vaporizing or humidification, fan, and heat. The best diffusers are atomizing and employ a cold air pump to force the essential oil through an atomizer, separating the oil into tiny particles that create a micro-fine vapor in the air. The essential oil bottle is, in some manner, directly connected to the diffuser, and no water is involved. Atomizing diffusers are normally more expensive and usually create a little bit of noise due to the mechanisms in action. Vaporizing or humidification diffusers employ water with the essential oil and use ultrasonic waves to emit the oil and water particles into the air. Fan and heat diffusers are usually low cost and mainly used for small areas such as cars. The amount of oil used varies with each diffuser type.

Different diffusers provide different capacities for covering the square footage of a room. Other features may include timers, some allowing both constant and intermittent distribution options. Essential oils can be added to water or alcohol *(such as vodka)* in a **spray bottle** *(preferably glass)*. The mixture can then be sprayed in the air *(e.g. air freshener)*, on surfaces *(e.g. counter-top)*, or on the body *(e.g.. for cooling and soothing benefits)*.

The best **dosage** for aromatic use of essential oils is smaller doses implemented multiple times throughout the day. It is best to avoid having infants and young children inhale oils at a close distance, as it is harder to determine dosage.

TOPICAL

Essential oils are fat-soluble. Because of their chemical compounds, they are readily absorbed and enter the bloodstream when they are **applied directly**. This is one reason why quality of oils is important. Many quality oils are safe to use NEAT *(i.e., applied topically to the skin with no carrier oil)*. One location that is most universally accepted as best for NEAT application is the bottoms of the feet.

The other primary method of distributing essential oils topically is to combine them with a carrier oil *(i.e., a different kind of oil used for dilution such as fractionated coconut oil)* for both dilution and prevention of evaporation. Using a carrier oil PRIOR to applying an oil slows down the absorption process *(does not prohibit)*, therefore slowing the therapeutic onset. Applying a carrier oil AFTER essential oil application enhances therapeutic onset. Either way, the carrier oil prevents potential rapid evaporation.

By taking the time to massage an essential oil thoroughly into the skin, absorption is enhanced by increasing the blood flow to the area thus allowing the skin to more efficiently absorb valued compounds. Applying essential oils with a carrier oil and then **massaging** the skin or applying warm heat such as a rice bag or moist cloth compress helps drive the oil deeper into the tissues. This is especially helpful for muscle pain, body aches, and injured tissue. Carrier oils also protect the skin from irritation. Children, the elderly, and those with sensitive skin or compromised systems are advised to always use a carrier oil.

Some of the more popular **carrier oils** are fractionated coconut oil, virgin coconut oil, jojoba oil, grapeseed oil, almond oil, avocado oil, and extra virgin olive oil. Competing aroma is one consideration when selecting the carrier oil of choice. Fractionated coconut oil is a favorite and is created by removing the fatty acids from regular coconut oil, which is solid at 76 degrees. Fractionating, or removing the fatty acids, keeps the oil in a liquid state, making it easier for use in application *(e.g., while giving a massage)* and to combine with essential oils in containers such as spray and roll-on bottles. The fractionating process also increases shelf life and makes it odorless and colorless. It's great on the skin and doesn't clog the pores.

Topical application methods can vary considerably. Most frequently, oils are simply placed either on the skin of any area of concern or on the bottoms of the feet. Additional methods of distribution can include combining oils in an unscented lotion, or with a carrier oil or water in a spray, balm, or roller bottle. Limiting the number of drops used and diluting is the best way to safely use essential oils topically. It's generally unnecessary to use exaggerated amounts to achieve a therapeutic effect. Every drop of essential oil contains a vast bouquet of potent chemical constituents made by nature to deliver powerful effects in sometimes as little as one or a few drops.

The appropriate **dosage** for topical use of essential oils is different for each individual and should be tailored to their personal circumstances. The age and size of an individual are the biggest considerations as is the individual's overall health status. It is best to use smaller amounts more often rather than greater amounts less often. Start with the lowest amount that makes sense, and then increase the dose as needed to achieve the desired outcome. A topical dose of essential oils can be repeated every twenty minutes in an acute situation or every two to six hours as needed otherwise.

A recommended ratio for dilution follows:

Babies	*0.3 % dilution*	*(1 drop to 1 tablespoon)*
Children	*1.0 % dilution*	*(1 drop to 1 teaspoon)*
Adults	*2.0–4.0% dilution*	*(3-6 drops to 1 teaspoon)*

When applying essential oils topically, avoid sensitive skin areas such as eyes, inner ears, genitals, and broken, damaged, or injured skin. After applying essential oils, the residue can be enjoyed and massaged into the palms for therapeutic benefit. However, if immediate contact with sensitive areas, such as the eyes, is predicted be sure to thoroughly wash hands.

A favorite use for essential oils is in a **bath**, which functions both as a topical and aromatic method. Using an emulsifier such as shampoo, bath gel, milk, or honey with an essential oil before placing in the bath water disperses the oil throughout the water rather than it floating on top. Or add 3 to 10 drops of essential oils to **bath salts** *(use amount per product instructions)* or 1 cup Epsom salts, and then dissolve in bath.

Essential oils can be applied to **reflex points** or nerve endings in the feet or hands. Oils can also be applied to various points on the rim and parts of the ears, referred to as **auricular therapy**, which are similar to the reflex points on the hands or feet. Refer to "Reflexology" later in this section.

Layering is the process of applying more than one oil to a desired location to intensify the effect of an oil or to address multiple concerns at once. For example, frankincense is often used as the first oil applied to an area on the skin to magnify the effects of subsequent oils layered on top. If an individual is sensitive to or dislikes the smell of an oil(s), they may resist its use. Applying an oil to the bottoms of one's feet *(perhaps the least preferred aroma is applied first)* and then layering a second and even third oil on top to "deodorize" and create a different aroma can be effective. Putting on socks after application can "contain" the aroma to a degree as an additional option. For example, apply vetiver then layer lavender on top. If satisfactory, then the process is complete. If not, add a third oil such as wild orange or invigorating blend. The last oil applied will be the strongest aroma initially. After time, a more base note oil lingers longer than a top note oil.

INTERNAL

Just as plants are eaten fresh, dried for herbs, used in hot water infusions *(tea)*, taken internally for therapeutic benefits, and used for improved flavor of foods, essential oils can be taken internally for these same uses. We consume essential oils when we eat food. Fresh aromatic plants normally contain 1 to 2 percent by weight of volatile compounds or essential oils. When plants are distilled for the extraction of their essential oils, the properties are concentrated. Essential oils are more potent than whole plant material. Small amounts should be used when taking oils internally.

Essential oils are fat-soluble, so they are readily delivered to all organs of the body, including the brain. They are then metabolized by the liver and other organs. Internal use of essential oils is the most potent method of use, and proper dosing for internal use should be followed according to labeling recommendations and other professional guidelines to avoid unnecessary overuse or toxicity. All ingested food can be toxic if taken in too high of doses. Some traditional essential oil users profess that internal use of essential oils is not safe. However, modern research as well as internal use by hundreds of thousands of users over many years indicates that internal use following appropriate and safe dosing guidelines is perfectly and appropriately safe. Dosage guidelines for internal use vary depending on the age and size of the person as well as an individual's health status.

Essentials oils can be **ingested** internally under the tongue *(1 to 2 drops sublingually)*, in a gelatin cap *(often referred to as a "gel cap")*, in a vegetable capsule *(often referred to as a "veggie cap")*, in a tea, in food, or in water. Some essential oils, such as cinnamon and oregano, are best used internally. Heat affects the compounds in an oil. Therefore, it is best to add oils to hot liquids after the heating process has occurred.

Another method of internal essential oil use is **vaginal insertion**. Oils can be diluted in a carrier oil, inserted using a vaginal syringe, and held in place using a tampon. Oils can also be diluted in a carrier oil and then absorbed into a tampon. The tampon is inserted and kept in usually overnight. Essential oils can also be diluted in water and used to irrigate the vaginal area with a vaginal syringe.

Rectal insertion is an appropriate and safe way to apply essential oils, especially for internal conditions. Oils can be deposited into the rectum using a rectal syringe, or oils can be placed in a capsule and the capsule then inserted and retained in the rectum overnight. Consult an aromatherapy professional for using essential oils in **suppositories**.

Keep in mind that a single drop of essential oil is obtained from a large amount of plant material. One drop of essential oil can contain hundreds of compound constituents and is very potent. These two facts should be considered in determining the amount of oil to ingest. For example, it takes one lemon to make about five drops of lemon essential oil. A common internal dose for an adult is 1 to 5 drops of essential oil every one or two to six hours *(depending on the oils selected)*, but preferably no more than 25 drops of essential oils divided into doses in a 24-hour period. This methodology allows the body, especially the liver, time to process each dosage. This dosage should be adjusted for a person's age, size, and health status. For extended internal use a lower daily dose is advised. If a higher dose is desired, consult a healthcare professional.

Some oils are not considered safe to ingest. Those include oils from the needles of trees such as pine essential oil and some bark oils such as cypress and some varieties of eucalyptus. Verifying a "Safe for Supplemental Use" or "Supplement Facts" label on an essential oil bottle serves as guide for oils that are appropriate to be taken internally. Other oils such as wintergreen and birch are required by law to have childproof lids on them, because the benefit of thinning blood could be hazardous to a young child or baby if ingested.

Oil Touch Technique

Essential oils have a powerful effect on well being. These effects are specific and unique to each oil that nature has provided. When we understand these healing properties and how our bodies naturally respond to them, we can use essential oils to promote a superior state of being. The Oil Touch technique provides a way to use these gifts to maximizes emotional and physical healing.

The Oil Touch technique is comprised of four stages. Each stage utilizes two oils or oil blends. Do not substitute other essential oils. Because these essential oils are applied full strength *(NEAT)* to the skin, it is very important that you use only the highest quality essential oil. Oils need to be both pure and potent. The method of distillation, growing and harvesting standards, plant species, even the region of the world from which it comes, greatly affect the content of the essential oil. Much like the raw materials entering a factory completely determine the end product, an Oil Touch is effective if the essential oil used has consistent and whole chemistry.

WHAT IS OIL TOUCH?

Oil Touch is an interaction between nature's chemistry and neurology *(brain and healing communication system)*. It supports the body to move toward a healing state. Health is created as the body achieves and maintains balance. This balance can be interrupted by heightened stress, environmental toxins, or traumas. Oil Touch promotes balance so healing can continue and is recommended as an integral part of preventive care even for healthy people.

Oil Touch is not a treatment for any specific disease or condition. The body's natural healing abilities are miraculous. Awakening these abilities in others is a simple and precious gift.

HOW DOES IT WORK?

Balance in your body looks something like a series of connected teeter-totters. To illustrate, consider the process of standing up. In order for you to stand and walk, your body is maintaining a delicate balance between falling forward and falling backwards. Just like leaning too much to either side will make you fall over, your body inside is maintaining similar delicate balances. For example, your nervous system is either in a stressed state or a rested state. Like a teeter-totter, both sides can't be high at the same time. Your immune system is the same and will mirror the nervous system's actions. It is either moving infection out of your body or it is pushing it in deeper for you to deal with later. Your body works this way with regard to your senses too. When injured your body sends pain; we call this nocioception. When it is not in pain, it sends good sensations we call proprioception. When all of these are in balance with each other you become more healthy and heal much better. Oil Touch can help restore this balance. It can be compared to re-booting a computer for optimal functioning. This condition is called homeostasis.

The Oil Touch Technique

Oil Touch technique is divided into four stages. Each stage supports a shift in how your body heals and adapts to stress and injury.

Step 1 shifts the nervous system from stress to rest. *Step 2* encourages the body to move from the secondary immune system to the primary immune system. *Step 3* reduces pain and inflammation. During the entire process, good feeling *(proprioception)* is stimulated. As the technique progresses, the effects compound, and a dramatic shift occurs in all three factors.

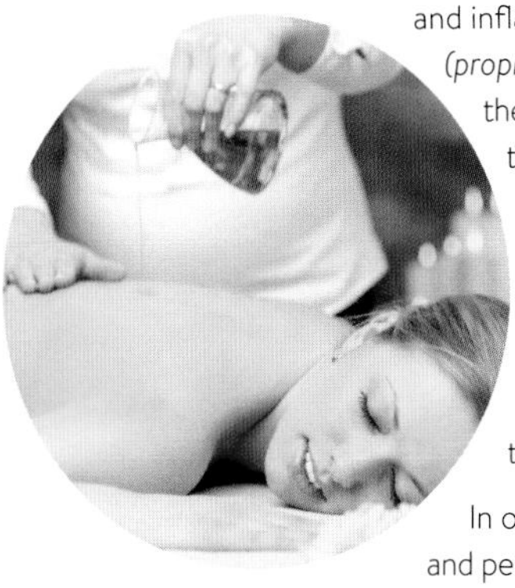

Once your recipient is in this state, they are ready for *step 4*. In this step, you nudge them back the other direction. The body takes over and finds its balance. This is why it is like re-booting a computer. You turn it off and then back on. The body knows where to stay to get the healing job done right.

In order to do this, you will need to learn a few easy skills and perform them in the right order.

Setting up for an Oil Touch:

You should find a quiet, comfortable place. Using a massage table is best. A headpiece that angles up and down can be helpful for comfort. You may wish to bolster the recipient's ankles with a rolled towel or blanket. Your goal is to make your recipient as comfortable as possible. Your recipient will need a blanket for warmth and modesty as they will need to remove their clothing from the waist up and lie face down on the table. They will have their arms at their sides with their shoes and socks off. They will remain in this position for the duration of the technique. Encourage the recipient to completely relax and receive.

Applying Oil:

When applying oil, hold the bottle at a 45-degree angle over the recipient and let a drop fall onto the back. You will typically apply 3 to 4 drops along the spine. It is preferable to start at the low back and move up to the neck. In stage 4 you will apply a couple of drops to each foot.

Distributing the Oil:

When distributing along the spine spread the oil from the base of the low back to the top of the head. This is done by gently using the pads of the finger tips. This is a very light touch and is complete when you have spread the oil along the spine with three passes.

Palm Circles through the Heart Area:

Making a triangle with the thumbs and first fingers, place your hands on the center of the back at the level of the heart. Slide the hands in a clockwise fashion over the skin, creating a circle about eight inches wide. Complete three circles and hold for a moment. After pausing, separate the hands, sliding them along the spine. One hand stops on back of the head while the other hand stops and rests just below the waistline. Pause, leaving your hands in this position. Connect with your recipient, and feel their breathing. Focus on being present with them to find a rhythm that is theirs and not yours.

The Alternating Palm Slide:

This movement is a rhythm created by sliding the hands along the surface of the skin. Stand to the side of the recipient, and place your hand on the low back with your fingers pointing away from you at the level just below their waistline. Place your palm against the far side of the spine. Slide your hand away from you with very mild pressure. That is the basic movement. Begin this motion with your fingertips at the spine and lower your palm to their skin as you slide your hand away from you. The slide ends when your hand starts to turn down the recipient's side. Follow your first slide with a second using your other hand and, while alternating hands, move up the body toward the head with each horizontal slide. Keep your touch very light and keep it rhythmic. It is kind of like mowing a lawn, one stroke overlapping the other as it moves up the back toward the head. This movement continues up the back, the shoulders, the neck, and finally up on the head until you reach the level just above the ears.

Repeat this three times, beginning each time at the waistline. Move to the recipient's other side, and complete three passes on the opposite side.

5 Zone Activation:

Imagine broad vertical pinstripes running from the waistline to the shoulders five to the left of the spine and five to the right running parallel with the spine. The two-inch area directly on either side of the spine is Zone 1. The spaces on both sides directly adjacent to Zone 1 are Zone 2 and so forth. Zone 5 is the farthest out, located on both sides at the angle of the ribs where they start to turn down to the recipient's sides. Standing at the head of the table, place both hands on either side of the spine at the waistline as close together as you can. Drag your palms with light pressure up the spine, allowing your fingers to trail behind like the train of a wedding dress. Continue this motion through the neck and head, allowing your hands to gently continue the motion lightly to the crown of the head. That completes Zone 1. Now move to Zone 2. Place your hands at the waistline again, but separate them about two inches *(this is Zone 2)*. Pull your palms up toward the shoulders in a straight line as you did for Zone 1. However, once your hands reach the shoulders, turn the fingertips in, drag your palms out along the shoulder blade, rotate the fingers out, and slide them under the front of the shoulders as you drag your palms lightly back to toward the spine, continue up the neck and head as you did for Zone 1. Repeat for Zones 3, 4, and 5 as you did for zone 2, starting with your hands on the zone just outside the previous one. Complete just one pass per zone.

Auricular Stress Reduction:

Stand at the head of the table. Using your thumbs and forefingers, take hold of both earlobes. Massage them in a circular motion, much like you might rub a penny. Massage along the edge of the ears from the lobe to the top. Drag your fingers back down to the earlobe and repeat three times.

Perform the Auricular Stress Reduction on both ears at the same time while the client is laying face down.

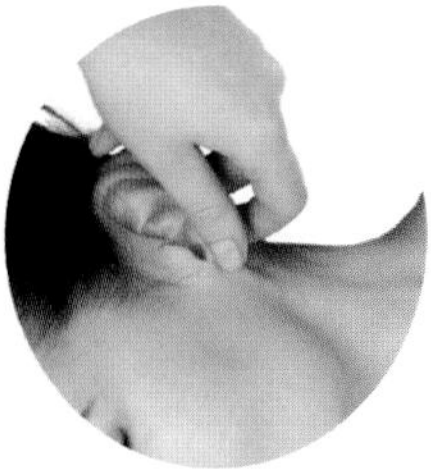

Thumb Walk Tissue Pull:

Stand at your recipient's side near the hips. Place your hands on the back at the waistline with your thumbs on the muscles running directly on either side of the spine. In a circular motion with your thumbs, massage the muscle on either side as you walk up the spine in an alternating fashion until you reach the back of the head. Repeat three times.

Autonomic Balance on the Feet:

There are three steps for the feet. Apply the oils *(wild orange and peppermint)* together, and spread on the bottom of the foot. You may wish to apply some fractionated coconut oil here as well.

Grip the foot with your hands and, using a circular motion with your thumbs similar to the thumb tissue pull, wipe the oil into the skin. Start at the side of the heel and move across it horizontally, then move down one half inch and work your way across the other direction almost like you are tilling a garden. Repeat this pattern until you reach the end of the forefoot. You will have just pushed the oil quickly into the skin.

Divide the foot into five zones, just like on the back. The strip running from the heal to the big toe is Zone 1, the strip including the second toe is Zone 2, and so forth. To trigger the reflexes in the foot, place one thumb near the other thumb, starting at the heel on the inside *(Zone 1)*, walk down the foot, pushing into the bottom of the foot with the thumbs using medium pressure. Let one thumb trail the other thumb, so each spot is triggered twice. Complete one pass for each of the five zones, continuing to the tips of the toes.

Gripping the foot, swipe down each zone with your thumb as you slightly compress the foot with your hand. Similar to lightly milking a cow, alternating your hands, swipe Zone 1 three times and then continue through all five zones. Make one pass.

Complete these steps again on the second foot.

The Lymphatic Pump:

If your recipient falls asleep let them sleep, or perform the Lymphatic Pump. This will help them get moving again and be less disoriented when they arise. Do this by taking both feet in the hands, saddling your thumbs just in front of the heel at the arch. Push toward the head crisply one time, giving them a forward shake. Their body will rebound back toward you. Repeat the motion, matching the rebound. Create a pulse going back and forth. Do this for about ten seconds and repeat a couple of times.

Tips

- If for some reason a particular essential oil cannot be used, do not substitute it with another oil. Just remove it from the technique and use fractionated coconut oil on that stage
- The Oil Touch technique is designed to be performed on a massage table. If you do not have access to one, adapt, and do the best you can.
- Once you establish contact with your recipient, stay in contact with at least one hand on the body at all times.
- You can use fractionated coconut oil at any time during this process, but if you are using it to lubricate the skin you are pressing too hard. You should be able to perform this on dry skin. Complete the following steps in order, referencing the descriptions above.

STEP 1 Grounding blend

- Apply & distribute oil
- Heart Area Circles

Lavender

- Apply & distribute oil
- Alternating Palm Slide
- 5-Zone Activation
- Auricular Stress Reduction

STEP 2 Melaleuca

- Apply & distribute oil
- Alternating Palm Slide
- 5-Zone Activation

Protective blend

- Apply & distribute oil
- Alternating Palm Slide
- 5-Zone Activation
- Thumb Walk Tissue Pull

STEP 3 Massage blend

- Apply & distribute oil
- Alternating Palm Slide
- 5-Zone Activation

Soothing blend

- Apply & distribute oil
- Alternating Palm Slide
- 5-Zone Activation
- Thumb Walk Tissue Pull

STEP 4 Wild orange & Peppermint

- Apply & distribute oil
- Alternating Palm Slide
- 5-Zone Activation
- Thumb Walk Tissue Pull

Improving Results

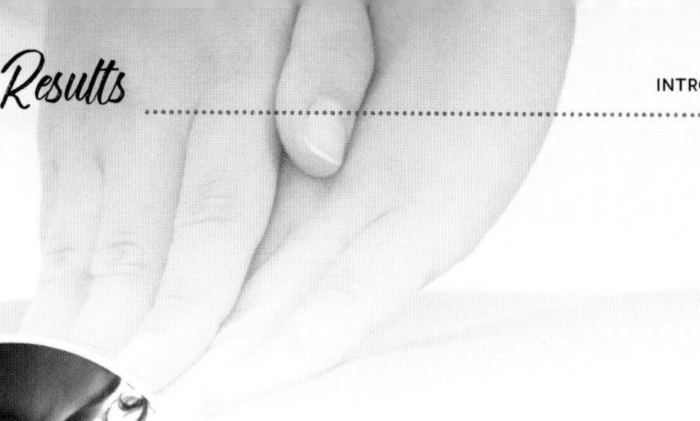

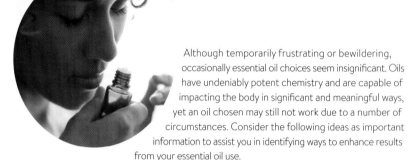

Although temporarily frustrating or bewildering, occasionally essential oil choices seem insignificant. Oils have undeniably potent chemistry and are capable of impacting the body in significant and meaningful ways, yet an oil chosen may still not work due to a number of circumstances. Consider the following ideas as important information to assist you in identifying ways to enhance results from your essential oil use.

Application Method – There are three basic ways to use essential oils: aromatic, topical, and internal. Each method impacts the body and its numerous layers and parts in different ways. For example, to eliminate a respiratory infection, both topical and internal use may be needed to address the multiple facets of that temporary issue. As the condition progresses, a change in application methods may be called for. Pay attention to body cues and adjust as needed. Take a moment to consider the variety of aspects of any situation and how you can address them by using more than one oil in more than one way. For further and detailed knowledge on how to use essential oils, refer to *Application Methods* on page 23. Also consider learning a special method, *The Oil Touch Technique*, taught on page 28.

Frequency Of Use – A best rule of essential oil use is: use less more often. With the powerful chemistry packed in every drop, a little goes a long way. For example, 1-2 drops of an oil every 20-30 minutes *(e.g. stomach flu or food poisoning, sprained ankle)* or every 1-2 hours *(e.g. cold & flu, exhaustion)* until desired relief is achieved, will likely far more effective and fast-acting then 10 drops used one time per day. The body can only chemically process so much at any given time. Therefore, repeated usage such as every 15-30 minutes for an acute condition and 2-4 times daily for a more chronic or long-lasting condition, is far more likely to drive the results you are looking for. Wondering where to start with your oil use for particular health goal? Consider: a couple drops, a couple times per day, in, on or around you.

Oil Selection – One of the most beautiful things about essential oils is if a legitimate reference or expert says, "This oil does that," it is likely true more than 80% of the time. For the occasional time that it doesn't work, it's often found that a user simply doesn't know the true nature of their issue and therefore made a less effective choice. Perhaps a stomach issue was suspected so a favorite digestion blend was used yet no effect. Really the gall bladder was the issue and grapefruit and geranium oils would have been the better selection. Additionally, as individual's body chemistry, composition, and level of health differ, effects differ as well. See the section in this book titled *How to Know Which Oils to Use* on page 21, to familiarize yourself with methods of selection. You will discover there are many ways to approach oil choices throughout the book. Dive in and become your own expert user!

Quality – The quality of essential oils offered in the marketplace radically differ. Many are adulterated and deceptively labeled. For example, it's common practice for a distributor to dilute pure oils with synthetic counterparts or add a less expensive oil *(e.g. add cypress to frankincense or lemongrass to melissa)* to extend oil yield. Though the dealer may have found momentary profit, their choice drastically reduces the effects for the end user. Because chemical profiles have some similarities, most methods of testing for quality are inferior and won't identify the adulterations, allowing for the deception to prevail. Choosing a reliable source is imperative to safe and successfully use. Be sure to read *Why Quality Matters* on page 18.

Body Health – What many people don't realize is that essential oils work chemically with and within the body. Acting as messenger molecules, or what is known as exogenous ligands, they enter the body like a hired outside management consulting firm, rapidly identifying what's needed and immediately sending instructions to whatever department need be involved. Imagine if no one were in the office, nothing would get done. If the body is void of necessary nutrition, then the oils have no way for their powerful instructions to be carried out. One of the most crucial habits for successful results from essential use is to make a healthy diet and use of high-quality dietary supplements vital daily wellness habits.

Lifestyle – Assessing lifestyle and self-care patterns may be necessary to find the culprits of compromise. Lack of sleep or proper consumption of water, poor quality drinking water, lack of regular exercise or movement, consumption of acid-producing beverages *(e.g. carbonated or caffeinated drinks)*, high levels of stress, etc. may be overriding the benefits of essential oils as the demands on the body are simply too high. It is possible the ratio of offense *(e.g. a bad habit)* is higher than the ratio of solutions *(e.g. good habits like essential oil use)* and frequency of oil use may need to be adjusted along with overall changes in personal choices. Oils can cover up for a myriad of sins, but lifestyle has a significant impact on the results you experience.

Safety and Storage

Essential oils are concentrated, potent plant extracts and should be used with reasonable care. Essential oils are very effective and safe when used appropriately. It takes a small amount to induce a powerful therapeutic benefit.

Never apply oils directly to the eyes or ear canals. After applying essential oils, avoid eye contact or the touching of sensitive areas. If essential oils enter the eyes, place a drop of carrier oil, such as fractionated coconut oil or olive oil, in the eye and blink until the oils clear. Never use water, as oils and water don't mix or help with dilution.

Some oils are "warm," creating a heat-like sensation on the skin, and should be diluted with a carrier oil when used topically. These oils can include birch, cassia, cinnamon, clove, eucalyptus, ginger, lemongrass, oregano, peppermint, thyme, and wintergreen. With babies, children, and those with sensitive skin or compromised health, it is particularly important to exercise caution or avoidance with these same oils, as they can be a temporary irritant or overly potent to delicate skin. When using these oils internally, it is best to consume in a gelatin or vegetable capsule.

Some oils contain furocoumarins, a constituent that can cause skin to be photosensitive. Photosensitive oils react to sources of UV rays. The higher the concentration of furanoids, the greater the sensitivity. Oils with concentrated amounts of furanoids include any cold pressed citrus oil such as bergamot, grapefruit, lemon, and lime, with lesser amounts in wild orange. Internal use of these oils is typically not a problem. It is best to wait a minimum of twelve hours after topical application of photosensitive oils before being exposed to UV rays.

Most essential oils applied topically and used reasonably are safe to be used during pregnancy and nursing. Some individuals prefer to avoid internal use during pregnancy and some use essential oils only aromatically during the first trimester. Several oils may be helpful during and after delivery. Internal use of peppermint essential oil should be avoided while nursing as it may reduce milk supply.

Persons with critical health conditions should consult a healthcare professional or qualified aromatherapist before using essential oils and may want to research individual oils prior to using them. In general, those with low seizure thresholds should be cautious in using or avoid altogether fennel, basil, rosemary, birch, and any digestive blend that contains fennel. Those with high blood pressure should be cautious with or avoid thyme and rosemary essential oils.

On occasion a person may experience a cleansing reaction, which takes place when the body is trying to rid itself of toxins faster than it is able. When this happens, increase water intake and decrease application of essential oils, or change the area of application.

The compounds in essential oils are best preserved when stored and kept from light, heat, air, and moisture. Long exposure to oxygen begins to break down and change the chemical makeup of an essential oil. This process is called oxidation and an oil is said to have "oxidative breakdown." This process is slow but can, over time, promote skin sensitivity with some oils. Citrus oils and blue tinted oils are especially prone to this breakdown.

For optimum storage of these types of oils for longer than a year, refrigeration is best. A carrier oil can also be added to slow the oxidation process. Keep air space in essential oil bottles to a minimum for those that are opened and kept for a long period of time. Consider combining partially used bottles. Some oils with compounds such as sesquiterpenes *(e.g. myrrh and sandalwood)* can actually get better with age. Essential oils can be flammable and should be kept clear of open flame, spark, or fire hazards.

Section 2

QUICK REFERENCE

HOW TO USE THIS SECTION

Ailments are indexed A-Z. Start by searching for the ailment in question, then note the recommended essential oils for each ailment. Oils are listed in order of most common use. Application methods are also recommended for each oil.

FREQUENTLY

For acute conditions use every fifteen to twenty minutes until symptoms subside, then apply every two to six hours as needed. For chronic or ongoing conditions, repeat one to two times per day, typically a.m. and p.m.

Safety Tips

- For adults, use 2-3 drops; for children, use 1-2 drops
- Avoid eyes, ears, and nose
- Avoid exposing area of application to sunlight for 12 hours after using citrus oils topically
- Dilute oils for children and sensitive skin with fractionated coconut oil
- Refer to the National Solutions section for specific oil safety and usage

= AROMATIC

- Diffuse with a diffuser.
- Inhale from cupped hands *(your personal diffuser).*
- Inhale from oil bottle.
- Wear an oil pendant.

= TOPICAL

- Apply to area of pain or concern *(dilute as needed).*
- Apply under nose, back of neck, forehead, or wrists.
- To affect entire body, apply to bottoms of feet, spine, or navel.
- To affect specific organs or body systems, apply to reflex points on the ears, hands, or feet *(See Reflexology pg 432).*

**Add warm compress or massage to drive oils deeper into body tissues*

= INTERNAL

- Put a drop or two of oil under tongue, hold a few seconds, and then swallow.
- Drink a few drops in a glass of water.
- Put a few drops of oil in an empty capsule and swallow.
- Put a drop of oil on the back of your hand and lick.

STEPS

1. Look up ailment.
2. Choose one or more of the recommended oils. *(Order of recommendation is left to right.)*
3. Use oil(s) as indicated.
4. Learn more in corresponding body system / focus area.
5. Find more solutions at ***essentiallife.com***

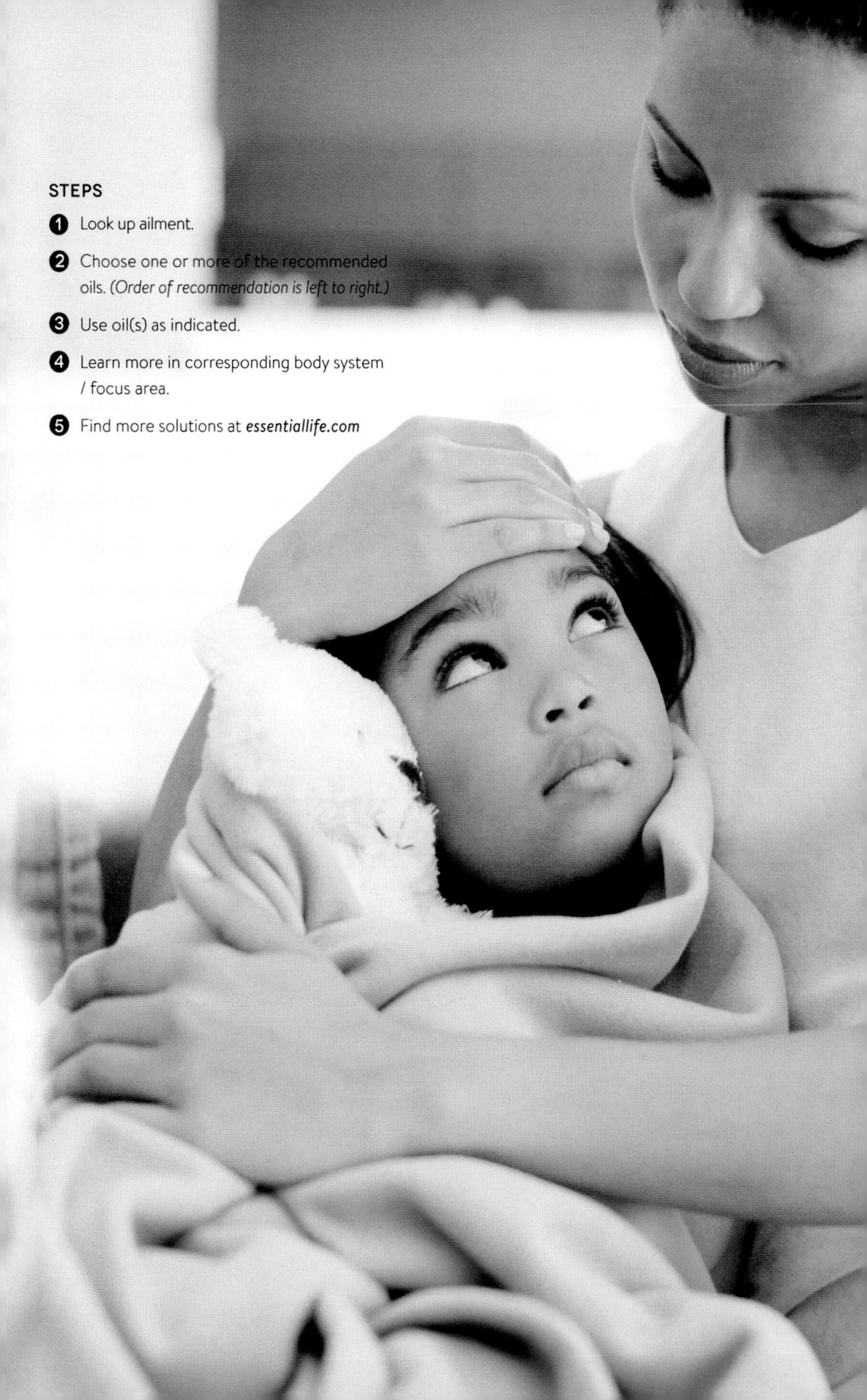

ABDOMINAL CRAMPS

Digestive & Intestinal (pg. 209), Women's Health (pg. 234), Pain & Inflammation (pg. 224)

digestion blend	peppermint	petitgrain	ginger	women's m. blend

ABNORMAL SPERM MORPHOLOGY

Men's Health (pg. 219)

thyme	rosemary	clary sage	cellular c. blend	detoxification blend

ABSCESS (TOOTH)

Oral Health (pg. 223)

clove	melaleuca	thyme	frankincense	cleansing blend

ABSENTMINDEDNESS

Brain (pg. 203), Focus & Concentration (pg. 214)

focus blend	cedarwood	peppermint	patchouli	vetiver

ABUSE TRAUMA

Mood & Behavior (pg. 220), Limbic (pg. 218)

melissa	Roman chamomile	comforting blend	frankincense	joyful blend

ACHE

Muscular (pg. 221), Skeletal (pg. 229), Pain & Inflammation (pg. 224), Immune & Lymphatic (pg. 215)

soothing blend	massage blend	peppermint	wintergreen	cypress

ACID REFLUX

Digestive & Intestinal (pg. 209)

digestion blend	fennel	peppermint	ginger	lemon

ACIDOSIS

Detoxification (pg. 208)

detoxification blend	helichrysum	lemon	fennel	cellular c. blend

ACNE

Integumentary (pg. 216), Endocrine (pg. 211), Detoxification (pg. 208)

skin clearing blend	melaleuca	sandalwood	anti-aging blend	arborvitae
topical	topical, internal	topical	topical	topical

ACROMEGALY

Endocrine (pg. 211)

frankincense	detoxification blend	grounding blend	reassuring blend	rosemary
topical, internal	topical, internal	topical	topical	topical

ACTINIC KERATOSIS

Integumentary (pg. 216)

anti-aging blend	lavender	frankincense	sandalwood	geranium
topical	topical	topical	topical	topical

ADD / ADHD

Focus & Concentration (pg. 214)

focus blend	vetiver	reassuring blend	lavender	encouraging blend
topical, aromatic	topical, aromatic	topical, aromatic	topical, aromatic	topical, aromatic

ADDICTIONS

Endocrine (pg. 211), Autoimmune (pg. 201)

copaiba	helichrysum	black pepper	bergamot	cinnamon
internal	internal	internal	internal, topical	internal

ADDISON'S DISEASE

Endocrine (pg. 211), Autoimmune (pg. 201)

clove	basil	cinnamon	detoxification blend	rosemary
internal, topical	internal, topical	internal, topical	internal, topical	topical, internal

ADRENAL FATIGUE

Endocrine (pg. 211), Energy & Vitality (pg. 212)

rosemary	basil	geranium	detoxification blend	ylang ylang
topical, internal, aromatic	topical, internal, aromatic	topical, internal, aromatic	topical, internal	topical, internal, aromatic

AGE SPOTS

Integumentary (pg. 216)

anti-aging blend	frankincense	sandalwood	spikenard	petitgrain
topical	topical	topical	topical	topical

AGITATION — *Mood & Behavior (pg. 220), Focus & Concentration (pg. 214)*

restful blend	*soothing blend*	*reassuring blend*	*grounding blend*	*lavender*

AIDS OR HIV — *Immune & Lymphatic (pg. 215)*

cinnamon	*protective blend*	*melissa*	*melaleuca*	*cellular c. blend*

ALCOHOL ADDICTION — *Addictions (pg. 198), Limbic (pg. 218)*

helichrysum	*renewing blend*	*cinnamon*	*detoxification blend*	*metabolic blend*

ALERTNESS — *Brain (pg. 203), Focus & Concentration (pg. 214), Energy & Vitality (pg. 212)*

peppermint	*rosemary*	*encouraging blend*	*respiration blend*	*focus blend*

ALKALOSIS — *Detoxification (pg. 208)*

geranium	*grounding blend*	*protective blend*	*invigorating blend*	*rosemary*

ALLERGIES (INSECT) — *First Aid (pg. 213), Integumentary (pg. 216), Allergies (pg. 199)*

lavender	*cleansing blend*	*Roman chamomile*	*arborvitae*	*blue tansy*

ALLERGIES (PET DANDER) — *Allergies (pg. 199)*

lavender	*Roman chamomile*	*detoxification blend*	*respiration blend*	*cleansing blend*

ALLERGIES (RESPIRATORY) — *Respiratory (pg. 228), Allergies (pg. 199), First Aid (pg. 213), Digestive & Intestinal (pg. 209)*

lavender	*lemon*	*peppermint*	*Roman chamomile*	*respiration blend*

ALZHEIMER'S DISEASE

Brain (pg. 203)

cellular c. blend	*frankincense*	*thyme*	*clove*	*cilantro*
Internal, Topical	Internal, Topical	Internal, Topical	Internal, Aromatic	Internal, Topical

AMENORRHEA

Women's Health (pg. 234)

women's m. blend	*basil*	*rosemary*	*cellular c. blend*	*clary sage*
Topical	Internal, Topical	Internal, Topical	Internal, Topical	Internal, Topical

AMNESIA

Brain (pg. 203)

peppermint	*focus blend*	*renewing blend*	*reassuring blend*	*frankincense*
Aromatic, Topical	Topical	Aromatic, Topical	Topical, Aromatic	Aromatic, Topical, Internal

AMYOTROPHIC LATERAL SCLEROSIS (ALS) / LOU GEHRIG'S DISEASE

Autoimmune (pg. 201), Nervous (pg. 222), Muscular (pg. 221)

cypress	*cellular c. blend*	*melissa*	*patchouli*	*frankincense*
Topical	Topical, Internal	Topical, Internal	Topical, Aromatic	Topical, Internal

ANEMIA

Cardiovascular (pg. 205)

detoxification blend	*cinnamon*	*helichrysum*	*geranium*	*cellular c. blend*
Internal, Topical	Internal, Topical	Internal, Topical	Internal, Topical	Internal, Topical

ANEURYSM

Cardiovascular (pg. 205)

helichrysum	*cypress*	*cellular c. blend*	*frankincense*	*marjoram*
Internal, Topical, Aromatic	Topical, Aromatic	Internal, Topical	Internal, Topical, Aromatic	Internal, Topical, Aromatic

ANGER

Mood & Behavior (pg. 220), Children (pg. 207), Focus & Concentration (pg. 214)

renewing blend	*grounding blend*	*helichrysum*	*reassuring blend*	*restful blend*
Aromatic, Topical	Topical, Aromatic	Topical, Aromatic	Aromatic, Topical	Topical, Aromatic

ANGINA

Cardiovascular (pg. 205)

Douglas fir	*thyme*	*basil*	*cinnamon*	*rosemary*
Topical, Aromatic	Internal, Aromatic, Topical	Internal, Topical	Internal, Topical	Internal, Topical, Aromatic

ANKYLOSING SPONDYLITIS — *Skeletal (pg. 229), Pain & Inflammation (pg. 224)*

wintergreen	massage blend	birch	grounding blend	soothing blend

ANOREXIA — *Eating Disorders (pg. 210), Addictions (pg. 198), Weight (pg. 233)*

grapefruit	patchouli	metabolic blend	bergamot	reassuring blend

ANOSMIA — *Respiratory (pg. 228)*

peppermint	basil	lemongrass	helichrysum	arborvitae

ANTHRAX — *Immune & Lymphatic (pg. 215)*

oregano	melissa	thyme	clove	frankincense

ANXIETY — *Mood & Behavior (pg. 220), Stress (pg. 231), Focus & Concentration (pg. 214)*

restful blend	lavender	reassuring blend	grounding blend	wild orange

APATHY — *Mood & Behavior (pg. 220)*

ginger	encouraging blend	inspiring blend	ylang ylang	invigorating blend

APPETITE (LOSS OF) — *Digestive & Intestinal (pg. 209), Stress (pg. 231), Eating Disorders (pg. 210), Weight (pg. 233)*

reassuring blend	metabolic blend	comforting blend	wild orange	cardamom

APPETITE (OVERACTIVE) — *Weight (pg. 233), Eating Disorders (pg. 210), Addictions (pg. 198)*

metabolic blend	grapefruit	ginger	cinnamon	peppermint

ARDS — *Respiratory (pg. 228)*

rosemary	melissa	eucalyptus	respiration blend	cardamom

ARRHYTHMIA — *Cardiovascular (pg. 205)*

lavender	ylang ylang	basil	rosemary	melissa

ARTERIOSCLEROSIS — *Cardiovascular (pg. 205)*

black pepper	lemongrass	cinnamon	juniper berry	protective blend

ARTHRITIC PAIN — *Skeletal (pg. 229), Pain & Inflammation (pg. 224)*

soothing blend	copaiba	turmeric	frankincense	black pepper

ARTHRITIS (REACTIVE) — *Immune & Lymphatic (pg. 215), Pain & Inflammation (pg. 224), Autoimmune (pg. 201), Skeletal (pg. 229)*

soothing blend	lemongrass	protective blend	massage blend	wintergreen

ASTHMA — *Respiratory (pg. 228), Allergies (pg. 199), Digestive & Intestinal (pg. 209)*

respiration blend	eucalyptus	rosemary	peppermint	cardamom

ATAXIA — *Brain (pg. 203), Muscular (pg. 221)*

frankincense	sandalwood	helichrysum	marjoram	cellular c. blend

ATHEROSCLEROSIS — *Cardiovascular (pg. 205)*

marjoram	lemongrass	metabolic blend	cinnamon	protective blend

ATHLETE'S FOOT

Athletes (pg. 200), Candida (pg. 204), Integumentary (pg. 216)

melaleuca	*cinnamon*	*oregano*	*skin clearing blend*	*arborvitae*

AUDITORY PROCESSING DISORDER

Brain (pg. 203), Nervous (pg. 222)

helichrysum	*basil*	*reassuring blend*	*Douglas fir*	*cellular c. blend*

AUTISM / ASPERGER'S

Brain (pg. 203), Mood & Behavior (pg. 220), Nervous (pg. 222)

clary sage	*restful blend*	*grounding blend*	*detoxification blend*	*frankincense*

AUTOIMMUNE DISORDER

Autoimmune (pg. 201)

cellular c. blend	*turmeric*	*lemongrass*	*detoxification blend*	*thyme*

AUTOINTOXICATION

Detoxification (pg. 208), Weight (pg. 233)

detoxification blend	*cilantro*	*clove*	*geranium*	*thyme*

AVOIDANT RESTRICTIVE FOOD INTAKE DISORDER

Eating Disorders (pg. 210)

metabolic blend	*patchouli*	*inspiring blend*	*renewing blend*	*bergamot*

BACK MUSCLE FATIGUE

Muscular (pg. 221)

massage blend	*soothing blend*	*ginger*	*wintergreen*	*marjoram*

BACK PAIN

Pain & Inflammation (pg. 224), Skeletal (pg. 229), Muscular (pg. 221)

soothing blend	*copaiba*	*wintergreen*	*Siberian fir*	*frankincense*

BACK STIFFNESS

Pain & Inflammation (pg. 224), Muscular (pg. 283), Skeletal (pg. 229)

massage blend	peppermint	soothing blend	Siberian fir	tension blend
topical	topical, internal	topical	topical	topical

BACTERIA

Immune & Lymphatic (pg. 215)

melaleuca	oregano	cinnamon	cleansing blend	cilantro
internal, topical	internal, topical	internal, topical	topical, aromatic	topical, internal

BAGS UNDER THE EYES

Integumentary (pg. 216), Sleep (pg. 230)

lime	anti-aging blend	juniper berry	cedarwood	Roman chamomile
internal, topical	topical	internal, topical	topical	topical, internal

BALANCE PROBLEMS

Brain (pg. 203), Cardiovascular (pg. 205), Immune & Lymphatic (pg. 215)

rosemary	cedarwood	frankincense	ylang ylang	Douglas fir
topical, aromatic, internal	topical, aromatic	topical, aromatic	topical, aromatic	topical, aromatic

BALDNESS

Integumentary (pg. 216), Men's Health (pg. 219)

cellular c. blend	ylang ylang	rosemary	thyme	clary sage
topical	topical	topical	topical	topical

BASAL CELL CARCINOMA

Cellular Health (pg. 206), Integumentary (pg. 216)

cellular c. blend	frankincense	sandalwood	detoxification blend	melissa
internal, topical	topical, internal	topical, internal	internal, topical	internal, topical

BED BUGS

First Aid (pg. 213)

repellent blend	arborvitae	eucalyptus	Siberian fir	peppermint
aromatic, topical	aromatic, topical	aromatic, topical	aromatic, topical	aromatic, topical

BED SORES

Integumentary (pg. 216)

lavender	myrrh	geranium	frankincense	cypress
topical	topical	topical	topical	topical

BED-WETTING

Children (pg. 207), Urinary (pg. 232), Mood & Behavior (pg. 220)

cypress | juniper berry | cinnamon | copaiba | reassuring blend

BEE STING

First Aid (pg. 213)

cleansing blend | lavender | Roman chamomile | clove | basil

BELL'S PALSY

Nervous (pg. 222), Immune & Lymphatic (pg. 215), Muscular (pg. 221)

frankincense | basil | thyme | protective blend | helichrysum

BENIGN PROSTATIC HYPERPLASIA

Cellular Health (pg. 206), Men's Health (pg. 219)

clary sage | thyme | cellular c. blend | juniper berry | sandalwood

BINGE EATING DISORDER (BED)

Eating Disorders (pg. 210), Digestive & Intestinal (pg. 209), Weight (pg. 233)

metabolic blend | cinnamon | joyful blend | comforting blend | cedarwood

BIPOLAR DISORDER

Limbic (pg. 218)

melissa | joyful blend | reassuring blend | restful blend | bergamot

BLADDER CONTROL

Urinary (pg. 232), Mood & Behavior (pg. 220)

renewing blend | thyme | rosemary | coriander | spearmint

BLADDER INFECTION (CYSTITIS)

Urinary (pg. 232), Candida (pg. 204)

lemongrass | wintergreen | oregano | thyme | lemon

BLEEDING

Cardiovascular (pg. 205), First Aid (pg. 213)

helichrysum	yarrow	geranium	lavender	frankincense
topical, internal	topical, internal	topical, internal	topical, internal	topical, internal

BLISTERS FROM SUN

Integumentary (pg. 216)

lavender	myrrh	anti-aging blend	helichrysum	sandalwood
topical	topical	topical	topical	topical

BLISTERS ON FEET

Integumentary (pg. 216)

myrrh	frankincense	patchouli	lavender	eucalyptus
topical	topical	topical	topical	topical

BLOATING

Digestive & Intestinal (pg. 209)

peppermint	ginger	digestion blend	fennel	metabolic blend
internal, topical	internal, topical	internal, topical	internal, topical	internal, topical

BLOOD CLOT

Cardiovascular (pg. 205)

coriander	cellular c. blend	fennel	helichrysum	massage blend
topical	topical	topical	topical	topical

BLOOD PRESSURE (HIGH) / HYPERTENSION

Cardiovascular (pg. 205), Urinary (pg. 232)

marjoram	ylang ylang	helichrysum	petitgrain	clove
internal, topical	topical	internal, topical	topical, internal	topical

BLOOD PRESSURE (LOW) / HYPOTENSION

Cardiovascular (pg. 205), Endocrine (pg. 211)

thyme	cellular c. blend	basil	rosemary	lime
topical, internal, aromatic	topical, internal	topical, internal, aromatic	topical, internal, aromatic	topical, internal, aromatic

BLOOD SUGAR (HIGH) HYPERGLYCEMIA

Blood Sugar (pg. 202), Endocrine (pg. 211)

coriander	cinnamon	cassia	metabolic blend	fennel
internal, topical	internal, topical	internal, topical	internal, topical	internal, topical

BLOOD SUGAR (LOW) HYPOGLYCEMIA

Blood Sugar (pg. 202), Endocrine (pg. 211)

cassia	lavender	detoxification blend	cypress	juniper berry

BLOOD TOXICITY

Cardiovascular (pg. 205), Detoxification (pg. 208)

geranium	detoxification blend	turmeric	cellular c. blend	frankincense

BODY DYSMORPHIC DISORDER

Brain (pg. 203), Limbic (pg. 218), Mood & Behavior (pg. 220)

clove	frankincense	arborvitae	cellular c. blend	rosemary

BODY MYOSITIS

Muscular (pg. 221), Pain & Inflammation (pg. 224)

marjoram	lemongrass	massage blend	cypress	wintergreen

BODY ODOR

Detoxification (pg. 208)

petitgrain	cilantro	cleansing blend	detoxification blend	arborvitae

BOILS

Integumentary (pg. 216)

myrrh	anti-aging blend	melaleuca	cleansing blend	lavender

BONE PAIN

Skeletal (pg. 229), Pain & Inflammation (pg. 224)

soothing blend	helichrysum	wintergreen	Siberian fir	birch

BONE SPURS

Skeletal (pg. 229)

cypress	eucalyptus	basil	lemongrass	wintergreen

BRAIN FOG

Brain (pg. 203), Focus & Concentration (pg. 214)

peppermint	encouraging blend	rosemary	lemon	Douglas fir
topical, aromatic	topical, aromatic	topical	topical, aromatic	topical, aromatic

BRAIN INJURY

Brain (pg. 203)

frankincense	grounding blend	cellular c. blend	renewing blend	bergamot
topical, internal, aromatic	topical, aromatic	topical, aromatic, internal	topical, aromatic	topical, aromatic

BREASTFEEDING (MILK SUPPLY)

Pregnancy, Labor & Nursing (pg. 226)

clary sage	women's m. blend	basil	fennel	geranium
topical, internal	topical	topical, internal	topical, internal	topical, internal

BREATHING PROBLEMS

Respiratory (pg. 228)

respiration blend	eucalyptus	Douglas fir	cardamom	peppermint
topical	topical	topical	topical, internal	topical, internal

BRITTLE NAILS

Integumentary (pg. 216)

myrrh	lemon	frankincense	grapefruit	eucalyptus
topical	topical	topical	topical	topical

BROKEN BONE

Skeletal (pg. 229)

Siberian fir	birch	helichrysum	soothing blend	wintergreen
topical	topical	topical, internal	topical	topical

BROKEN CAPILLARIES

Cardiovascular (pg. 205)

cypress	geranium	helichrysum	yarrow	lavender
topical	internal, topical	internal, topical	internal, topical	internal, topical

BROKEN HEART SYNDROME

Cardiovascular (pg. 205), Mood & Behavior (pg. 220), Emotional (pg. 236)

comforting blend	ylang ylang	geranium	lime	clary sage
aromatic, topical	aromatic, topical, internal	aromatic, topical, internal	aromatic, topical, internal	aromatic, topical, internal

BRONCHITIS — *Respiratory (pg. 228), Immune & Lymphatic (pg. 215)*

respiration blend	eucalyptus	cardamom	thyme	protective blend

BRUISE — *Cardiovascular (pg. 205), Integumentary (pg. 216), First Aid (pg. 213)*

Siberian fir	Roman chamomile	geranium	helichrysum	soothing blend

BRUISED MUSCLES — *Muscular (pg. 221)*

soothing blend	helichrysum	birch	massage blend	Siberian fir

BUERGER'S DISEASE — *Cardiovascular (pg. 205)*

clary sage	arborvitae	cypress	lemongrass	cinnamon

BULIMIA — *Eating Disorders (pg. 210), Addictions (pg. 198)*

melissa	cinnamon	grapefruit	renewing blend	patchouli

BUNIONS — *Skeletal (pg. 229)*

eucalyptus	cypress	ginger	wintergreen	basil

BURNS — *Integumentary (pg. 216), First Aid (pg. 213)*

lavender	peppermint	anti-aging blend	myrrh	helichrysum

BURSITIS — *Skeletal (pg. 229)*

soothing blend	birch	wintergreen	Siberian fir	cypress

CALCIFIED SPINE

Skeletal (pg. 229)

birch	*cellular c. blend*	*lemongrass*	*soothing blend*	*wintergreen*

CALLUSES

Integumentary (pg. 216)

Roman chamomile	*cypress*	*skin clearing blend*	*Siberian fir*	*oregano*

CANCER (BLADDER)

Cellular Health (pg. 206)

frankincense	*cellular c. blend*	*lemongrass*	*rosemary*	*cinnamon*

CANCER (BLOOD)

Cellular Health (pg. 206)

frankincense	*cellular c. blend*	*turmeric*	*hellichrysum*	*Siberian fir*

CANCER (BONE)

Cellular Health (pg. 206)

frankincense	*cellular c. blend*	*helichrysum*	*lemongrass & turmeric*	*Siberian fir*

CANCER (BRAIN)

Cellular Health (pg. 206)

arborvitae	*cellular c. blend*	*clove*	*frankincense*	*thyme*

CANCER (BREAST)

Cellular Health (pg. 206)

frankincense	*thyme*	*grapefruit*	*cellular c. blend*	*eucalyptus*

CANCER (CERVICAL)

Cellular Health (pg. 206)

frankincense	*cellular c. blend*	*Siberian fir*	*tangerine*	*sandalwood*

CANCER (COLON)
Cellular Health (pg. 206)

geranium	*detoxification blend*	*rosemary*	*turmeric*	*cellular c. blend*

CANCER (FOLLICULAR THYROID)
Cellular Health (pg. 206)

rosemary	*clary sage*	*frankincense*	*tangerine*	*sandalwood*

CANCER (HURTHLE CELL THYROID)
Cellular Health (pg. 206)

melissa	*frankincense*	*cellular c. blend*	*clary sage*	*thyme*

CANCER (LIVER)
Cellular Health (pg. 206)

detoxification blend	*turmeric*	*tangerine*	*cellular c. blend*	*clove*

CANCER (LUNG)
Cellular Health (pg. 206)

frankincense	*respiration blend*	*cellular c. blend*	*rosemary*	*thyme*

CANCER (LYMPH)
Cellular Health (pg. 206)

lemongrass	*frankincense*	*cellular c. blend*	*tangerine*	*turmeric*

CANCER (MOUTH)
Cellular Health (pg. 206)

myrrh	*turmeric*	*cellular c. blend*	*frankincense*	*black pepper*

CANCER (OVARIAN)
Cellular Health (pg. 206)

frankincense	*tangerine*	*detoxification blend*	*grapefruit*	*cellular c. blend*

CANCER (PANCREATIC)

Cellular Health (pg. 206)

turmeric	*cellular c. blend*	*cinnamon*	*detoxification blend*	*frankincense*
internal, topical	internal, topical	internal, topical	internal, topical	internal, topical

CANCER (PROSTATE)

Cellular Health (pg. 206)

thyme	*detoxification blend*	*oregano*	*turmeric*	*cellular c. blend*
internal	internal, topical	internal	internal, topical	internal, topical

CANCER (SKIN)

Cellular Health (pg. 206)

anti-aging blend	*sandalwood*	*turmeric*	*tangerine*	*frankincense*
topical	topical	topical, internal	topical, internal	topical, internal

CANCER (THROAT)

Cellular Health (pg. 206)

frankincense	*cellular c. blend*	*thyme*	*lavender*	*cinnamon*
internal, topical, aromatic	internal, topical	internal, topical	topical, aromatic	internal, topical

CANCER (THYROID)

Cellular Health (pg. 206)

cellular c. blend	*turmeric*	*thyme*	*lemongrass*	*frankincense*
internal, topical	topical, internal	internal, topical	internal, topical	internal, topical

CANCER (TONGUE)

Cellular Health (pg. 206)

geranium	*cellular c. blend*	*turmeric*	*frankincense*	*detoxification blend*
internal, topical	internal, topical	internal, topical	internal, topical	internal, topical, aromatic

CANCER (UTERINE)

Cellular Health (pg. 206)

clary sage	*cellular c. blend*	*turmeric*	*frankincense*	*geranium*
internal, topical	internal, topical	internal, topical	internal, topical	internal, topical

CANDIDA

Candida (pg. 204)

thyme	*oregano*	*cellular c.*	*p. pepper & melaleuca*	*arborvitae*
internal, topical	internal, topical	topical, internal	internal, topical	topical

CANKER SORES — *Oral Health (pg. 223)*

protective blend · *myrrh* · *black pepper* · *melaleuca* · *birch*

CARDIOVASCULAR DISEASE — *Cardiovascular (pg. 205)*

massage blend · *black pepper* · *basil* · *cypress* · *tension blend*

CARPAL TUNNEL SYNDROME — *Nervous (pg. 222)*

soothing blend · *lemongrass* · *cypress* · *ginger* · *copaiba*

CARTILAGE INJURY — *Skeletal (pg. 229), Athletes (pg. 200)*

soothing blend · *lemongrass* · *helichrysum* · *birch* · *wintergreen*

CATARACTS — *Nervous (pg. 222)*

lemongrass · *clary sage* · *cardamom* · *anti-aging blend* · *black pepper*

CAVITIES — *Oral Health (pg. 223)*

clove · *protective blend* · *birch* · *wintergreen* · *helichrysum*

CELIAC DISEASE — *Autoimmune (pg. 201), Digestive & Intestinal (pg. 209)*

lemongrass · *digestion blend* · *cardamom* · *metabolic blend* · *detoxification blend*

CELLULITE — *Detoxification (pg. 208), Weight (pg. 233)*

eucalyptus · *grapefruit* · *metabolic blend* · *spikenard* · *lemongrass*

CHAPPED SKIN *Integumentary (pg. 216), Children (pg. 207)*

Roman chamomile	*petitgrain*	*sandalwood*	*anti-aging blend*	*myrrh*
topical	topical	topical	topical	topical

CHEMICAL IMBALANCE *Brain (pg. 203), Mood & Behavior (pg. 220)*

detoxification blend	*joyful blend*	*cilantro*	*cellular c. blend*	*melissa*
internal, topical	aromatic, topical	internal, topical	internal, topical	internal, topical, aromatic

CHEMICAL SENSITIVITY REACTION *Allergies (pg. 199)*

detoxification blend	*cilantro*	*cleansing blend*	*coriander*	*arborvitae*
internal, topical	internal, topical	topical, aromatic	internal, topical	topical, aromatic

CHEST INFECTION *Immune & Lymphatic (pg. 215)*

detoxification blend	*protective blend*	*respiration blend*	*eucalyptus*	*melaleuca*
internal, topical	internal, topical, aromatic	internal, topical	topical	topical, internal

CHEST PAIN *Cardiovascular (pg. 205), Stress (pg. 231), Respiratory (pg. 228), Pain & Inflammation (pg. 224)*

marjoram	*Douglas fir*	*massage blend*	*basil*	*protective blend*
internal, topical	topical	topical	internal, topical	internal, topical

CHICKEN POX *Immune & Lymphatic (pg. 215)*

melaleuca	*patchouli*	*blue tansy*	*protective blend*	*thyme*
internal, topical	internal, topical	topical	internal	internal, topical

CHIGGERS *Parasites (pg. 225), First Aid (pg. 213)*

lemongrass	*cleansing blend*	*repellent blend*	*lavender*	*clove*
topical	aromatic, topical	topical	topical	topical, internal

CHOLERA *Immune & Lymphatic (pg. 215)*

cinnamon	*rosemary*	*detoxification blend*	*respiration blend*	*melissa*
internal, topical, aromatic	internal, topical, aromatic	internal, topical, aromatic	topical, aromatic	topical, internal, aromatic

CHOLESTEROL (HIGH)				Cardiovascular (pg. 205)
metabolic blend	lemongrass	coriander	cinnamon	lemon

CHONDROMALACIA PATELLA				Skeletal (pg. 229)
massage blend	helichrysum	birch	Siberian fir	sandalwood

CHRONIC FATIGUE				Energy & Vitality (pg. 212), Limbic (pg. 218), Endocrine (pg. 211)
rosemary	inspiring blend	geranium	black pepper	basil

CHRONIC PAIN				Pain & Inflammation (pg. 224), Muscular (pg. 283), Skeletal (pg. 229), Sleep (pg. 230)
soothing blend	helichrysum	copaiba	wintergreen	peppermint

CIRCULATION (POOR)				Cardiovascular (pg. 205)
cypress	massage blend	geranium	cassia	peppermint

CIRRHOSIS				Digestive & Intestinal (pg. 209)
detoxification blend	geranium	myrrh	helichrysum	marjoram

CLOGGED PORES				Integumentary (pg. 216)
skin clearing blend	cedarwood	juniper berry	cellular c. blend	petitgrain

CLUB FOOT				Skeletal (pg. 229), Muscular (pg. 221)
basil	massage blend	wintergreen	marjoram	helichrysum

COLD (COMMON)

Immune & Lymphatic (pg. 215)

protective blend	*black pepper*	*respiration blend*	*thyme*	*yarrow*
topical, internal, aromatic	topical, internal	topical, aromatic	topical, internal, aromatic	topical, internal, aromatic

COLD BODY TEMPERATURE

Cardiovascular (pg. 205)

inspiring blend	*cypress*	*massage blend*	*wintergreen*	*eucalyptus*
topical	topical	topical	topical	topical

COLD HANDS / FEET / NOSE

Cardiovascular (pg. 205)

massage blend	*encouraging blend*	*cassia*	*cellular c. blend*	*inspiring blend*
topical	topical, aromatic	topical, internal	topical, internal	topical, aromatic

COLD SORES / FEVER BLISTERS

Oral Health (pg. 223), Immune & Lymphatic (pg. 215)

melaleuca	*melissa*	*arborvitae*	*protective blend*	*bergamot*
topical, internal	topical, internal	topical	topical, internal	topical, internal

COLIC

Children (pg. 207), Digestive & Intestinal (pg. 209)

digestion blend	*fennel*	*Roman chamomile*	*restful blend*	*ylang ylang*
topical, internal	topical, internal	topical	topical	topical

COLITIS

Digestive & Intestinal (pg. 209)

cardamom	*digestion blend*	*peppermint*	*copaiba*	*ginger*
internal, topical	internal, topical	internal, topical	topical, internal	topical, internal

COMA

Brain (pg. 203), Blood Sugar (pg. 202)

frankincense	*spikenard*	*vetiver*	*ginger*	*cedarwood*
topical, aromatic, internal	topical, aromatic, internal	topical, aromatic	topical, aromatic, internal	topical, aromatic

CONCENTRATION (POOR)

Focus & Concentration (pg. 214), Brain (pg. 203)

focus blend	*vetiver & lavender*	*reassuring blend*	*cedarwood*	*encouraging blend*
topical, aromatic	topical, aromatic	topical, aromatic	topical, aromatic	topical, aromatic

CONCUSSION — Athletes (pg. 200), Brain (pg. 203)

frankincense · sandalwood · cedarwood · clove · petitgrain

CONFIDENCE (LACK OF) — Mood & Behavior (pg. 220)

bergamot · encouraging blend · patchouli · jasmine · inspiring blend

CONFUSION — Mood & Behavior (pg. 220), Focus & Concentration (pg. 214)

peppermint · frankincense · rosemary · Douglas fir · encouraging blend

CONGENITAL HEART DISEASE — Cardiovascular (pg. 205)

geranium · ylang ylang · helichrysum · basil · inspiring blend

CONGESTION — Respiratory (pg. 228), Allergies (pg. 199), Digestive & Intestinal (pg. 209)

lemon · peppermint · digestion blend · respiration blend · eucalyptus

CONJUNCTIVITIS (PINK EYE) — Immune & Lymphatic (pg. 215), Children (pg. 207)

lavender · melaleuca · Douglas fir · rosemary · melissa

CONNECTIVE TISSUE INJURY — Skeletal (pg. 229), Muscular (pg. 221)

lemongrass · helichrysum · wintergreen · Siberian fir · clove

CONSTIPATION — Digestive & Intestinal (pg. 209), Children (pg. 207)

digestion blend · marjoram · detoxification blend · ginger · peppermint

CONVALESCENCE

Brain (pg. 203)

petitgrain	frankincense	spikenard	comforting blend	myrrh
topical, internal	topical, internal	internal, topical	topical, aromatic	topical, internal

CONVULSIONS

Brain (pg. 203)

petitgrain	sandalwood	spikenard	frankincense	clary sage
topical, internal	topical	topical, internal	topical, internal	topical

CORNS

Integumentary (pg. 216)

arborvitae	lemon	cellular c. blend	clove	ylang ylang
topical	topical	topical	topical	topical

CORTISOL IMBALANCE

Endocrine (pg. 211)

geranium	basil	ylang ylang	neroli	petitgrain
internal, topical	internal, topical	internal, topical	topical	internal, topical

COUGH

Respiratory (pg. 228)

respiration blend	rosemary	digestion blend	cardamom	lemon
topical, aromatic	topical, aromatic, internal	internal, topical, aromatic	internal, topical, aromatic	internal, topical, aromatic

COUGH (WHOOPING)

Respiratory (pg. 228)

clary sage	Roman chamomile	respiration blend	blue tansy	cardamom
internal, topical, aromatic	topical, internal, aromatic	topical, aromatic	topical	topical, internal

CRADLE CAP

Children (pg. 207)

lavender	melaleuca	sandalwood	frankincense	anti-aging blend
topical	topical	topical	topical	topical

CRAMPS (INTESTINAL)

Digestive & Intestinal (pg. 209)

digestion blend	marjoram	ginger	turmeric	cardamom
topical, internal	topical, internal	topical, internal	internal, topical	topical, internal

CREUTZFELDT-JAKOB DISEASE *Brain (pg. 203), Immune & Lymphatic (pg. 215)*

spikenard	frankincense	cellular c. blend	clove	detoxification blend

CROHN'S DISEASE *Autoimmune (pg. 201), Digestive & Intestinal (pg. 209)*

digestion blend	copaiba	frankincense	peppermint	pink pepper

CROUP *Children (pg. 207), Respiratory (pg. 228)*

thyme	lemon	eucalyptus	marjoram	respiration blend

CRYING BABY *Children (pg. 207)*

restful blend	Roman chamomile	reassuring blend	lavender	comforting blend

CUSHING'S SYNDROME *Endocrine (pg. 211)*

clove	black pepper	cellular c. blend	geranium	invigorating blend

CUTS *First Aid (pg. 213), Integumentary (pg. 216)*

melaleuca	frankincense	geranium	lavender	helichrysum

CYST *Integumentary (pg. 216)*

Douglas fir	protective blend	lemon	thyme	cardamom

CYSTIC FIBROSIS *Respiratory (pg. 228)*

eucalyptus	lemon	Douglas fir	respiration blend	frankincense

DANDRUFF

Integumentary (pg. 216)

melaleuca	wintergreen	patchouli	rosemary	petitgrain
Topical	Topical	Topical	Topical	Topical

DEEP VEIN THROMBOSIS

Cardiovascular (pg. 205)

frankincense	cypress	wintergreen	cellular c. blend	detoxification blend
Topical, Internal	Topical	Topical	Topical, Internal	Topical, Internal

DEHYDRATION

First Aid (pg. 213), Athletes (pg. 200), Urinary (pg. 232)

wild orange	lemon	metabolic blend	detoxification blend	juniper berry
Internal, Topical	Internal, Topical	Internal, Topical	Internal, Topical	Internal, Topical

DEMENTIA

Brain (pg. 203)

cellular c. blend	frankincense	thyme	sandalwood	clove
Internal, Topical	Internal, Topical	Internal, Topical	Internal, Topical	Internal, Topical

DENGUE FEVER

Immune & Lymphatic (pg. 215)

eucalyptus	melissa	protective blend	thyme	melaleuca
Topical, Aromatic	Internal, Topical	Topical, Internal	Topical, Internal	Topical, Internal, Aromatic

DENTAL INFECTION

Oral Health (pg. 223)

clove	protective blend	myrrh	melaleuca	cinnamon
Topical, Internal	Topical, Internal	Topical, Internal	Topical, Internal	Topical, Internal

DEPRESSION

Mood & Behavior (pg. 220), Limbic (pg. 218), Pregnancy, Labor & Nursing (pg. 226)

melissa	joyful blend	uplifting blend	frankincense	neroli
Topical, Internal, Aromatic	Topical, Aromatic	Topical, Aromatic	Topical, Aromatic, Internal	Topical, Aromatic

DETERIORATING SPINE

Skeletal (pg. 229)

wintergreen	birch	cellular c. blend	helichrysum	Siberian fir
Topical	Topical	Topical, Internal	Topical	Topical

DETOXIFICATION — *Detoxification (pg. 208)*

detoxification blend	grapefruit	metabolic blend	clove	lemon

DIABETES — *Blood Sugar (pg. 202)*

cinnamon	coriander	metabolic blend	juniper berry	cassia

DIABETES (GESTATIONAL) — *Pregnancy, Labor & Nursing (pg. 226), Blood Sugar (pg. 202)*

cinnamon	detoxification blend	coriander	cassia	juniper berry

DIABETIC SORES — *Integumentary (pg. 216), Blood Sugar (pg. 202)*

myrrh	lavender	patchouli	sandalwood	geranium

DIAPER RASH — *Children (pg. 207)*

grounding blend	Roman chamomile	lavender	myrrh	patchouli

DIARRHEA — *Digestive & Intestinal (pg. 209)*

digestion blend	cardamom	black pepper	melaleuca	ginger

DIGESTIVE DISCOMFORT — *Digestive & Intestinal (pg. 209)*

digestion blend	cardamom	peppermint	ginger	fennel

DIPHTHERIA — *Respiratory (pg. 228), Immune & Lymphatic (pg. 215)*

eucalyptus	respiration blend	protective blend	digestion blend	thyme

DIVERTICULITIS

Digestive & Intestinal (pg. 209)

digestion blend	metabolic blend	basil	cellular c. blend	massage blend
Internal, Topical	Internal, Topical	Internal, Topical	Internal, Topical	Topical

DIZZINESS

Cardiovascular (pg. 205)

rosemary	peppermint	cedarwood	arborvitae	detoxification blend
Topical, Aromatic, Internal	Topical, Aromatic, Internal	Topical, Aromatic	Aromatic, Topical	Topical, Internal

DO QUERVAIN'S TENOSYNOVITIS

Muscular (pg. 221), Skeletal (pg. 229)

lemongrass	cypress	massage blend	soothing blend	birch
Topical	Topical	Topical	Topical	Topical

DOWN SYNDROME

Brain (pg. 203)

grounding blend	frankincense	melissa	cellular c. blend	cedarwood
Aromatic, Topical	Topical, Internal	Internal, Topical	Topical, Internal	Topical, Aromatic

DRUG ADDICTION

Addictions (pg. 198)

detoxification blend	restful blend	peppermint	encouraging blend	cleansing blend
Internal, Topical	Aromatic, Topical	Internal, Topical, Aromatic	Aromatic, Topical	Topical

DRY SKIN

Integumentary (pg. 216)

myrrh	petitgrain	patchouli	sandalwood	anti-aging blend
Topical	Topical	Topical	Topical	Topical

DUMPING SYNDROME

Digestive & Intestinal (pg. 209)

fennel	ginger	frankincense	helichrysum	digestion blend
Internal, Topical	Internal, Topical	Internal, Topical	Internal, Topical	Internal, Topical

DYSENTERY

Digestive & Intestinal (pg. 209)

peppermint	ginger	protective blend	myrrh	spearmint
Internal, Topical	Internal, Topical	Internal, Topical	Topical, Internal	Topical, Internal

DYSMENORRHEA — *Women's Health (pg. 234)*

women's m. blend	*clary sage*	*massage blend*	*marjoram*	*thyme*

DYSPHAGIA — *Digestive & Intestinal (pg. 209), Oral Health (pg. 223)*

peppermint	*arborvitae*	*black pepper*	*restful blend*	*lavender*

E. COLI — *Immune & Lymphatic (pg. 215)*

cinnamon	*protective blend*	*cassia*	*oregano*	*clove*

EAR INFECTION — *Respiratory (pg. 228)*

protective blend	*thyme*	*basil*	*melaleuca*	*helichrysum*

EAR MITES — *Parasites (pg. 225), Respiratory (pg. 228)*

cleansing blend	*cedarwood*	*thyme*	*clove*	*melaleuca*

EARACHE — *Respiratory (pg. 307)*

melaleuca	*helichrysum*	*basil*	*lavender*	*rosemary*

ECZEMA — *Integumentary (pg. 216), Candida (pg. 204)*

cedarwood	*neroli*	*skin clearing blend*	*yarrow*	*myrrh*

EDEMA — *Cardiovascular (pg. 205), Pregnancy, Labor & Nursing (pg. 226)*

cypress	*lemon*	*lemongrass*	*juniper berry*	*grapefruit*

EHRLICHIOSIS

Immune & Lymphatic (pg. 215)

oregano	*protective blend*	*thyme*	*detoxification blend*	*rosemary*
internal, topical	internal, topical	internal, topical	internal, topical	topical, internal

ELECTRICAL HYPERSENSITIVITY SYNDROME

Limbic (pg. 218)

vetiver	*frankincense*	*detoxification blend*	*grounding blend*	*cleansing blend*
topical, internal, aromatic	internal, topical, aromatic	internal, topical	topical	topical

EMOTIONAL TRAUMA

Mood & Behavior (pg. 220), Limbic (pg. 218)

frankincense	*melissa*	*helichrysum*	*renewing blend*	*reassuring blend*
topical	topical	topical	topical	topical

EMPHYSEMA

Respiratory (pg. 228)

Douglas fir	*respiration blend*	*eucalyptus*	*black pepper*	*frankincense*
topical, aromatic	topical, aromatic	topical, aromatic	topical, internal	topical, internal

ENDOMETRIOSIS

Women's Health (pg. 234)

clary sage	*thyme*	*geranium*	*cellular c. blend*	*rosemary*
topical, internal	topical, internal	topical, internal	internal, topical	topical, internal

ENDURANCE (POOR)

Energy & Vitality (pg. 212)

peppermint	*basil*	*metabolic blend*	*respiration blend*	*encouraging blend*
topical, internal, aromatic	topical, aromatic	internal, topical	topical, aromatic	aromatic, topical

ENERGY (LACK OF)

Energy & Vitality (pg. 212)

peppermint	*pink pepper*	*invigorating blend*	*encouraging blend*	*inspiring blend*
topical, internal, aromatic	topical, aromatic, internal	topical, aromatic	aromatic, topical	aromatic, topical

ENGORGEMENT

Pregnancy, Labor & Nursing (pg. 226)

peppermint	*massage blend*	*soothing blend*	*tension blend*	*ginger*
topical	topical	topical	topical	topical

EPILEPSY

Brain (pg. 203)

spikenard	frankincense	clary sage	cedarwood	cellular c. blend

EPSTEIN-BARR (EBV)

Immune & Lymphatic (pg. 215), Energy & Vitality (pg. 212)

detoxification blend	rosemary	basil	ylang ylang	inspiring blend

ERECTILE DYSFUNCTION

Men's Health (pg. 219), Intimacy (pg. 217)

cypress	detoxification blend	sandalwood	ylang ylang	inspiring blend

ESOPHAGITIS

Digestive & Intestinal (pg. 209)

peppermint	digestion blend	frankincense	fennel	coriander

ESTROGEN IMBALANCE

Women's Health (pg. 234), Detoxification (pg. 208)

grapefruit	thyme	women's m. blend	detoxification blend	basil

EXHAUSTION

Energy & Vitality (pg. 212), Endocrine (pg. 211), Athletes (pg. 200)

encouraging blend	inspiring blend	basil	invigorating blend	wild orange

EYES (DRY)

Respiratory (pg. 228)

sandalwood	frankincense	lavender	wild orange	detoxification blend

EYES (SWOLLEN)

Nervous (pg. 222)

anti-aging blend	cypress	lemon	frankincense	detoxification blend

FAINTING

Cardiovascular (pg. 205), First Aid (pg. 213)

peppermint	rosemary	invigorating blend	sandalwood	frankincense
topical, aromatic	topical	topical, aromatic	internal, topical, aromatic	internal, topical

FATIGUE

Energy & Vitality (pg. 212)

encouraging blend	inspiring blend	basil	invigorating blend	wild orange
topical, aromatic	topical, aromatic	topical, internal	topical, aromatic	topical, internal, aromatic

FEAR

Mood & Behavior (pg. 220)

reassuring blend	encouraging blend	comforting blend	bergamot	inspiring blend
aromatic, topical	aromatic, topical	aromatic, topical	aromatic, topical	aromatic, topical

FEAR OF FLYING

Mood & Behavior (pg. 220)

reassuring blend	grounding blend	restful blend	cassia	protecting blend
aromatic, topical	aromatic, topical	aromatic, topical	topical, aromatic, internal	topical, aromatic, internal

FEVER

Immune & Lymphatic (pg. 215)

peppermint	spearmint	eucalyptus	pink pepper	yarrow
topical, internal	topical	topical	topical	topical, internal

FIBRILLATION

Cardiovascular (pg. 205)

ylang ylang	black pepper	lime	marjoram	massage blend
topical, internal	topical	topical, internal	topical	topical

FIBROCYSTIC BREASTS

Endocrine (pg. 211), Women's Health (pg. 234)

frankincense	thyme	grapefruit	sandalwood	geranium
topical, internal	topical, internal	topical, internal	topical, internal	topical, internal

FIBROIDS (UTERINE)

Immune & Lymphatic (pg. 215), Women's Health (pg. 234)

sandalwood	frankincense	thyme	lemongrass	cellular c. blend
topical, internal	topical, internal	topical, internal	topical, internal	topical, internal

FIBROMYALGIA	*Muscular (pg. 221)*

cellular c. blend	*massage blend*	*ginger*	*soothing blend*	*oregano*

FIFTH'S DISEASE (HUMAN PARVOVIRUS B19)	*Children (pg. 207), Immune & Lymphatic (pg. 215)*

protective blend	*cellular c. blend*	*black pepper*	*oregano*	*cleansing blend*

FLEAS	*Parasites (pg. 225), First Aid (pg. 213)*

eucalyptus	*arborvitae*	*cedarwood*	*repellent blend*	*lavender*

FLOATERS	*Nervous (pg. 222)*

anti-aging blend	*sandalwood*	*frankincense*	*lavender*	*cellular c. blend*

FLU (INFLUENZA)	*Immune & Lymphatic (pg. 215), Children (pg. 207)*

protective blend	*thyme*	*melissa*	*yarrow*	*oregano*

FOCAL BRAIN DYSFUNCTION (BRAIN INJURY)	*Brain (pg. 203), Limbic (pg. 218)*

helichrysum	*frankincense*	*cellular c. blend*	*sandalwood*	*grounding blend*

FOCUS	*Focus & Concentration (pg. 214)*

focus blend	*frankincense & wild orange*	*vetiver & lavender*	*cedarwood*	*peppermint*

FOOD ADDICTION	*Addictions (pg. 198), Weight (pg. 233)*

grapefruit	*metabolic blend*	*peppermint*	*ginger*	*basil*

FOOD POISONING

Digestive & Intestinal (pg. 209), Parasites (pg. 225), Immune & Lymphatic (pg. 215)

digestion blend	detoxification blend	melaleuca	clove	lemon
topical, internal	internal, topical	internal, topical	internal, topical	topical, internal

FRAGILE HAIR

Integumentary (pg. 216)

rosemary	cellular c. blend	thyme	cedarwood	geranium
topical	topical, internal	topical	topical	topical

FROZEN SHOULDER

Skeletal (pg. 229), Muscular (pg. 221)

soothing blend	wintergreen	Siberian fir	lemongrass	birch
topical	topical	topical	topical	topical

FUNGAL SKIN INFECTION

Integumentary (pg. 216), Candida (pg. 204)

melaleuca	skin clearing blend	cellular c. blend	turmeric	myrrh
topical, internal	topical	topical, internal	topical	topical, internal

FUNGUS

Immune & Lymphatic (pg. 215), Candida (pg. 204), Integumentary (pg. 216)

oregano	cellular c. blend	cinnamon	melaleuca	arborvitae
topical, internal, aromatic	topical, internal, aromatic	topical, internal, aromatic	topical, internal, aromatic	topical, aromatic

GALLBLADDER INFECTION

Digestive & Intestinal (pg. 209)

detoxification blend	metabolic blend	protective blend	cinnamon	rosemary
topical, internal	topical, internal	topical, internal	topical, internal	topical, internal

GALLBLADDER ISSUES

Digestive & Intestinal (pg. 209), Detoxification (pg. 208)

geranium	grapefruit	detoxification blend	metabolic blend	turmeric
topical, internal	internal, topical	topical, internal	internal, topical	internal, topical

GALLSTONES

Digestive & Intestinal (pg. 209)

geranium	juniper berry	lemon & grapefruit	detoxification blend	wintergreen
internal, topical	internal, topical	internal, topical	internal, topical	topical

GANGLION CYST

Skeletal (pg. 229), Cellular Health (pg. 206)

cellular c. blend	frankincense	lemongrass	lemon	basil

GANGRENE

Cardiovascular (pg. 205), Immune & Lymphatic (pg. 215), Blood Sugar (pg. 202)

cypress	massage blend	metabolic blend	cinnamon	myrrh

GAS (FLATULENCE)

Digestive & Intestinal (pg. 209)

ginger	digestion blend	black pepper	coriander	peppermint

GASTRITIS

Digestive & Intestinal (pg. 209)

peppermint	digestion blend	coriander	petitgrain	fennel

GASTROENTERITIS / STOMACH FLU

Digestive & Intestinal (pg. 209), Children (pg. 207)

cardamom	peppermint	ginger	digestion blend	thyme

GASTROESOPHAGEAL REFLUX DISEASE (GERD)

Digestive & Intestinal (pg. 209)

detoxification blend	lemon	digestion blend	ginger	coriander

GENITAL WARTS

Immune & Lymphatic (pg. 215), Women's Health (pg. 234), Men's Health (pg. 219), Integumentary (pg. 216)

frankincense	arborvitae	thyme	melissa	geranium

GIARDIA

Parasites (pg. 225), Digestive & Intestinal (pg. 209)

thyme	oregano	rosemary	cardamom	protective blend

GINGIVITIS

Oral Health (pg. 223)

myrrh	clove	protective blend	frankincense	black pepper

GLAUCOMA

Nervous (pg. 222)

lemongrass	cellular c. blend	frankincense	black pepper	anti-aging blend

GOITER

Autoimmune (pg. 201), Endocrine (pg. 211)

myrrh	lemongrass	cellular c. blend	frankincense	patchouli

GOUT

Skeletal (pg. 229), Pain & Inflammation (pg. 224)

copaiba	lemongrass	turmeric	wintergreen	soothing blend

GRAVE'S DISEASE

Endocrine (pg. 211)

myrrh	frankincense	lemongrass	rosemary	detoxification blend

GRIEF

Mood & Behavior (pg. 220)

comforting blend	joyful blend	reassuring blend	restful blend	magnolia

GROWING PAINS

Children (pg. 207), Muscular (pg. 221)

cypress	massage blend	Siberian fir	marjoram	soothing blend

GULF WAR SYNDROME

Limbic (pg. 218), Nervous (pg. 222), Pain & Inflammation (pg. 224), Digestive & Intestinal (pg. 209)

frankincense	clove	thyme	patchouli	inspiring blend

GUM DISEASE — *Oral Health (pg. 223)*

protective blend	*myrrh*	*clove*	*melaleuca*	*cinnamon*

GUMS (BLEEDING) — *Oral Health (pg. 223)*

myrrh	*helichrysum*	*frankincense*	*clove*	*melaleuca*

H. PYLORI — *Immune & Lymphatic (pg. 215), Digestive & Intestinal (pg. 209)*

cassia or cinnamon	*black pepper*	*oregano*	*ginger*	*thyme*

HAIR (DRY) — *Integumentary (pg. 216)*

sandalwood	*patchouli*	*geranium*	*copaiba*	*rosemary*

HAIR (OILY) — *Integumentary (pg. 216)*

petitgrain	*lemon*	*arborvitae*	*rosemary*	*joyful blend*

HAIR LOSS — *Integumentary (pg. 216)*

clary sage	*cellular c. blend*	*thyme*	*rosemary*	*arborvitae*

HALITOSIS — *Oral Health (pg. 223)*

peppermint	*spearmint*	*metabolic blend*	*protective blend*	*cardamom*

HALLUCINATIONS — *Limbic (pg. 218)*

grounding blend	*frankincense*	*cedarwood*	*reassuring blend*	*restful blend*

HAND, FOOT & MOUTH DISEASE

Immune & Lymphatic (pg. 215)

thyme	cinnamon	melaleuca	melissa	wintergreen
internal, topical	internal, topical	internal, topical	internal, topical	topical

HANGOVER

Addictions (pg. 198), Detoxification (pg. 208)

detoxification blend	metabolic blend	lemon	geranium	tension blend
internal, topical	internal	internal	internal	topical

HARDENING OF ARTERIES

Cardiovascular (pg. 205)

black pepper	lemongrass	cinnamon	grapefruit	lemon
internal, topical	internal, topical	internal, topical	internal, topical	internal, topical

HASHIMOTO'S DISEASE

Endocrine (pg. 211), Autoimmune (pg. 201)

cellular c. blend	myrrh	detoxification blend	lemongrass	peppermint
internal, topical	topical, internal	topical, internal	topical, internal	topical, internal, aromatic

HAY FEVER

Allergies (pg. 199), Respiratory (pg. 228)

lavender	lemon	respiration blend	cleansing blend	cilantro
internal, topical, aromatic	internal, topical, aromatic	aromatic, topical	topical, aromatic	internal, topical, aromatic

HEAD LICE

Parasites (pg. 225), Integumentary (pg. 216), First Aid (pg. 213)

cinnamon	arborvitae	eucalyptus	rosemary	thyme
topical	topical	topical	topical	topical, internal

HEADACHE

Pain & Inflammation (pg. 224), Nervous (pg. 222), Muscular (pg. 283), Women's Health (pg. 234)

tension blend	peppermint	Siberian fir	copaiba	frankincense
topical	topical, aromatic	internal, topical	topical, internal	topical, aromatic

HEADACHE (SINUS)

Pain & Inflammation (pg. 224), Respiratory (pg. 228)

basil	cedarwood	rosemary	peppermint	eucalyptus
topical, aromatic, internal	topical, aromatic	topical, internal, aromatic	topical, aromatic, internal	topical, aromatic

HEADACHE (TENSION) — *Muscular (pg. 221), Pain & Inflammation (pg. 224)*

tension blend · *peppermint* · *soothing blend* · *massage blend* · *frankincense*

HEADACHES (BLOOD SUGAR) — *Blood Sugar (pg. 202)*

cassia · *detoxification blend* · *metabolic blend* · *protective blend* · *coriander*

HEARING IN A TUNNEL — *Respiratory (pg. 228)*

helichrysum · *lemon* · *clary sage* · *cardamom* · *cleansing blend*

HEARING PROBLEMS — *Respiratory (pg. 228)*

helichrysum · *basil* · *lemon* · *frankincense* · *patchouli*

HEART FAILURE — *Cardiovascular (pg. 205)*

lemongrass · *marjoram* · *ylang ylang* · *thyme* · *rosemary*

HEART ISSUES — *Cardiovascular (pg. 205)*

ylang ylang · *cypress* · *marjoram* · *geranium* · *massage blend*

HEARTBURN — *Digestive & Intestinal (pg. 209), Pregnancy, Labor & Nursing (pg. 301)*

digestion blend · *peppermint* · *cardamom* · *black pepper* · *detoxification blend*

HEAT EXHAUSTION — *First Aid (pg. 213), Athletes (pg. 200)*

peppermint · *lime* · *lemon* · *petitgrain* · *eucalyptus*

HEATSTROKE

First Aid (pg. 213), Athletes (pg. 200)

peppermint	petitgrain + lemon	black pepper	detoxification blend	spearmint
topical, internal	internal, topical	topical, internal	internal, topical	topical, internal

HEAVY METAL TOXICITY

Detoxification (pg. 208)

cilantro	detoxification blend	arborvitae	thyme	black pepper
internal	internal, topical	internal	internal, topical	internal, topical

HEMATOMA

Cardiovascular (pg. 205)

cypress	helichrysum	geranium	massage blend	lemongrass
topical	topical	topical	topical	topical

HEMOCHROMATOSIS

Digestive & Intestinal (pg. 209)

detoxification blend	cellular c. blend	arborvitae	geranium	helichrysum
internal, topical	internal, topical	topical	internal	topical, internal

HEMOPHILIA

Cardiovascular (pg. 205)

geranium	helichrysum	lavender	Roman chamomile	vetiver
internal, topical	topical	internal, topical	topical	topical

HEMORRHAGE

Cardiovascular (pg. 205)

helichrysum	yarrow	geranium	wild orange	lavender
topical, internal	topical	topical, internal	topical, internal	topical, internal

HEMORRHOIDS

Cardiovascular (pg. 205), Digestive & Intestinal (pg. 209), Integumentary (pg. 216), Pregnancy, Labor & Nursing (pg. 226)

cypress	helichrysum	yarrow	myrrh	grounding blend
topical	topical, internal	internal	topical	topical

HEPATITIS

Digestive & Intestinal (pg. 209), Immune & Lymphatic (pg. 215)

detoxification blend	melaleuca	myrrh	helichrysum	geranium
internal, topical	internal, topical	internal, topical	internal, topical	topical, internal

HERNIA, HIATAL — Digestive & Intestinal (pg. 209)

basil	arborvitae	helichrysum	ginger	juniper berry

HERNIA, INCISIONAL — Integumentary (pg. 216)

helichrysum	geranium	basil	arborvitae	cypress

HERNIATED DISC — Skeletal (pg. 229), Pain & Inflammation (pg. 224)

birch	wintergreen	Siberian fir	eucalyptus	massage blend

HERPES SIMPLEX — Immune & Lymphatic (pg. 215), Autoimmune (pg. 201)

melissa	melaleuca	peppermint	protective blend	basil

HICCUPS — Respiratory (pg. 228), Children (pg. 207)

detoxification blend	peppermint	restful blend	arborvitae	basil

HIVES — Allergies (pg. 199), Children (pg. 207)

Roman chamomile	rosemary	frankincense	peppermint	lavender

HOARSE VOICE — Oral Health (pg. 223)

lemon or lime	ginger	frankincense or myrrh	peppermint	cinnamon

HODGKIN'S DISEASE — Cellular Health (pg. 206)

cardamom	cellular c. blend	lemongrass	myrrh	frankincense

HORMONAL IMBALANCE (FEMALE)

Women's Health (pg. 234), Detoxification (pg. 208)

women's m. blend	geranium	clary sage	women's blend	ylang ylang
topical	internal, topical	topical, internal	topical, aromatic	topical, aromatic

HORMONE IMBALANCE (MALE)

Men's Health (pg. 219), Detoxification (pg. 208)

sandalwood	juniper berry	rosemary	grounding blend	ylang ylang
topical, aromatic	internal, topical	topical, internal, aromatic	topical, aromatic	aromatic, topical, internal

HOT FLASHES

Women's Health (pg. 234)

women's m. blend	peppermint	eucalyptus	clary sage	tension blend
topical	topical, internal	topical	topical, internal	topical

HUNTINGTON'S DISEASE

Brain (pg. 203), Nervous (pg. 222), Autoimmune (pg. 201)

cellular c. blend	frankincense	clove	thyme	rosemary
internal, topical	internal, topical	internal, topical	internal, topical	internal, topical

HYDROCEPHALUS

Brain (pg. 203)

spikenard	frankincense	basil	juniper berry	sandalwood
topical, internal	topical, internal, aromatic	topical, internal	topical, internal, aromatic	topical, internal

HYPERACTIVITY

Focus & Concentration (pg. 214), Children (pg. 207), Energy & Vitality (pg. 212)

vetiver	lavender	focus blend	petitgrain	reassuring blend
topical, aromatic	aromatic, topical	topical, aromatic	topical, aromatic, internal	aromatic, topical

HYPERPNEA

Respiratory (pg. 228)

peppermint	cardamom	patchouli	respiration blend	ylang ylang
topical, internal, aromatic	topical, internal, aromatic	topical, aromatic	topical, aromatic	topical, aromatic

HYPERSOMNIA

Sleep (pg. 230), Focus & Concentration (pg. 214), Energy & Vitality (pg. 212)

detoxification blend	peppermint	lemon	Douglas fir	eucalyptus
topical, internal	topical, internal, aromatic	topical, internal, aromatic	topical, aromatic	topical, aromatic

HYPERTHYROIDISM — *Endocrine (pg. 211)*

cellular c. blend	rosemary	myrrh	ginger	juniper berry

HYPOGLYCEMIA — *Blood Sugar (pg. 202)*

cassia	lavender	detoxification blend	cypress	juniper berry

HYPOTHERMIA — *First Aid (pg. 213)*

cinnamon	clove	ginger	wintergreen	massage blend

HYPOTHYROIDISM — *Endocrine (pg. 211)*

clove	peppermint	blue tansy	lemongrass	myrrh

HYSTERIA — *Mood & Behavior (pg. 220), Women's Health (pg. 234)*

Roman chamomile	melissa	neroli	grounding blend	petitgrain

ICHTHYOSIS VULGARIS — *Integumentary (pg. 216)*

frankincense	geranium	sandalwood	patchouli	cedarwood

IMPETIGO — *Integumentary (pg. 216)*

geranium	oregano	vetiver	cleansing blend	lavender

IMPOTENCE — *Men's Health (pg. 219), Intimacy (pg. 217)*

cypress	inspiring blend	ylang ylang	ginger	massage blend

INCONTINENCE

Urinary (pg. 232), Men's Health (pg. 219), Women's Health (pg. 234)

cypress	basil	thyme	massage blend	lemongrass
topical	topical, internal	topical, internal	topical	topical, internal

INDIGESTION

Digestive & Intestinal (pg. 209), Weight (pg. 233), Detoxification (pg. 208)

digestion blend	peppermint	black pepper	metabolic blend	cardamom
internal, topical	internal, topical	internal, topical	internal, topical	internal, topical

INFANT REFLUX

Children (pg. 207)

fennel	digestion blend	peppermint	lavender	Roman chamomile
topical, internal	topical	internal, topical	topical	topical, internal

INFECTED WOUNDS

Integumentary (pg. 216), First Aid (pg. 213)

melaleuca	cleansing blend	frankincense	copaiba	protective blend
topical	topical	topical	topical	topical

INFECTION

Immune & Lymphatic (pg. 215)

oregano	protective blend	cinnamon	thyme	melissa
topical, internal	topical, internal, aromatic	topical, internal	topical, internal	internal, topical, aromatic

INFERTILITY

Men's Health (pg. 219), Women's Health (pg. 234)

thyme	clary sage	spikenard	ylang ylang	grapefruit & detoxification
internal, topical	topical, internal	internal, topical	topical, internal	internal, topical

INFLAMMATION

Pain & Inflammation (pg. 224)

frankincense	peppermint	massage & soothing b.	cellular c. blend	turmeric
topical, internal	topical, internal	topical	topical, internal	topical

INFLAMMATORY BOWEL DISEASE

Digestive & Intestinal (pg. 209), Autoimmune (pg. 201)

digestion blend	ginger	marjoram	copaiba	basil
internal, topical	internal, topical	topical, internal	internal, topical	topical, internal

INFLAMMATORY MYOPATHIES

Muscular (pg. 221), Autoimmune (pg. 201)

lemongrass · *massage blend* · *soothing blend* · *Siberian fir* · *wintergreen*

INGROWN TOENAIL

Integumentary (pg. 216)

arborvitae · *cellular c. blend or lemongrass* · *eucalyptus* · *myrrh* · *melaleuca*

INJURY (MUSCLE, BONE, CONNECTIVE TISSUE, BRUISING (SKIN))

First Aid (pg. 213), Muscular (pg. 283), Skeletal (pg. 229)

helichrysum · *soothing blend* · *lemongrass* · *wintergreen* · *copaiba*

INSECT BITES

First Aid (pg. 213), Allergies (pg. 199)

lavender · *cleansing blend* · *Roman chamomile* · *blue tansy* · *basil*

INSECT REPELLENT

First Aid (pg. 213)

repellent blend · *cedarwood* · *eucalyptus* · *arborvitae* · *cleansing*

INSOMNIA

Sleep (pg. 230)

restful blend · *lavender* · *petitgrain* · *Roman chamomile* · *vetiver*

INSULIN IMBALANCES

Blood Sugar (pg. 202)

coriander · *cinnamon* · *metabolic blend* · *cassia* · *geranium*

INSULIN RESISTANCE

Blood Sugar (pg. 202)

lavender · *metabolic blend* · *ginger* · *detoxification blend* · *oregano*

IRIS INFLAMMATION

Nervous (pg. 222)

juniper berry	*helichrysum*	*patchouli*	*frankincense*	*arborvitae*

IRRITABLE BOWEL SYNDROME

Digestive & Intestinal (pg. 209)

digestion blend	*ginger*	*peppermint*	*cardamom*	*detoxification blend*

ITCHING

Integumentary (pg. 216), Allergies (pg. 199)

Roman chamomile	*detoxification blend*	*blue tansy*	*lavender*	*myrrh*

JAUNDICE

Digestive & Intestinal (pg. 209)

frankincense	*lemon*	*geranium*	*detoxification blend*	*juniper berry*

JET LAG

Sleep (pg. 230), Energy & Vitality (pg. 212), First Aid (pg. 213)

peppermint	*restful blend*	*rosemary*	*invigorating blend*	*metabolic blend*

JOCK ITCH

Men's Health (pg. 219), Candida (pg. 204)

melaleuca	*myrrh*	*cedarwood*	*thyme*	*patchouli*

JOINT PAIN

Skeletal (pg. 229), Pain & Inflammation (pg. 224)

turmeric & copaiba	*soothing blend*	*Siberian fir*	*pink & black pepper*	*wintergreen*

KIDNEY INFECTION

Urinary (pg. 232)

lemongrass	*juniper berry*	*thyme*	*cinnamon*	*cardamom*

KIDNEY STONES
Urinary (pg. 232)

lemon	eucalyptus	wintergreen	lemongrass	birch

KIDNEYS
Urinary (pg. 232)

juniper berry	lemon	cellular c. blend	rosemary	eucalyptus

KNEE CARTILAGE INJURY
Skeletal (pg. 229)

lemongrass	wintergreen or birch	helichrysum	copaiba	Siberian fir

LABOR
Pregnancy, Labor & Nursing (pg. 226)

ylang ylang	women's m. blend	restful blend	clary sage	frankincense

LACTATION PROBLEMS
Pregnancy, Labor & Nursing (pg. 226)

fennel	basil	clary sage	ylang ylang	soothing blend

LACTOSE INTOLERANCE
Digestive & Intestinal (pg. 209), Allergies (pg. 199)

cardamom	digestion blend	ginger	metabolic blend	coriander

LARYNGITIS
Respiratory (pg. 228), Oral Health (pg. 223)

lemon	protective blend	myrrh	sandalwood	frankincense

LEAD POISONING
Detoxification (pg. 208)

cilantro	detoxification blend	helichrysum	rosemary	frankincense

LEAKY GUT SYNDROME

Digestive & Intestinal (pg. 209)

myrrh	*lemongrass*	*cardamom*	*dill*	*digestion blend*

LEARNING DIFFICULTIES

Focus & Concentration (pg. 214), Brain (pg. 203)

vetiver & lavender	*grounding blend*	*focus blend*	*peppermint*	*cedarwood*

LEG CRAMPS

Muscular (pg. 221), Pregnancy, Labor & Nursing (pg. 226)

massage blend	*marjoram*	*basil*	*soothing blend*	*Douglas fir*

LEGG-CALVE-PERTHES DISEASE

Children (pg. 207), Skeletal (pg. 229)

massage blend	*lemongrass*	*peppermint*	*cypress*	*cassia*

LEGIONNAIRES' DISEASE

Respiratory (pg. 228), Immune & Lymphatic (pg. 215)

melaleuca	*black pepper*	*thyme*	*eucalyptus*	*birch*

LEUKEMIA

Cellular Health (pg. 206)

frankincense	*cellular c. blend*	*lemongrass*	*detoxification blend*	*geranium*

LIBIDO (LOW) FOR MEN

Intimacy (pg. 217), Men's Health (pg. 219)

ylang ylang	*patchouli*	*inspiring blend*	*cinnamon*	*neroli*

LIBIDO (LOW) FOR WOMEN

Intimacy (pg. 217), Women's Health (pg. 234)

ylang ylang	*women's blend*	*jasmine*	*inspiring blend*	*neroli*

LICHEN NITIDUS

Integumentary (pg. 216)

cleansing blend	patchouli	cellular c. blend	detoxification blend	geranium

LIPOMA

Cellular Health (pg. 206)

cellular c. blend	clove	arborvitae	frankincense	eucalyptus

LIPS (DRY)

Integumentary (pg. 216)

myrrh	geranium	sandalwood	lavender	frankincense

LISTERIA INFECTION

Immune & Lymphatic (pg. 215)

cinnamon	oregano	protective blend	melaleuca	cleansing blend

LIVER DISEASE

Digestive & Intestinal (pg. 209)

detoxification blend	geranium	copaiba	turmeric	lemon & grapefruit

LOCKJAW (TETANUS)

Immune & Lymphatic (pg. 215), Nervous (pg. 222), Muscular (pg. 221)

soothing blend	cypress	rosemary	clove	eucalyptus

LONG QT SYNDROME

Cardiovascular (pg. 205)

ylang ylang	melissa	rosemary	protective blend	detoxification blend

LOU GEHRIG'S DISEASE (ALS)

Nervous (pg. 222), Autoimmune (pg. 201), Muscular (pg. 221)

melissa	cellular c. blend	frankincense	copaiba	cypress

LUMBAGO

Muscular (pg. 221), Skeletal (pg. 229)

soothing blend	massage blend	frankincense	Siberian fir	cardamom
topical	topical	topical	topical	topical

LUPUS

Autoimmune (pg. 201)

cellular c. blend	detoxification blend	clove	copaiba	massage blend
internal, topical	internal, topical	internal, topical	internal, topical	topical

LYME DISEASE

Immune & Lymphatic (pg. 215)

oregano	thyme	clove	cassia	frankincense
internal	topical, internal	topical, internal	internal, topical	internal, topical, aromatic

LYMPHOMA

Cellular Health (pg. 206)

cellular c. blend	frankincense	thyme	clove	wild orange
internal, topical	internal, topical	internal, topical	internal, topical	internal, topical, aromatic

MACULAR DEGENERATION

Nervous (pg. 222)

anti-aging blend	helichrysum	coriander	juniper berry	frankincense
topical	topical, internal	topical, internal	internal, topical	topical, internal

MALABSORPTION SYNDROME

Digestive & Intestinal (pg. 209)

sandalwood	fennel	invigorating blend	digestion blend	ginger
topical, internal	topical, internal	topical	topical, internal	topical, internal

MALARIA

Immune & Lymphatic (pg. 215), Parasites (pg. 225)

thyme	cinnamon	detoxification blend	eucalyptus	repellent blend (to avoid)
internal, topical	internal, topical	topical, internal	topical, aromatic	topical, aromatic

MARFAN SYNDROME (CONNECTIVE TISSUE DISORDER)

Cardiovascular (pg. 205), Skeletal (pg. 229), Muscular (pg. 221)

lemongrass	helichrysum	massage blend	Siberian fir	basil
topical, internal	topical, internal	topical	topical	topical, internal

QUICK REFERENCE

MASTITIS — *Pregnancy, Labor & Nursing (pg. 226)*

lavender	cellular c. blend	thyme	peppermint	oregano

MEASLES — *Immune & Lymphatic (pg. 215)*

protective blend	yarrow	melaleuca	coriander	blue tansy

MELANOMA
PIGMENT-CONTAINING CELLS — *Cellular Health (pg. 206)*

frankincense	sandalwood	cellular c. blend	anti-aging blend	lemongrass

MELATONIN IMBALANCES / INSUFFICIENCIES — *Endocrine (pg. 211), Sleep (pg. 230)*

vetiver	lavender	restful blend	petitgrain	Roman chamomile

MEMORY (POOR) — *Focus & Concentration (pg. 214), Brain (pg. 203)*

peppermint	rosemary	frankincense	thyme	sandalwood

MENIERE'S DISEASE — *Women's Health (pg. 234)*

helichrysum	frankincense	juniper berry	ginger	basil

MENINGITIS — *Immune & Lymphatic (pg. 215)*

melaleuca	protective blend	clove	cellular c. blend	basil

MENOPAUSE — *Women's Health (pg. 234)*

women's m. blend	detoxification blend	inspiring blend	thyme	clary sage

MENORRHAGIA (EXCESSIVE MENSTRUAL BLEEDING)

Women's Health (pg. 234)

women's m. blend	*helichrysum*	*detoxification blend*	*geranium*	*cellular c. blend*
Topical	Topical, Internal	Internal, Topical	Topical, Internal	Internal

MENSTRUAL CYCLE (IRREGULAR OR SCANTY)

Women's Health (pg. 234)

women's m. blend	*geranium*	*rosemary*	*yarrow*	*detoxification blend*
Topical	Internal, Topical	Internal, Topical	Internal, Topical	Internal, Topical

MENSTRUAL PAIN / CRAMPS

Women's Health (pg. 234)

women's m. blend	*clary sage*	*marjoram*	*tension blend*	*copaiba*
Topical	Topical, Internal	Topical, Internal	Topical	Topical, Internal

MENTAL FATIGUE

Brain (pg. 203)

rosemary	*basil*	*peppermint*	*encouraging blend*	*invigorating blend*
Aromatic, Topical, Internal	Aromatic, Topical, Internal	Aromatic, Topical, Internal	Aromatic, Topical	Aromatic, Topical

MESENTERIC LYMPHADENTIS

Immune & Lymphatic (pg. 215)

cleansing blend	*cellular c. blend*	*basil*	*cardamom*	*detoxification blend*
Topical	Internal, Topical	Topical, Internal	Internal, Topical	Internal, Topical

MESOTHELIOMA

Cellular Health (pg. 206)

detoxification blend	*basil*	*black pepper*	*cellular c. blend*	*skin clearing blend*
Internal, Topical	Topical, Internal	Topical, Internal, Aromatic	Internal, Topical	Topical, Aromatic

METABOLIC MUSCLE DISORDERS

Muscular (pg. 221)

basil	*cypress*	*ginger*	*peppermint*	*cassia*
Internal, Topical	Topical	Internal, Topical	Internal, Topical	Internal, Topical

METABOLISM (LOW)

Weight (pg. 233)

grapefruit	*metabolic blend*	*cinnamon*	*cellular c. blend*	*clove*
Internal	Internal	Internal	Internal	Internal

MIGRAINE

Pain & Inflammation (pg. 224), Muscular (pg. 221)

peppermint · *copaiba* · *frankincense* · *lavender* · *tension blend*

MILK SUPPLY (LOW)

Pregnancy, Labor & Nursing (pg. 226)

fennel · *dill* · *cardamom* · *lavender* · *clary sage*

MISCARRIAGE (PREVENTION)

Pregnancy, Labor & Nursing (pg. 226)

comforting blend · *patchouli* · *anti-aging blend* · *thyme* · *cellular c. blend*

MISCARRIAGE (RECOVERY)

Pregnancy, Labor & Nursing (pg. 226)

detoxification blend · *cellular c. blend* · *clary sage* · *comforting blend* · *women's m. blend*

MITRAL VALVE PROLAPSE

Cardiovascular (pg. 205)

helichrysum · *marjoram* · *tension blend* · *massage blend* · *cellular c. blend*

MOLD / MILDEW

Allergies (pg. 199), Detoxification (pg. 208)

melaleuca · *oregano* · *thyme* · *cleansing blend* · *arborvitae*

MOLES

Integumentary (pg. 216)

frankincense · *skin clearing blend* · *cellular c. blend* · *detoxification blend* · *juniper berry*

MONONUCLEOSIS

Immune & Lymphatic (pg. 215)

melissa · *thyme* · *cinnamon* · *eucalyptus* · *protective blend*

MOOD SWINGS

Mood & Behavior (pg. 220), Candida (pg. 204), Women's Health (pg. 234)

grounding blend	*uplifting blend*	*renewing blend*	*neroli*	*joyful blend*

MORNING SICKNESS

Pregnancy, Labor & Nursing (pg. 226)

ginger	*basil*	*peppermint*	*cassia*	*digestion blend*

MOSQUITO BITES

First Aid (pg. 213)

cleansing blend	*lavender*	*Roman chamomile*	*blue tansy*	*melaleuca*

MOTION SICKNESS

Digestive & Intestinal (pg. 209), First Aid (pg. 213)

ginger	*basil*	*peppermint*	*cassia*	*digestion blend*

MOUTH ULCERS

Oral Health (pg. 223), Autoimmune (pg. 201)

clove	*protective blend*	*cinnamon*	*melaleuca*	*myrrh*

MRSA

Immune & Lymphatic (pg. 215)

cinnamon	*oregano*	*thyme*	*protective blend*	*clove*

MUCUS

Respiratory (pg. 228), Digestive & Intestinal (pg. 209), Allergies (pg. 199)

lemon	*digestion blend*	*fennel*	*eucalyptus*	*cardamom*

MULTIPLE CHEMICAL SENSITIVITY REACTION

Allergies (pg. 199)

cilantro	*detoxification blend*	*Douglas fir*	*geranium*	*coriander*

MULTIPLE SCLEROSIS	*Nervous (pg. 222), Autoimmune (pg. 201)*

detoxification blend · *frankincense* · *sandalwood* · *cellular c. blend* · *cypress*

MUMPS	*Immune & Lymphatic (pg. 215)*

protective blend · *cellular c. blend* · *detoxification blend* · *yarrow* · *lavender*

MUSCLE PAIN	*Muscular (pg. 221), Athletes (pg. 200), Pain & Inflammation (pg. 224),*

massage blend · *soothing blend* · *Siberian fir* · *marjoram* · *peppermint*

MUSCLE PULLS, STRAINS	*Muscular (pg. 221), Athletes (pg. 200), Pain & Inflammation (pg. 224)*

copaiba · *lemongrass* · *soothing blend* · *marjoram* · *massage blend*

MUSCLE SPASMS	*Muscular (pg. 221), Athletes (pg. 200), Sleep (pg. 230)*

massage blend · *marjoram* · *copaiba* · *Roman chamomile* · *basil*

MUSCLE STIFFNESS	*Muscular (pg. 221), Athletes (pg. 200)*

tension blend · *massage blend* · *Siberian fir* · *ginger* · *marjoram*

MUSCLE WEAKNESS / LACK OF GROWTH	*Muscular (pg. 221), Athletes (pg. 200)*

wintergreen or birch · *helichrysum* · *ginger* · *lemongrass* · *Siberian fir*

MUSCULAR CRAMPS / CHARLEY HORSE	*Athletes (pg. 200), Muscular (pg. 221)*

marjoram · *massage blend* · *soothing blend* · *tension blend* · *Siberian fir*

MUSCULAR DYSTROPHY

Muscular (pg. 221)

lemongrass	frankincense	tension blend	cellular c. blend	marjoram
topical, internal	topical, internal	topical	topical, internal	topical, internal

MYASTHENIA GRAVIS

Muscular (pg. 221), Autoimmune (pg. 201)

helichrysum	ginger	lemongrass	cypress	cellular c. blend
internal, topical	internal, topical	internal, topical	topical	internal, topical

MYELOFIBROSIS

Skeletal (pg. 229)

helichrysum	detoxification blend	ginger	frankincense	Siberian fir
topical, internal	topical, internal	topical, internal	topical, internal	topical

MYOTONIC DYSTROPHY

Muscular (pg. 221)

Douglas fir	cellular c. blend	helichrysum	Siberian fir	lemongrass
topical	internal, topical	internal, topical	topical	internal, topical

NAILS

Integumentary (pg. 216)

sandalwood	lemon	wild orange	arborvitae	women's m. blend
topical	topical	topical	topical	topical

NARCOLEPSY

Sleep (pg. 230), Brain (pg. 203)

sandalwood	comforting blend	encouraging blend	wild orange	focus blend
internal, topical, aromatic	topical, aromatic	topical, aromatic	aromatic, internal, topical	topical, aromatic

NASAL POLYP

Respiratory (pg. 228), Cellular Health (pg. 206)

rosemary	melissa	respiration blend	protective blend	sandalwood
topical, aromatic	topical	topical, aromatic	topical, aromatic	topical, aromatic

NAUSEA

Digestive & Intestinal (pg. 209)

digestion blend	ginger	peppermint	pink pepper	detoxification blend
internal, topical, aromatic	internal, topical, aromatic	internal, topical, aromatic	internal, topical, aromatic	internal, topical, aromatic

NECK PAIN

Muscular (pg. 221)

soothing blend	*tension blend*	*copaiba*	*massage blend*	*wintergreen*

NERVES, WEAKENED / DAMAGED

Nervous (pg. 222)

vetiver	*helichrysum*	*petitgrain*	*copaiba*	*patchouli*

NERVOUS FATIGUE

Energy & Vitality (pg. 212), Stress (pg. 231)

peppermint	*invigorating blend*	*basil*	*yarrow*	*detoxification blend*

NERVOUSNESS

Mood & Behavior (pg. 220), Stress (pg. 231)

reassuring blend	*grounding blend*	*restful blend*	*encouraging blend*	*petitgrain*

NEURALGIA

Nervous (pg. 222), Muscular (pg. 283), Pain & Inflammation (pg. 224)

helichrysum	*tension blend*	*wintergreen*	*clove or neroli*	*Douglas fir*

NEURITIS

Nervous (pg. 222)

cardamom	*patchouli*	*helichrysum*	*ginger*	*soothing blend*

NEUROMUSCULAR DISORDERS

Muscular (pg. 221)

marjoram	*arborvitae*	*ginger*	*basil*	*massage blend*

NEUROPATHY

Nervous (pg. 222)

cypress	*massage blend*	*soothing blend*	*basil*	*wintergreen*

NIGHT EATING SYNDROME (NES)

Eating Disorders (pg. 210), Weight (pg. 233)

cinnamon	metabolic blend	grapefruit	ginger	peppermint
internal, aromatic	internal, aromatic	internal, aromatic, topical	internal, aromatic, topical	internal, aromatic, topical

NIGHT SWEATS

Women's Health (pg. 234)

peppermint	cellular c. blend	women's m. blend	women's blend	spearmint
topical, internal	internal, topical	topical	topical	topical, internal

NIGHTTIME URINATION

Children (pg. 207)

rosemary	cypress	juniper berry	metabolic blend	thyme
internal	topical	internal, topical	internal	internal

NIPPLES, SORE

Pregnancy, Labor & Nursing (pg. 226)

myrrh	melaleuca	sandalwood	frankincense	geranium
topical	topical	topical	topical	topical

NOSE (DRY)

Respiratory (pg. 228)

myrrh	wild orange	geranium	sandalwood	lavender
topical	topical	topical	topical	topical

NOSEBLEED

Respiratory (pg. 228)

helichrysum	geranium	myrrh	protective blend	lavender
topical	topical	topical	topical	topical

NUMBNESS

Nervous (pg. 222), Cardiovascular (pg. 205)

peppermint	cypress	tension blend	ginger	basil
topical	topical	topical	topical	topical

OBESITY

Weight (pg. 233), Endocrine (pg. 211), Stress (pg. 231), Blood Sugar (pg. 202)

metabolic blend	cinnamon	grapefruit	ginger	bergamot
internal, topical	internal, topical	internal, topical	internal, topical	aromatic, topical, internal

QUICK REFERENCE

OBSESSIVE-COMPULSIVE DISORDER (OCD) — *Mood & Behavior (pg. 220), Limbic (pg. 218)*

cedarwood · restful blend · renewing blend · focus blend · ylang ylang

OCULAR ROSACEA — *Nervous (pg. 222), Integumentary (pg. 216), Respiratory (pg. 228)*

myrrh · frankincense · detoxification blend · anti-aging blend · sandalwood

OLFACTORY LOSS — *Respiratory (pg. 228), Allergies (pg. 199)*

helichrysum · peppermint · basil · cellular c. blend · arborvitae

OPPOSITIONAL DEFIANT DISORDER — *Mood & Behavior (pg. 220)*

reassuring blend · tension blend · renewing blend · cardamom · uplifting blend

ORAL HEALTH — *Oral Health (pg. 223)*

myrrh · clove · peppermint · protective blend · turmeric

OSGOOD-SCHLATTER DISEASE — *Skeletal (pg. 229)*

cypress · ginger · lemongrass · massage blend · birch

OSTEOARTHRITIS — *Skeletal (pg. 229), Pain & Inflammation (pg. 224)*

black pepper · frankincense · Siberian fir · soothing blend · wintergreen

OSTEOMYELITIS — *Immune & Lymphatic (pg. 215), Skeletal (pg. 229)*

thyme · melissa · lemongrass · wintergreen · clove

OSTEOPOROSIS

Skeletal (pg. 229)

Siberian fir	clove	wintergreen	geranium	lemongrass
Topical	Internal, Topical	Topical	Topical, Internal	Topical, Internal

OVARIAN CYST

Women's Health (pg. 234), Cellular Health (pg. 206)

detoxification blend	cellular c. blend	clary sage	basil	rosemary
Internal, Topical	Internal, Topical	Internal, Topical	Internal, Topical, Aromatic	Topical, Internal

OVER-EXERCISED

Muscular (pg. 221), Athletes (pg. 200)

peppermint	soothing blend	massage blend	marjoram	eucalyptus
Topical	Topical	Topical	Topical	Topical

OVERACTIVE BLADDER (OAB)

Urinary (pg. 232)

cypress	thyme	juniper berry	ginger	detoxification blend
Topical	Internal, Topical	Topical, Internal	Topical, Internal	Topical, Internal

OVEREATING

Weight (pg. 233), Stress (pg. 231), Eating Disorders (pg. 210)

metabolic blend	coriander	grapefruit	cinnamon	ginger
Topical, Internal	Topical, Internal, Aromatic	Topical, Internal, Aromatic	Topical, Internal, Aromatic	Topical, Internal

OVERHEATED

First Aid (pg. 213), Athletes (pg. 200)

peppermint	eucalyptus	tension blend	petitgrain	spearmint
Topical, Internal	Topical	Topical	Topical, Internal	Topical

OVERWHELMED

Mood & Behavior (pg. 220)

reassuring blend	focus blend	rosemary	restful blend	lemon
Aromatic, Topical	Aromatic, Topical	Aromatic, Topical	Aromatic, Topical	Aromatic, Topical

OVULATION (LACK OF)

Women's Health (pg. 234), Blood Sugar (pg. 202)

basil	women's m. blend	thyme	ylang ylang	clary sage
Topical, Internal	Topical, Aromatic	Topical, Internal	Topical, Aromatic	Topical

PAGET'S DISEASE

Skeletal (pg. 229), Cellular Health (pg. 206)

cellular c. blend	myrrh	wintergreen	clove	women's m. blend

PAIN

Pain & Inflammation (pg. 224)

turmeric or copaiba	peppermint	soothing blend	helichrysum	wintergreen or birch

PALPITATIONS

Cardiovascular (pg. 205)

ylang ylang	petitgrain	lavender	neroli	rosemary

PANCREATITIS

Endocrine (pg. 211)

coriander	rosemary	geranium	cinnamon	detoxification blend

PANIC ATTACKS

Mood & Behavior (pg. 220)

petitgrain	restful blend	neroli	magnolia	grounding blend

PARALYSIS

Nervous (pg. 222), Muscular (pg. 283), Cardiovascular (pg. 205), Immune & Lymphatic (pg. 215), Autoimmune (pg. 201)

frankincense	cypress	melissa	ginger	cellular c. blend

PARASITES

Parasites (pg. 225), Detoxification (pg. 208), Digestive & Intestinal (pg. 209), Integumentary (pg. 216)

clove	oregano	thyme	turmeric	lemongrass

PARATHYROID DISORDER

Endocrine (pg. 211)

women's m. blend	detoxification blend	melissa	ginger	invigorating blend

PARKINSON'S DISEASE

Brain (pg. 203), Nervous (pg. 222), Muscular (pg. 283), Addictions (pg. 198)

frankincense	*detoxification blend*	*marjoram*	*melissa*	*cellular c. blend*

PELVIC PAIN SYNDROME

Women's Health (pg. 234), Digestive & Intestinal (pg. 209)

ginger	*geranium*	*thyme*	*copaiba*	*rosemary*

PERFORATED EAR DRUM

Respiratory (pg. 228)

basil	*ylang ylang*	*protective blend*	*arborvitae*	*patchouli*

PERICARDIAL DISEASE

Cardiovascular (pg. 205)

rosemary	*juniper berry*	*marjoram*	*lemongrass*	*detoxification blend*

PERIMENOPAUSE

Women's Health (pg. 234)

detoxification blend	*women's blend*	*cellular c. blend*	*clary sage*	*rosemary*

PERINEAL TEARING, LACK OF ELASTICITY

Pregnancy, Labor & Nursing (pg. 226)

geranium	*frankincense*	*sandalwood*	*Roman chamomile*	*lavender*

PERIODIC LIMB MOVEMENT DISORDER

Sleep (pg. 230)

massage blend	*tension blend*	*marjoram*	*basil*	*lavender*

PERNICIOUS ANEMIA

Autoimmune (pg. 201), Cardiovascular (pg. 205)

helichrysum	*geranium*	*detoxification blend*	*cinnamon*	*lemon*

PERSPIRATION (EXCESSIVE) — *Endocrine (pg. 211), Athletes (pg. 200), Urinary (pg. 232), Detoxification (pg. 208)*

coriander · geranium · petitgrain · detoxification blend · Douglas fir

PHANTOM PAINS — *Pain & Inflammation (pg. 224), Nervous (pg. 222)*

helichrysum · basil · frankincense · soothing blend · massage blend

PHLEBITIS — *Cardiovascular (pg. 205)*

cypress · helichrysum · detoxification blend · basil · lemongrass

PICA — *Eating Disorders (pg. 210), Children (pg. 207)*

multivitamin supplements · patchouli · cilantro · cinnamon · peppermint

PINKEYE — *Immune & Lymphatic (pg. 215), Children (pg. 207)*

frankincense · melaleuca · spikenard · lavender · clary sage

PINWORMS — *Parasites (pg. 225)*

clove · oregano · thyme · lemongrass · protective blend

PLANTAR FASCIITIS — *Skeletal (pg. 229), Muscular (pg. 221)*

copaiba · lemongrass · massage blend · wintergreen · Siberian fir

PLANTAR WARTS — *Integumentary (pg. 216)*

cinnamon · melissa · cleansing blend · oregano · frankincense

PLAQUE

Oral Health (pg. 223), Cardiovascular (pg. 205)

protective blend	clove	thyme	myrrh	lemon
topical	topical	topical	topical	topical

PLEURISY

Respiratory (pg. 228)

cinnamon	respiration blend	rosemary	eucalyptus	melissa
topical, internal, aromatic	topical, aromatic	topical, internal, aromatic	topical, aromatic	topical, aromatic

PNEUMONIA

Respiratory (pg. 228)

respiration blend	arborvitae	copaiba	Roman chamomile	eucalyptus
topical, aromatic	topical, aromatic	topical, internal, aromatic	topical, aromatic	topical, aromatic

POISON IVY

First Aid (pg. 213), Integumentary (pg. 216)

geranium	cleansing blend	Roman chamomile	lavender	frankincense
topical	topical	topical	topical, internal	topical

POLIO

Immune & Lymphatic (pg. 215), Nervous (pg. 222)

melissa	lemongrass	patchouli	spikenard	frankincense
internal, topical	topical, internal	topical, internal	topical, internal	topical, internal

POLYCYSTIC OVARY SYNDROME (PCOS)

Women's Health (pg. 234), Blood Sugar (pg. 202), Cellular Health (pg. 206)

thyme	basil	geranium	detoxification blend	cellular c. blend
topical, internal	topical, internal	topical, internal	internal, topical	topical, internal

POLYMYOSITIS

Muscular (pg. 221), Pain & Inflammation (pg. 224)

ginger	black pepper	grounding blend	soothing blend	cellular c. blend
topical, internal	topical, internal	topical	topical	topical, internal

POLYPS

Digestive & Intestinal (pg. 209), Cellular Health (pg. 206), Women's Health (pg. 234), Respiratory (pg. 228)

rosemary	ginger	peppermint	clove	lemongrass
topical, internal	internal, topical	internal, topical	topical, internal	topical, internal

PORPHYRIA — *Nervous (pg. 222), Integumentary (pg. 216), Detoxification (pg. 208)*

detoxification blend · *frankincense* · *lemongrass* · *geranium* · *cellular c. blend*

POST-TRAUMATIC STRESS DISORDER (PTSD) — *Limbic (pg. 218), Mood & Behavior (pg. 220)*

melissa · *Roman chamomile* · *helichrysum & vetiver* · *grounding blend* · *neroli*

POSTPARTUM DEPRESSION — *Pregnancy, Labor & Nursing (pg. 226)*

uplifting blend · *frankincense* · *clary sage* · *detoxification blend* · *joyful blend*

PRE-WORKOUT MUSCLE PREP — *Athletes (pg. 200)*

soothing blend · *peppermint* · *marjoram* · *wild orange* · *metabolic blend*

PRECOCIOUS PUBERTY — *Endocrine (pg. 211), Women's Health (pg. 234), Men's Health (pg. 219)*

detoxification blend · *frankincense* · *women's blend* · *women's m. blend* · *cellular c. blend*

PREECLAMPSIA — *Pregnancy, Labor & Nursing (pg. 226)*

marjoram · *frankincense* · *detoxification blend* · *massage blend* · *cypress*

PREGNANCY — *Pregnancy, Labor & Nursing (pg. 226), Women's Health (pg. 234)*

digestion blend · *lavender* · *geranium* · *ylang ylang* · *metabolic blend*

PREGNANCY (POST-TERM) — *Pregnancy, Labor & Nursing (pg. 226)*

myrrh · *clary sage* · *detoxification blend* · *basil* · *women's blend*

PREMENSTRUAL SYNDROME BETWEEN OVULATION & A PERIOD

Women's Health (pg. 234), Mood & Behavior (pg. 220)

women's m. blend	geranium	cellular c. blend	clary sage	women's blend
Topical	Internal, Topical	Internal, Topical	Internal, Topical	Topical

PRETERM LABOR

Pregnancy, Labor & Nursing (pg. 226)

marjoram	ylang ylang & wild orange	lavender & neroli	grounding blend	restful blend
Topical, Internal	Topical	Topical, Internal	Topical	Topical, Aromatic

PROSTATITIS

Men's Health (pg. 219), Cardiovascular (pg. 205)

rosemary	grounding blend	juniper berry	cellular c. blend	cypress
Topical, Internal	Topical	Topical, Internal	Internal	Topical

PSORIASIS

Integumentary (pg. 216), Digestive & Intestinal (pg. 209), Candida (pg. 204), Parasites (pg. 225)

detoxification blend	Roman chamomile	turmeric	copaiba	geranium
Internal	Topical, Internal	Topical, Internal	Internal, Topical	Topical, Internal

PURGING DISORDER

Eating Disorders (pg. 210)

melissa	cinnamon	grounding blend	patchouli	metabolic blend
Internal, Topical	Internal, Topical, Aromatic	Aromatic, Topical	Aromatic, Internal, Topical	Internal, Topical

PYORRHEA

Oral Health (pg. 223)

clove	myrrh	cedarwood	frankincense	protective blend
Topical	Topical, Internal	Topical	Topical, Internal	Topical, Aromatic

Q FEVER

Immune & Lymphatic (pg. 215)

oregano	protective blend	thyme	eucalyptus	arborvitae
Internal, Topical	Topical, Internal	Internal, Topical	Topical	Topical

RADIATION DAMAGE

Cellular Health (pg. 206), Detoxification (pg. 208)

peppermint	detoxification blend	patchouli	cilantro	geranium
Internal, Topical	Internal, Topical	Topical	Internal, Topical	Internal, Topical

RASHES — *Integumentary (pg. 216), Allergies (pg. 199), Autoimmune (pg. 201), Parasites (pg. 225)*

cedarwood	*detoxification blend*	*neroli*	*lavender*	*anti-aging blend*

RAYNAUD'S DISEASE — *Cardiovascular (pg. 205), Endocrine (pg. 211)*

black pepper	*cypress*	*massage blend*	*lemongrass*	*comforting blend*

REACTIVE ATTACHMENT DISORDER (RAD) — *Limbic (pg. 218), Mood & Behavior (pg. 220), Stress (pg. 231)*

frankincense	*grounding blend*	*renewing blend*	*comforting blend*	*reassuring blend*

REITER'S ARTHRITIS — *Immune & Lymphatic (pg. 215), Digestive & Intestinal (pg. 209), Skeletal (pg. 229)*

basil	*thyme*	*soothing blend*	*massage blend*	*renewing blend*

RENAL ARTERY STENOSIS — *Cardiovascular (pg. 205), Urinary (pg. 232)*

detoxification blend	*ylang ylang*	*lemon*	*invigorating blend*	*lemongrass*

RESPIRATORY ISSUES — *Respiratory (pg. 228)*

respiration blend	*cardamom*	*rosemary*	*arborvitae*	*eucalyptus*

RESTLESS LEG SYNDROME — *Cardiovascular (pg. 205), Sleep (pg. 230)*

massage blend	*soothing blend*	*tension blend*	*cypress*	*restful blend*

RESTLESSNESS — *Sleep (pg. 230), Energy & Vitality (pg. 212), Mood & Behavior (pg. 220)*

grounding blend	*lavender*	*reassuring blend*	*patchouli*	*restful blend*

RETINITIS PIGMENTOSA

Nervous (pg. 222)

patchouli	*helichrysum*	*juniper berry*	*cellular c. blend*	*cardamom*
topical, internal	topical, internal	internal, topical	internal	internal, topical

RHEUMATIC FEVER

Immune & Lymphatic (pg. 215), Pain & Inflammation (pg. 224)

oregano	*ginger*	*wintergreen*	*eucalyptus*	*thyme*
internal, topical	internal, topical	topical	topical, aromatic	topical, internal

RHEUMATISM

Muscular (pg. 221), Skeletal (pg. 229)

tumeric	*soothing blend*	*spikenard*	*lemongrass*	*Siberian fir*
topical	topical, internal	internal	topical, internal	topical, internal

RHEUMATOID ARTHRITIS

Skeletal (pg. 229), Pain & Inflammation (pg. 224), Autoimmune (pg. 201)

soothing blend	*frankincense*	*massage blend*	*Siberian fir*	*marjoram*
topical	internal, topical	topical	topical, aromatic	internal, topical

RHINITIS

Respiratory (pg. 228)

respiration blend	*protective blend*	*peppermint*	*eucalyptus*	*oregano*
topical, aromatic	internal, aromatic, topical	internal, topical, aromatic	topical, aromatic	internal, topical

RINGWORM

Integumentary (pg. 216), Immune & Lymphatic (pg. 215)

petitgrain	*skin clearing blend*	*melaleuca*	*cleansing blend*	*myrrh*
internal, topical	topical	topical, internal	topical, internal	topical

ROSACEA

Integumentary (pg. 216), Nervous (pg. 222), Parasites (pg. 225)

Roman chamomile	*sandalwood*	*helichrysum*	*myrrh*	*cellular c. blend*
topical, internal	topical, internal	internal, topical	topical, internal	topical, internal

ROSEOLA

Children (pg. 207), Immune & Lymphatic (pg. 215)

melissa	*melaleuca*	*protective blend*	*copaiba*	*myrrh*
topical, internal	topical, internal	topical, internal	topical, internal	topical, internal, aromatic

RSV (RESPIRATORY SYNCYTIAL VIRUS) — *Children (pg. 207), Respiratory (pg. 228)*

rosemary	eucalyptus	melissa	Siberian fir	respiration blend

RUBELLA — *Immune & Lymphatic (pg. 215)*

protective blend	melaleuca	lime	thyme	clove

RUMINATION DISORDER — *Eating Disorders (pg. 210)*

digestion blend	detoxification blend	grapefruit	grounding blend	peppermint

SCABIES — *Parasites (pg. 225), Integumentary (pg. 216)*

cleansing blend	peppermint	thyme	arborvitae	protective blend

SCARLET FEVER — *Children (pg. 207), Immune & Lymphatic (pg. 215)*

oregano	protective blend	melaleuca	sandalwood	thyme

SCARRING — *Integumentary (pg. 216)*

frankincense	helichrysum	lavender	sandalwood & neroli	anti-aging blend

SCHIZOPHRENIA — *Brain (pg. 203), Limbic (pg. 218), Mood & Behavior (pg. 220)*

frankincense	Roman chamomile	juniper berry	spikenard	patchouli

SCHMIDT'S SYNDROME — *Autoimmune (pg. 201), Endocrine (pg. 211), Nervous (pg. 222)*

detoxification blend	spikenard	encouraging blend	cardamom	protective blend

SCIATICA

Nervous (pg. 222), Pain & Inflammation (pg. 224), Athletes (pg. 200)

soothing blend	Douglas fir	frankincense	Siberian fir	basil
Topical	Topical	Topical	Topical	Topical

SCLERODERMA

Autoimmune (pg. 201), Integumentary (pg. 216), Skeletal (pg. 229), Muscular (pg. 221)

sandalwood	helichrysum	Douglas fir	ginger	coriander
Topical, Internal	Topical, Internal	Topical, Aromatic	Topical, Internal	Topical, Internal

SCOLIOSIS

Skeletal (pg. 229)

soothing blend	lemongrass	helichrysum	massage blend	wintergreen
Topical	Topical	Topical	Topical	Topical

SCURVY

Immune & Lymphatic (pg. 215), Energy & Vitality (pg. 212)

cypress	detoxification blend	lemon	helichrysum	ginger
Topical	Internal, Topical	Internal, Topical	Internal, Topical	Internal, Topical

SEASONAL AFFECTIVE DISORDER (SAD)

Mood & Behavior (pg. 220), Limbic (pg. 218)

uplifting blend	bergamot	encouraging blend	joyful blend	inspiring blend
Topical, Aromatic	Topical, Aromatic, Internal	Topical, Aromatic	Topical, Aromatic	Topical, Aromatic

SEBACEOUS CYST

Integumentary (pg. 216)

fennel	cedarwood	basil	black pepper	coriander
Internal	Topical, Internal	Topical, Internal	Topical, Internal	Topical, Internal

SEIZURES

Brain (pg. 203), Children (pg. 207)

spikenard	frankincense	petitgrain	cedarwood	sandalwood
Topical, Internal, Aromatic	Topical, Internal, Aromatic	Internal, Topical, Aromatic	Aromatic, Topical	Aromatic, Topical, Internal

SEPSIS

Immune & Lymphatic (pg. 215)

oregano	marjoram	thyme	copaiba	protective blend
Topical, Internal	Topical, Internal	Topical, Internal	Topical, Internal	Topical, Internal, Aromatic

SEX DRIVE (EXCESSIVE) / HYPERSEXUALITY — *Intimacy (pg. 217)*

marjoram	*arborvitae*	*detoxification blend*	*neroli*	*comforting blend*

SEX DRIVE (LOW) — *Intimacy (pg. 217), Men's Health (pg. 219), Women's Health (pg. 234)*

inspiring blend	*jasmine*	*cinnamon*	*ylang ylang*	*women's blend*

SHIGELLA INFECTION — *Immune & Lymphatic (pg. 215), Digestive & Intestinal (pg. 209)*

eucalyptus	*clove*	*black pepper*	*thyme*	*protective blend*

SHIN SPLINTS — *Skeletal (pg. 229), Athletes (pg. 200)*

massage blend	*soothing blend*	*lemongrass*	*wintergreen*	*basil*

SHINGLES — *Immune & Lymphatic (pg. 215), Nervous (pg. 222)*

patchouli	*melissa*	*yarrow*	*melaleuca*	*black pepper*

SHOCK — *First Aid (pg. 213), Nervous (pg. 222), Stress (pg. 231)*

peppermint	*reassuring blend*	*lavender*	*Roman chamomile*	*grounding blend*

SICKLE CELL ANEMIA — *Cardiovascular (pg. 205), Detoxification (pg. 208)*

detoxification blend	*frankincense*	*lemongrass*	*geranium*	*cassia*

SILENT THYROIDITIS — *Autoimmune (pg. 201), Endocrine (pg. 211)*

detoxification blend	*basil*	*cellular c. blend*	*massage blend*	*comforting blend*

SINUS CONGESTION

Respiratory (pg. 228), Digestive & Intestinal (pg. 209)

respiration blend	*eucalyptus*	*rosemary*	*protective blend*	*helichrysum*
aromatic, topical	topical, aromatic	aromatic, topical	internal, topical, aromatic	topical, aromatic, internal

SINUSITIS

Respiratory (pg. 228)

peppermint	*respiration blend*	*cedarwood*	*inspiring blend*	*thyme*
aromatic, topical, internal	topical, aromatic	aromatic, topical	aromatic, topical	internal, topical

SJOGREN'S SYNDROME

Autoimmune (pg. 201)

cinnamon	*black pepper*	*detoxification blend*	*Roman chamomile*	*cellular c. blend*
internal, topical	internal, topical	internal, topical	internal, topical	internal, topical

SKIN (DRY)

Integumentary (pg. 216)

sandalwood	*cedarwood*	*copaiba*	*anti-aging blend*	*myrrh*
topical	topical	topical	topical	topical

SKIN (OILY)

Integumentary (pg. 216)

skin clearing blend	*petitgrain*	*lemon*	*wild orange*	*ylang ylang*
topical	topical, internal	topical, internal	topical, internal	internal, topical

SKIN ISSUES

Integumentary (pg. 216)

lavender	*anti-aging blend*	*geranium*	*sandalwood*	*frankincense*
topical	topical	topical	topical	topical

SKIN ULCERS

Integumentary (pg. 216)

frankincense	*helichrysum*	*lavender*	*geranium*	*myrrh*
topical, internal	topical	topical	topical	topical

SLEEP APNEA

Sleep (pg. 230), Respiratory (pg. 228)

respiration blend	*thyme*	*rosemary*	*peppermint*	*lemongrass*
topical, aromatic	topical, internal	topical, aromatic	topical, aromatic, internal	topical, aromatic, internal

SLEEPWALKING

Sleep (pg. 230)

vetiver	restful blend	lavender	reassuring blend	grounding blend

SMELL (LOSS OF)

Immune & Lymphatic (pg. 215), Respiratory (pg. 228)

sandalwood	peppermint	arborvitae	basil	helichrysum

SMOKING ADDICTION

Addictions (pg. 198), Mood & Behavior (pg. 220)

black pepper	clove	protective blend	cilantro	detoxification blend

SNAKE BITES

First Aid (pg. 213)

basil	cleansing blend	protective blend	myrrh	detoxification blend

SNORING

Respiratory (pg. 228), Sleep (pg. 230)

respiration blend	peppermint	rosemary	eucalyptus	Douglas fir

SOCIAL ANXIETY DISORDER

Brain (pg. 203), Mood & Behavior (pg. 220)

reassuring blend	bergamot & patchouli	Douglas fir	restful blend	comforting blend

SORE FEET

Athletes (pg. 200), Muscular (pg. 283), Skeletal (pg. 229)

massage blend	soothing blend	ginger	copaiba	wintergreen

SORE MUSCLES

Muscular (pg. 221), Pain & Inflammation (pg. 224), Athletes (pg. 200)

massage blend	soothing blend	peppermint	tension blend	marjoram

SORE THROAT

Oral Health (pg. 223), Immune & Lymphatic (pg. 215), Respiratory (pg. 228)

protective blend	melaleuca	myrrh	lime	thyme
internal, topical	internal, topical	internal	internal, topical	internal

SPINA BIFIDA

Skeletal (pg. 229), Nervous (pg. 222)

Siberian fir	clove	cellular c. blend	wintergreen	soothing blend
topical	topical	topical, internal	topical	topical

SPRAINS

Muscular (pg. 221), Pain & Inflammation (pg. 224), First Aid (pg. 213)

soothing blend	lemongrass	marjoram	copaiba	wintergreen
topical	topical	topical	topical	topical

STAPH INFECTION

Immune & Lymphatic (pg. 215)

protective blend	cleansing blend	geranium	oregano	myrrh
topical, internal	topical, internal	topical, internal	topical, internal	topical, internal

STEVENS-JOHNSON SYNDROME

Integumentary (pg. 216)

detoxification blend	melaleuca	frankincense	myrrh	arborvitae
topical, internal	topical, internal	topical, internal	topical	topical

STOMACH ACHE

Digestive & Intestinal (pg. 209)

digestion blend	peppermint	ginger	wild orange	black pepper
internal, topical	internal, topical	internal, topical	internal, topical, aromatic	topical, aromatic

STREP THROAT

Immune & Lymphatic (pg. 215)

oregano	protective blend	melaleuca	lemon	cinnamon
internal, topical	internal, topical	internal, topical	internal, topical	internal, topical

STRESS

Stress (pg. 231)

reassuring blend	grounding blend	lavender	restful blend	neroli
topical, aromatic	topical, aromatic	topical, aromatic	aromatic, topical	topical

STRESS FRACTURES — *Skeletal (pg. 229)*

birch	*helichrysum*	*Siberian fir*	*wintergreen*	*soothing blend*

STRETCH MARKS — *Integumentary (pg. 216), Pregnancy, Labor & Nursing (pg. 226), Weight (pg. 233)*

anti-aging blend	*geranium*	*sandalwood*	*lavender*	*frankincense*

STROKE — *Brain (pg. 203)*

cassia	*helichrysum*	*cypress*	*basil*	*fennel*

STYE — *Respiratory (pg. 228)*

melaleuca	*cellular c. blend*	*patchouli*	*frankincense*	*myrrh*

SUNBURN — *Integumentary (pg. 216), First Aid (pg. 213)*

lavender	*peppermint*	*anti-aging blend*	*frankincense*	*helichrysum*

SWIMMER'S EAR — *Respiratory (pg. 228)*

rosemary	*clove*	*protective blend*	*lavender*	*oregano*

SWIMMER'S ITCH — *Parasites (pg. 225), Integumentary (pg. 216)*

cleansing blend	*lemongrass*	*detoxification blend*	*frankincense*	*Roman chamomile*

TACHYCARDIA — *Cardiovascular (pg. 205)*

grounding blend	*ylang ylang*	*lavender*	*rosemary*	*melissa*

TASTE, LOSS

Respiratory (pg. 228), Nervous (pg. 222)

peppermint	*lime*	*detoxification blend*	*melissa*	*helichrysum*
internal, topical, aromatic	internal, topical, aromatic	internal, topical	internal, topical, aromatic	internal, topical, aromatic

TEAR DUCT (BLOCKED)

Respiratory (pg. 228)

myrrh	*lavender*	*clary sage*	*eucalyptus*	*melaleuca*
topical	topical	topical	topical	topical

TEETH GRINDING

Oral Health (pg. 223)

Roman chamomile	*lavender*	*marjoram*	*restful blend*	*geranium*
topical, internal, aromatic	aromatic, topical, internal	topical, aromatic	topical, aromatic	topical, aromatic

TEETH, DISCOLORED

Oral Health (pg. 223)

wintergreen	*lemon*	*peppermint*	*lime*	*detoxification blend*
topical	topical	topical	topical	topical

TEETHING PAIN

Oral Health (pg. 223), Children (pg. 207)

clove	*Roman chamomile*	*myrrh*	*protective blend*	*helichrysum*
topical	topical	topical	topical	topical

TENDONITIS

Muscular (pg. 221), Athletes (pg. 200)

soothing blend	*massage blend*	*copaiba & marjoram*	*lemongrass*	*Siberian fir*
topical	topical	topical	topical	topical

TENNIS ELBOW

Skeletal (pg. 229), Muscular (pg. 221)

massage blend	*soothing blend*	*basil*	*ginger*	*lemongrass*
topical	topical	topical	topical	topical

TENSION (MUSCLE)

Muscular (pg. 221),

tension blend	*massage blend*	*peppermint*	*marjoram*	*ginger*
topical	topical	topical	topical	topical

TESTOSTERONE (LOW) — Men's Health (pg. 219)

rosemary	sandalwood	inspiring blend	ylang ylang	detoxification blend

THRUSH — Candida (pg. 204), Children (pg. 207), Pregnancy, Labor & Nursing (pg. 226), Women's Health (pg. 234)

spikenard	arborvitae	clary sage	melaleuca	myrrh

TICK BITES — Parasites (pg. 225), First Aid (pg. 213)

cleansing blend	skin clearing blend	melaleuca	eucalyptus	peppermint

TINNITIS — Respiratory (pg. 228)

helichrysum	basil	cypress	detoxification blend	juniper berry

TMJ (TEMPOROMANDIBULAR JOINT DYSFUNCTION) — Muscular (pg. 221), Oral Health (pg. 223)

massage blend	marjoram	tension blend	Siberian fir	soothing blend

TOE FUNGUS — Athletes (pg. 200), Candida (pg. 204), Integumentary (pg. 216)

melaleuca	cinnamon	copaiba	skin clearing blend	arborvitae

TONSILLITIS — Immune & Lymphatic (pg. 215), Oral Health (pg. 223)

protective blend	myrrh	lemon	melaleuca	eucalyptus

TOOTHACHE — Oral Health (pg. 223)

clove	birch	helichrysum	protective blend	melaleuca

TOURETTE SYNDROME

Nervous (pg. 222), Brain (pg. 203), Mood & Behavior (pg. 220)

spikenard	cellular c. blend	patchouli	frankincense	vetiver
topical, internal	internal, topical	topical, internal	topical, internal	topical

TOXEMIA

Pregnancy, Labor & Nursing (pg. 226)

detoxification blend	metabolic blend	patchouli	cypress	frankincense
internal, topical	internal, topical	internal, topical	internal, topical	internal, topical

TOXICITY

Detoxification (pg. 208), First Aid (pg. 213)

detoxification blend	lemongrass	lemon	cellular c. blend	petitgrain
internal	internal	internal	internal	internal

TRANSVERSE MYELITIS

Nervous (pg. 222)

patchouli	clove	spikenard	wintergreen	Roman chamomile
topical	topical, internal	topical, internal	topical	internal, topical

TRIGEMINAL NEURALGIA

Nervous (pg. 222)

wintergreen	juniper berry	helichrysum	spikenard	Roman chamomile
topical	topical	topical	topical	topical

TUBERCULOSIS

Respiratory (pg. 228), Immune & Lymphatic (pg. 215)

thyme	black pepper	rosemary	eucalyptus	respiration blend
topical, internal	internal, topical	topical, aromatic, internal	topical, aromatic	topical, aromatic

TULAREMIA

Immune & Lymphatic (pg. 215)

oregano	melaleuca	detoxification blend	rosemary	thyme
internal, topical	internal, topical	internal, topical	internal, topical	internal, topical

TUMOR

Cellular Health (pg. 206)

cellular c. blend	frankincense	thyme	copaiba	sandalwood
internal, topical	internal, topical	internal, topical	internal, topical	internal, topical

Body System / Focus Areas

TURNER SYNDROME				Endocrine (pg. 211)
thyme	*clary sage*	*myrrh*	*ylang ylang*	*frankincense*

TYPHOID				Immune & Lymphatic (pg. 215)
clove	*oregano*	*eucalyptus*	*cinnamon*	*peppermint*

ULCERS (DUODENAL)				Digestive & Intestinal (pg. 209)
frankincense	*myrrh*	*wintergreen*	*digestion blend*	*fennel*

ULCERS (GASTRIC)				Digestive & Intestinal (pg. 209)
digestion blend	*peppermint*	*bergamot*	*yarrow*	*geranium*

ULCERS (LEG)				Integumentary (pg. 216), Cardiovascular (pg. 205)
geranium	*frankincense*	*massage blend*	*yarrow*	*helichrysum*

ULCERS (PEPTIC)				Digestive & Intestinal (pg. 209)
cinnamon	*fennel*	*peppermint*	*digestion blend*	*juniper berry*

ULCERS (VARICOSE)				Cardiovascular (pg. 205), Integumentary (pg. 216)
tension blend	*helichrysum*	*cypress*	*geranium*	*coriander*

URETER INFECTION				Urinary (pg. 232), Immune & Lymphatic (pg. 215)
coriander	*protective blend*	*lemongrass*	*cellular c. blend*	*cinnamon*

URINARY TRACT INFECTION (UTI)

Urinary (pg. 232), Immune & Lymphatic (pg. 215)

lemon	geranium	lemongrass	juniper berry	cypress
topical, internal	topical, internal	internal, topical	topical, internal	topical

URINATION (PAINFUL / FREQUENT)

Urinary (pg. 232)

cinnamon	melaleuca	lemongrass	detoxification blend	protective blend
internal, topical	internal, topical	internal, topical	internal, topical	topical, internal

URINE FLOW (POOR)

Urinary (pg. 232)

detoxification blend	metabolic blend	juniper berry	cypress	massage blend
internal, topical	internal	topical, internal	topical	topical

UTERINE BLEEDING

Pregnancy, Labor & Nursing (pg. 226), Women's Health (pg. 234)

women's m. blend	helichrysum	geranium	frankincense	lavender
topical	internal, topical	internal, topical	internal, topical	internal, topical

UVETITIS

Nervous (pg. 222)

myrrh	juniper berry	frankincense	anti-aging blend	sandalwood
topical, internal	topical, internal	topical, internal	topical	topical, internal

VAGINAL YEAST INFECTION

Candida (pg. 204), Women's Health (pg. 234)

melaleuca	spikenard	thyme	frankincense or myrrh	cellular c. blend
topical, internal	topical, internal	internal, topical	internal, topical	internal, topical

VAGINITIS

Candida (pg. 204), Women's Health (pg. 234)

melaleuca	patchouli	spikenard	yarrow	rosemary
topical, internal	internal, topical	topical, internal	internal, topical	topical, internal

VARICOSE VEINS

Cardiovascular (pg. 205), Integumentary (pg. 216)

cypress	helichrysum	coriander	yarrow	bergamot
topical	topical	internal, topical	internal, topical	internal, topical

VERTIGO				Brain (pg. 203), Cardiovascular (pg. 205)
frankincense	rosemary	ylang ylang	ginger	grounding blend

VIRUS				Immune & Lymphatic (pg. 215)
melissa	thyme	black pepper	yarrow	oregano

VISION (BLURRED)				Nervous (pg. 222)
cellular c. blend	lemongrass	helichrysum	frankincense	anti-aging blend

VISION (POOR)				Nervous (pg. 222)
cellular c. blend	anti-aging blend	cypress	lemongrass	juniper berry

VITILIGO				Autoimmune (pg. 201), Integumentary (pg. 216)
detoxification blend	women's blend	vetiver	cellular c. blend	sandalwood

VOMITING				Digestive & Intestinal (pg. 209), Immune & Lymphatic (pg. 215), Eating Disorders (pg. 210)
digestion blend	peppermint	fennel	ginger	pink pepper

WARTS				Integumentary (pg. 216)
melissa	arborvitae	oregano	frankincense	lemongrass

WASP STING				First Aid (pg. 213)
cleansing blend	Roman chamomile	lavender	peppermint	cedarwood

WATER RETENTION

Urinary (pg. 232), Cardiovascular (pg. 205), Pregnancy, Labor & Nursing (pg. 226)

lemon	cypress	metabolic blend	juniper berry	grapefruit
internal, topical	topical	internal, topical	internal, topical	internal, topical

WEIGHT ISSUES

Weight (pg. 233)

metabolic blend	grapefruit	detoxification blend	bergamot	cellular c. blend
internal, topical	internal	internal	aromatic, topical, internal	internal

WHIPLASH

Muscular (pg. 221)

tension blend	Siberian fir	lemongrass	soothing blend	massage blend
topical	topical	topical	topical	topical

WITHDRAWAL SYMPTOMS

Addictions (pg. 198), Mood & Behavior (pg. 220), Focus & Concentration (pg. 214)

encouraging blend	frankincense	spikenard	detoxification blend	uplifting blend
topical, aromatic	internal, topical	internal, topical	internal, topical	aromatic, topical

WORKOUT RECOVERY

Athletes (pg. 200), Muscular (pg. 221)

massage blend	lemon	soothing blend	peppermint	tension blend
topical	internal	topical	topical	topical

WORMS

Parasites (pg. 225), Digestive & Intestinal (pg. 209)

clove	oregano	thyme	lemongrass	blue tansy
internal, topical	internal, topical	internal, topical	internal, topical	topical

WOUNDS

Integumentary (pg. 216), First Aid (pg. 213)

melaleuca	lavender	yarrow	helichrysum	frankincense
topical	topical	topical	topical	topical

WRINKLES

Integumentary (pg. 216)

anti-aging blend	petitgrain	spikenard	geranium & neroli	sandalwood
topical	topical	topical	topical	topical

QUICK REFERENCE

XENOESTROGENS *Women's Health (pg. 234), Detoxification (pg. 208)*

lemon · *women's m. blend* · *detoxification blend* · *thyme* · *ginger*

XEROPHTHALMIA *Respiratory (pg. 228)*

lavender · *sandalwood* · *lemon* · *anti-aging blend* · *detoxification blend*

YEAST *Candida (pg. 204), Women's Health (pg. 234), Children (pg. 207)*

melaleuca · *thyme* · *oregano* · *cellular c. blend* · *lemongrass*

3

NATURAL SOLUTIONS

Becoming familiar with the qualities and common benefits of essential oils is a key part of living THE ESSENTIAL LIFE. As you become versed in the powerful qualities of each oil, blend, and supplement, you will find confidence in turning to nature as your first resource for wellness. Nature's vast diversity provides answers for any health interest, be it physical, mental, or emotional.

Single Oils

Oil Blends

Supplements

Single Oils

Becoming familiar with the qualities and common benefits of essential oils is a key part of living THE ESSENTIAL LIFE. As you become versed in the powerful qualities of each oil, blend, and supplement, you will find confidence in turning to nature as your first resource for wellness. Nature's vast diversity provides answers for any health interest, be it physical, mental, or emotional.

This section provides a detailed reference for the origins, qualities, purposes, and safety of individual essential oils. The top uses of each oil are intended to be a succinct guide, as more detailed uses are highlighted in Body Systems.

Please note the symbols = aromatic = topical = internal that specify recommended usage. While all oils are meant to be used aromatically and most topically, only verified pure therapeutic essential oils are intended for internal use. *(See "Why Quality Matters," page 18 and "How to Use Essential Oils" page 23 for further detail.)*

Following symbols for Safety:

N = NEAT application = avoid sunlight for 12 hours = dilute as needed

= if pregnant or nursing, consult your physician = caution with epilepsy

= avoid contact with eyes, inner ears, and sensitive areas

ARBORVITAE

Thuja plicata

woody · majestic · strong

TOP USES

Candida & Fungal Issues – Apply to bottoms of feet or area of concern.

Viruses – Apply to bottoms of feet.

Cold Sores & Warts – Apply to sore or wart frequently.

Respiratory Issues – Apply to chest with fractionated coconut oil.

Repellent – Diffuse, spray on surfaces, or apply to repel bugs and insects.

Cancer – Apply to bottoms of feet.

Stimulant – Apply under nose and back of neck to stimulate body systems and awareness.

Bacterial Support – Apply to bottoms of feet or spine with fractionated coconut oil. Spray diluted in water on surfaces or diffuse to kill airborne pathogens.

Skin Complaints – Apply with lavender to troubled skin.

Sunscreen – Apply with helichrysum or lavender to protect against sun exposure.

Emotional Balance –
Use aromatically & topically to get from Overzealous ⟶ Composed.

TOP PROPERTIES – Antiviral, Antifungal, Antibacterial, Stimulant *(for more, see pg 260)*.

SAFETY –

BASIL

Ocimum basilicum

regenerating · uplifting · stimulating

TOP USES

Adrenal Fatigue – Apply under nose, to bottoms of feet, back of neck, forehead, and / or over the adrenal area.

Earache – Apply behind and down beneath ear area: swab ear canal to relieve pain and infection.

Loss Of Sense Of Smell – Apply under nose and to toes to regain or increase sense of smell.

Migraines & Dizziness – Apply with wintergreen or peppermint to temples and back of neck.

Mental Fatigue & Focus – Breathe in, diffuse or apply across forehead.

Nausea & Cramping – Take in a capsule or apply to abdomen to ease discomfort.

Gout & Rheumatism – Apply to spine, bottoms of feet, ears, ankles, or area over heart.

PMS & Menstrual Issues – Apply to lower abdomen to stimulate menstrual flow and assist with menstrual cramping.

Emotional Balance –
Use aromatically & topically to get from Inundated ⟶ Relieved.

TOP PROPERTIES – Stimulant, Neurotonic, Steroidal, Regenerative, Antispasmodic, Anti-inflammatory, Antibacterial, Digestive *(for more, see pg 260)*.

SAFETY –

BERGAMOT

Citrus bergamia

uplifting · assuring · restoring

TOP USES

Addictions – Apply to back of neck and bottoms of feet or diffuse.

Skin Issues – Apply diluted to affected areas.

Insomnia – Apply under nose or diffuse before sleep.

Stress – Apply to back of neck and bottoms of feet or diffuse.

Joint Issues & Muscle Cramps – Apply to affected areas.

Fungal Issues – Apply to affected areas or take in a capsule.

Coughs, Infections & Bronchitis – Apply to chest.

Acne, Oily Skin, Eczema & Psoriasis – Apply diluted to affected area.

Appetite Loss – Breathe in and / or take in a capsule.

Self-Worth Issues – Apply to belly button and over heart to enhance feelings of worth.

Emotional Balance – Use aromatically & topically to get from Inadequate ⟶ Worthy.

TOP PROPERTIES – Neurotonic, Anti-inflammatory, Antidepressant, Antibacterial, Antifungal, Digestive Stimulant *(for more, see pg 260).*

SAFETY –

BIRCH

Betula lenta

invigorate · activate · soothe

TOP USES

Connective Tissue & Muscles Injuries – Apply to affected area.

Arthritis, Rheumatism & Gout – Apply to affected area.

Muscle Pain & Spasms – Apply to area of concern for steroidal support.

Fever – Apply on spine.

Bone Spurs, Gallstones, Kidney Stones & Cataracts – Apply to bottoms of feet or areas of concern.

Ulcers & Cramps – Apply to abdomen as needed.

Broken Bones & Tooth Pain – Apply to area of concern.

Emotional Balance – Use aromatically & topically to get from Cowardly ⟶ Courageous.

TOP PROPERTIES – Analgesic, Neurotonic, Anti-rheumatic, Stimulant, Steroidal, Warming *(for more, see pg 260).*

SAFETY –

BLACK PEPPER

Piper nigrum

spicy · warming · uplifting

TOP USES

Constipation, Diarrhea & Gas – Take in capsule or apply to abdomen.

Respiratory & Lymphatic Drainage & Cleansing – Use a drop under tongue or inhale / diffuse.

Poor Circulation & Cold Extremities – Apply with a warm compress to increase circulation and blood flow to muscles and nerves.

Cold, Flu, Aches & Chills – Use in a capsule or apply to bottoms of feet or along spine.

Congested Airways – Diffuse or apply to chest with white fir to clear airways.

Food Flavor – Enhance your favorite foods by adding a drop as seasoning to add flavor and support digestion.

Anxiety – Diffuse or apply under nose or on bottoms of feet.

Cramps, Sprains & Muscle Spasms – Apply to affected area.

Emotional Balance – Use aromatically & topically to get from Repressed ⟶ Honest.

TOP PROPERTIES – Antioxidant, Anti-spasmodic, Digestive, Expectorant, Neurotonic, Stimulant, Rubefacient *(for more, see pg 260)*.

SAFETY –

BLUE TANSY

Tanacetum annuum

eliminating · relieving · defending

TOP USES

Allergies, Itching, Rashes, Watery Eyes & Sneezing – Apply to bottoms of feet and / or affected area(s).

Acne, Eczema, Psoriasis & Sunburn – Apply to affected area(s) with helichrysum.

Fibromyalgia, Sciatica, Arthritis, & Rheumatism – Apply to affected area(s).

Fungal & Skin Infections, Spores – Apply to affected area(s).

Asthma & Respiratory Issues, Hiccups – Combine with eucalyptus or peppermint and apply to chest and / or under nose.

Tension & Sinus Headaches, Migraines, Toothache – Massage into temples, sides of nose, or gums.

Indigestion, Stomach Ulcer & Intestinal Worms – Massage into abdomen.

Cold, Flu, Mumps, Chicken Pox, & Muscle Aches – Apply to affected area(s) or bottoms of feet.

Emotional Balance – Use aromatically & topically to get from Inundated ⟶ Relieved.

TOP PROPERTIES – Anti-histamine, Insect Repellent, Anti-allergenic, Antifungal, Vermicide, Antiviral, Stomachic *(for more, see pg 260)*.

SAFETY –

invigorate · relax · cleanse

★ **TOP USES**

Congestion – Apply to chest and bridge of nose or diffuse.

Stomach Ache & Constipation – Take in a capsule or apply to abdomen.

Colitis & Diarrhea – Apply to abdomen.

Gastritis & Stomach Ulcers – Use in a capsule.

Menstrual & Muscular Pain – Apply to area of concern to relieve pain and inflammation.

Sore Throat & Fevers – Gargle a drop in water or apply to throat and back of neck.

Mental Fatigue & Confusion – Apply under nose and to back of neck to clear your mind and ease fatigue.

Pancreatitis – Apply to area over pancreas and bottoms of feet to cleanse and restore pancreatic function.

Bad Breath & Household Odors – Take in a capsule for breath or diffuse A to clear air of odors.

★ **Emotional Balance** –
Use aromatically & topically to get from Self-centered ⟶ Charitable.

★ **TOP PROPERTIES** – Digestive, Antispasmodic, Anti-inflammatory, Decongestant, Expectorant, Tonic, Stomachic, Carminative *(for more, see pg 260).*

⚠ **SAFETY** – N

spicy · strong · warming

★ **TOP USES**

Cold Extremities – Apply diluted to bottoms of feet to increase blood flow and bring warmth.

Upset Stomach & Vomiting – Take in a capsule to resolve and restore digestion.

Detox for Ear, Nose, Throat, & Lungs – Use in a capsule to clear yeast, phlegm and plaque.

Water Retention & Kidney Infection – Take in a capsule or apply to bottoms of feet to kidney reflex points.

Viruses & Bacteria – Take in a capsule and diffuse.

Blood Sugar Balance – Take in a capsule with meals.

Metabolism Boost – Take in a capsule.

Sexual Drive – Diffuse or inhale aroma from bottle or apply to bottoms of feet to increase sexual desire.

Cooking – Add a drop to your favorite recipe for a sweet cinnamon-like flavor.

★ **Emotional Balance** –
Use aromatically & topically to get from Uncertain ⟶ Bold.

★ **TOP PROPERTIES** – Decongestant, Carminative, Detoxifier, Cardiotonic, Anti-microbial, Antiviral, Antifungal, Antispasmodic *(for more, see pg 260).*

⚠ **SAFETY** – N

CEDARWOOD

Juniperus virginiana

connecting · strong · deep

TOP USES

ADD, ADHD, & Low Gaba Levels – Apply to back of neck, across forehead, and / or diffuse / inhale to soothe anxious feelings, and regain focus & concentration.

Psoriasis & Eczema – Apply a drop with a drop of lavender to affected areas.

Calming & Anxiety – Put on palm of hands and inhale or apply to back of neck or bottoms of feet.

Cough & Sinus Issues – Apply to chest and forehead and inhale from cupped hands.

Stroke & Seizures – Apply on back of neck and bottoms of feet.

Urinary Tract, Bladder & Vaginal Infection – Apply to lower abdomen for infection support.

Gum Issues – Apply to gums.

Insect Repellent – Apply diluted or use in diffuser to deter insects.

Acne – Apply with a drop of melaleuca to blemishes.

Emotional Balance – Use aromatically & topically to get from Alone ⟶ Connected.

TOP PROPERTIES – Anti-inflammatory, Diuretic, Astringent, Antiseptic, Insecticidal, Sedative *(for more, see pg 260).*

SAFETY –

CILANTRO

Coriandrum sativum

fresh · awakening · cleansing

TOP USES

Heavy Metal Detox & Antioxidant – Use in a capsule to detox from heavy metals and free radicals.

Gas, Bloating & Constipation – Apply over abdomen.

Allergies – Apply over liver or on bottoms of feet to ease allergies by reducing liver toxicity.

Liver & Kidney Support – Take in a capsule or apply over liver and kidney area.

Fungal & Bacterial Infections – Use in a capsule and apply to infected area.

Cooking – Dip toothpick and add to your favorite salad, dip, or guacamole.

Body Odor – Combine with peppermint in a capsule.

Anxiety – Inhale or diffuse.

Emotional Balance – Use aromatically & topically to get from Obsessed ⟶ Expansive.

TOP PROPERTIES – Antioxidant, Antifungal, Detoxifying, Antibacterial *(for more, see pg 260).*

SAFETY – N

protecting · spicy · awakening

TOP USES

Diabetes & High Blood Sugar – Take in capsule to balance blood sugar.

Cold & Flu – Take in a capsule or apply to bottoms of feet. Diffuse to cleanse air.

Cholesterol & Heart Issues – Apply diluted to bottoms of feet or take in a capsule for increased blood flow.

Oral Health – Gargle a drop in water to combat oral infection.

Fungus & Bacteria – Take in a capsule.

Kidney Infection – Take in a capsule.

Vaginal Health – Take in a capsule.

Low Libido & Sexual Stimulant – Take in a capsule or dilute and apply to warm and stimulate.

Muscle Strain & Pain – Apply diluted to relieve.

Cooking – Add to your favorite baking recipe for a spicy twist.

Emotional Balance – Use aromatically & topically to get from Denied ⟶ Receptive.

TOP PROPERTIES – Antiseptic, Antimicrobial, Antioxidant, Antifungal, Antiviral, Aphrodisiac *(for more, see pg 260).*

SAFETY –

balancing · musky · feminine

TOP USES

Endometriosis & Breast Cancer – Apply diluted to breasts or take in capsule to regulate estrogen.

Breast Enlargement – Apply diluted to each breast for natural enlargement.

Parkinson's, Seizures & Convulsions – Apply to back of neck to support healthy brain function.

Child Birth & Low Milk Supply – Apply diluted down spine or over abdomen to help bring on labor. Apply to each breast for increased lactation.

Infertility & Prostate / Uterine Health – Use in a capsule or apply to abdomen and uterine reflex points.

PMS & Menopause – Take in a capsule or apply on abdomen or bottoms of feet.

Postpartum Depression & Anxiety – Inhale / diffuse or apply to the heart area and bottoms of feet.

Emotional Balance – Use aromatically & topically to get from Limited ⟶ Enlightened.

TOP PROPERTIES – Emmenagogue, Galactagogue, Neurotonic, Mucolytic, Anti-coagulant, Sedative, Antispasmodic *(for more, see pg 260).*

SAFETY –

CLOVE

Eugenia caryophyllata

warm · spicy · protective

TOP USES

Liver & Brain Support – Dilute and apply to bottom of feet or take in a capsule.

Immune Boost – Apply diluted to bottoms of feet or take in a capsule.

Circulation & Hypertension – Apply diluted to spine and bottoms of feet to increase blood flow.

Tooth Pain & Cavities – Dilute and apply to affected area to numb and ease pain.

Thyroid Issues & Metabolism Support – Apply diluted to big toe and take in a capsule.

Infection & Parasites – Take in a capsule.

Smoking Addiction – Apply with black pepper along tongue to decrease nicotine cravings.

Virus & Cold – Apply diluted along spine or take in a capsule.

Emotional Balance –
Use aromatically & topically to get from Dominated ⟶ Supported.

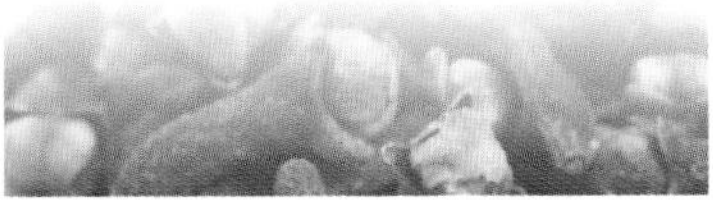

TOP PROPERTIES – Antioxidant, Antiviral, Antibacterial, Antifungal, Expectorant, Nervine, Anti-parasitic, Regenerative, Vermicide *(for more, see pg 260).*

SAFETY –

COPAIBA

Copaiba offincinalis

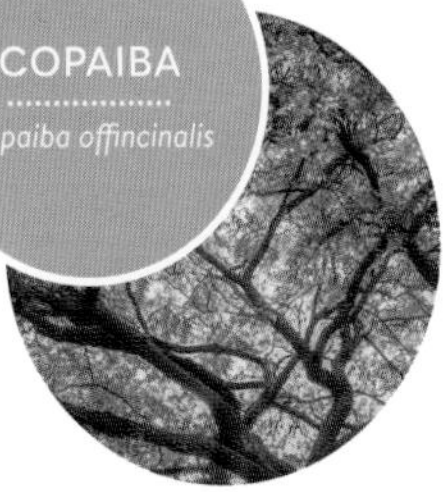

commanding · comforting · magnifying

TOP USES

Pain & Inflammation, Arthritis, Gout & Muscle Cramps – Diffuse A, inhale from cupped hands, and /or apply to area of concern.

Liver Toxicity & Issues – Take in a capsule or in water.

Tendonitis, Plantar Fasciitis & Heel Spurs – Apply to area of concern.

Respiratory Issues, Sore Throat & Tonsils – Diffuse, inhale from cupped hands, apply under nose, and/or to chest.

Bedwetting & Incontinence – Apply to abdomen and / or take in a capsule.

Colitis & Intestinal Infections – Apply to abdomen and/or take in a capsule.

Cancer & Autoimmune Disorders – Take in a capsule, apply to bottoms of feet, and / or along spine.

Fungal, Bacterial & Viral Infections – Take in a capsule, apply to area(s) of concern, bottoms of feet, and / or along spine.

Emotional Balance –
Use aromatically & topically to get from Plagued ⟶ Directed.

TOP PROPERTIES – Anti-inflammatory, Anti-arthritic, Analgesic, Antifungal, Antibacterial, Antioxidant, Anti-carcinoma, Carminative, Anti-microbial *(for more, see pg 260).*

SAFETY –

SINGLE OILS

CORIANDER

Coriandrum sativum

calming · green · stimulating

TOP USES

Gas & Nausea – Rub over abdomen or take in a capsule or glass of water.

High Blood Sugar & Diabetes – Use with cinnamon internally in a capsule with meals to help regulate blood sugar.

Itchy Skin & Rashes – Apply to area of concern.

Joint Pain – Apply directly to area of concern for soothing relief.

Neuropathy– Use in a capsule.

No Appetite – Take in a capsule or inhale from cupped hands.

Food Poisoning & Diarrhea – Use in a capsule or apply to abdomen.

Body Odor – Take in a capsule.

Low Energy & Nervous Exhaustion – Inhale from cupped hands or apply to bottoms of feet.

Emotional Balance –
Use aromatically & topically to get from Apprehensive ⟶ Participating.

TOP PROPERTIES – Analgesic, Antioxidant, Anti-inflammatory, Digestive, Antibacterial, Antispasmodic *(for more, see pg 260).*

SAFETY – N

CYPRESS

Cupressus sempervirens

lively · clean · energizing

TOP USES

Restless Leg & Poor Circulation – Apply to area(s) of concern to restore circulation and ease chronic pain.

Poor Urine Flow, Edema & Toxemia – Apply to clear lymph, promote blood & urine flow, and circulation.

Bed Wetting & Incontinence – Apply over bladder and / or bladder reflex point on foot.

Varicose Veins & Hemorrhoids – Rub over area of concern.

Cellulite – Apply diluted with eucalyptus over area followed by hot compress to break up and release cellulite.

Whooping & Spastic Cough – Apply over lungs followed by a hot compress.

Prostate, Pancreas & Ovary Issues – Massage over area of concern or corresponding reflex point.

Liver & Gallbladder Decongestant – Apply to liver reflex point on foot and over liver area.

Emotional Balance –
Use aromatically & topically to get from Stalled ⟶ Progressing.

TOP PROPERTIES – Antibacterial, Anti-septic, Anti-rheumatic, Stimulant, Vasoconstrictor, Tonifying *(for more, see pg 260).*

SAFETY –

DILL

Anethum graveolens

detoxing · disinfecting · cleansing

★ **TOP USES**

Muscle Spasms – Apply to calm muscles.

Nervousness – Inhale from cupped hands or apply under nose or back of neck with roman chamomile to calm nervousness.

Sugar Addiction & Pancreas Support – Take in a capsule to decrease addiction and lower glucose levels.

Low Breast Milk Supply – Apply to chest or take in a capsule.

Detox & Electrolyte Balance – Take in a capsule as part of a detox.

Cholesterol & High Blood Pressure – Take in a capsule.

Respiratory Issues – Apply diluted to chest or take in a capsule to dislodge and break up mucus.

Gas, Bloating & Indigestion – Take in a capsule or in water.

Lack Of Menstruation – Apply diluted over abdomen.

★ **Emotional Balance** –
Use aromatically & topically to get from Avoiding ⟶ Intentional.

★ **TOP PROPERTIES** – Antispasmodic, Expectorant, Stimulant, Galactagogue, Carminative, Emmenagogue, Hypertensive, Antibacterial *(for more, see pg 260)*.

⚠ **SAFETY** – N

DOUGLAS FIR

Pseudotsuga menziesii

cleansing · promoting · grounding

★ **TOP USES**

Mental Fog & Low Energy – Apply to temples and forehead or diffuse to clear mind and revive enthusiasm.

Congestion & Sinus Issues – Apply to chest or bridge of nose.

Respiratory Infection & Cough – Apply to throat, chest or diffuse.

Muscle & Joint Soreness – Apply with wintergreen to affected area for soothing relief.

Rheumatic & Arthritic Conditions – Apply to affected areas.

Constipation – Apply diluted to abdomen.

Skin Irritations & Cuts – Apply diluted to affected areas.

Cellulite & Skin Cleansing – Massage diluted with grapefruit to desired area.

★ **Emotional Balance** –
Use aromatically & topically to get from Upset ⟶ Renewed.

★ **TOP PROPERTIES** – Antioxidant, Analgesic, Antimicrobial, Antiseptic, Anticatarrhal, Astringent, Diuretic, Expectorant, Laxative, Sedative, Stimulant, Tonic *(for more, see pg 260)*.

⚠ **SAFETY** –

SINGLE OILS

EUCALYPTUS

Eucalyptus radiata

enlivening · fresh · clearing

TOP USES

Congestion, Cough, Bronchitis & Pneumonia – Apply to chest and over the bridge of nose. Diffuse or inhale from cupped hands.

Shingles, Malaria, Cold & Flu – Apply to bottoms of feet or along spine and diffuse.

Asthma, Sinusitis & Respiratory – Put in palms of hands and inhale from cupped hands or apply diluted to chest and feet.

Fever & Heat Sensitivity – Apply with peppermint down the spine for cooling effect.

Muscle Fatigue & Pain – Dilute and rub into overused muscles.

Kidney Stones – Gently massage over kidneys or areas of pain.

Cellulite – Dilute and massage over areas of concern.

Earaches – Dilute and apply to outer ear and bone behind the ear.

Breast Issues & Cancer – Dilute and massage into breast tissues.

Emotional Balance –
Use aromatically & topically to get from Congested ⟶ Stimulated.

TOP PROPERTIES – Antiviral, Antibacterial, Expectorant, Analgesic, Insecticidal, Hypotensive, Disinfectant, Catalyst *(for more, see pg 260).*

SAFETY –

FENNEL

Foeniculum vulgare

strong · purifying · supporting

TOP USES

Nausea, Colic & Flatulence – Take in a capsule or massage into abdomen.

Menstrual Issues & PMS – Take in a capsule or apply to abdomen to balance and tone female organs.

Menopause & Premenopause Issues – Take in a capsule or massage over abdomen.

Cramps & Spasms – Dilute and rub onto distressed muscles.

Breast Feeding Or Low Milk Supply – Use in a capsule or in water to increase milk supply.

Edema & Fluid Retention – Combine with grapefruit and massage over affected areas or take in a capsule.

Cough & Congestion – Apply diluted to chest and throat.

Intestinal Parasites & Sluggish Bowels – Take with lemon in a capsule.

Blood Sugar Imbalance – Take in a capsule or add to glass of water.

Emotional Balance –
Use aromatically & topically to get from Unproductive ⟶ Flourishing.

TOP PROPERTIES – Antispasmodic, Emmenagogue, Galactagogue, Diuretic, Mucolytic, Digestive, Anti-inflammatory *(for more, see pg 260).*

SAFETY –

royal · resin · woody

TOP USES

Cancer & Tumors – Take in a capsule with oil(s) that target area of interest or massage over affected area.

Seizures & Trauma – Put a drop under the tongue and apply along hairline.

Alzheimer's Disease, Dementia & Brain Injury – Use or apply under nose and back of neck, or diffuse.

Depression – Diffuse or put under the tongue to ease the effects of depression.

Wound Healing & Wrinkles – Apply to wounds or wrinkles to support skin regeneration.

Scars & Stretch Marks – Combine with myrrh and apply to reduce the appearance of scars and stretch marks.

Sciatica, Back Pain & Headaches – Apply over affected area or take in a capsule to reduce inflammation.

Immune System & Cellular Health – Take in a capsule or apply to bottoms of feet.

Emotional Balance – Use aromatically & topically to get from Separated ⟶ Unified.

TOP PROPERTIES – Immunostimulant, Anticancer, Anti-inflammatory, Antidepressant, Restorative *(for more, see pg 260)*.

SAFETY – N

strengthening · releasing · stabilizing

TOP USES

Liver, Gallbladder, Pancreas & Kidney Issues – Apply over area of concern or take in a capsule.

Blood Issues & Bleeding – Apply to troubled area to restore healthy blood or stop bleeding.

Cuts & Wounds – Apply to area of concern to keep wounds clean, stop bleeding, and regenerate tissue.

PMS & Hormone Balancing – Massage on abdomen or take a drop under tongue.

Low Libido – Massage diluted over abdomen or take a drop under tongue to increase sexual drive.

Dry Or Oily Hair & Skin – Apply to scalp or troubled skin to retain oil balance.

Moisturizer – Apply diluted and use as a moisturizer for skin hydration and balance.

Body Odor – Apply under arms as a deodorant.

Emotional Balance – Use aromatically & topically to get from Neglected ⟶ Mended.

TOP PROPERTIES – Haemostatic, Detoxifier, Regenerative, Anti-allergenic, Antihemorrhagic, Antitoxic *(for more, see pg 260)*.

SAFETY –

SINGLE OILS

GINGER

Zingiber officinale

warming · accelerating · stimulating

TOP USES

Spasms, Cramps & Sore Muscles – Dilute and massage into area of discomfort for warming relief.

Nausea, Morning Sickness & Loss Of Appetite – Diffuse, take a drop in a glass with warm water, apply diluted to wrists, or apply to bottoms of feet.

Motion Sickness & Vertigo – Inhale from cupped hands or take in a capsule.

Memory & Brain Support – Inhale from cupped hands or take in a capsule.

Heartburn & Reflux – Take in a capsule with lemon.

Alcohol Addiction – Take in a capsule as needed to ease cravings.

Hormone & Blood Sugar Imbalances – Take in a capsule.

Colic & Constipation – Apply diluted over abdomen or take I in a glass of warm water.

Emotional Balance – Use aromatically & topically to get from Apathetic ⟶ Activated.

TOP PROPERTIES – Anti-inflammatory, Antispasmodic, Digestive, Laxative, Analgesic, Stimulant, Decongestant, Neurotonic *(for more, see pg 260).*

SAFETY –

GRAPEFRUIT

Citrus X paradisi

citrus · detoxifying · fresh

TOP USES

Weight Loss & Obesity – Drink a few drops in water or take in a capsule. Apply to areas of concern to breakdown fat cells.

Breast & Uterine Issues & Progesterone Balance – Take in a capsule or apply diluted to area of concern.

Addictions & Sugar Cravings – Diffuse or take in a capsule.

Oily Skin & Acne – Apply to areas of concern to better manage breakouts.

Detoxification & Cellulite – Rub on bottoms of feet or drink in water for an overall detox. Apply diluted to problem areas to breakdown cellulite.

Lymphatic & Kidney Toxicity – Drink in water or apply diluted over lymph nodes, kidney area, or bottoms of feet.

Adrenal Fatigue – Apply diluted with basil over adrenal area, on bottoms of feet or back of neck. Take in a capsule.

Emotional Balance – Use aromatically & topically to get from Divided ⟶ Validated.

TOP PROPERTIES – Diuretic, Antioxidant, Antiseptic, Astringent, Antitoxic, Purifier, Expectorant *(for more, see pg 260).*

SAFETY –

GREEN MANDARIN

Citrus nobilis

composing · reclaiming · resolving

TOP USES

Depressed, Agitated, Nervous, Inner Child Work – Diffuse. Take 1 drop under tongue. Apply to pulse points. Especially good for children. Combine with lavender, vetiver, rose, and/or neroli.

Situational Anxiety – Apply 1-2 drops under nose, diffuse or inhale, or take.

Gas, Sluggish Digestion, Constipation, Heartburn & Ulcers – Apply 1-2 drops over area of concern or take.

Poor Circulation, Congested Lymphs, Water Retention – Take 1-2 drops with black pepper 2x's daily under tongue or in a capsule.

Liver & Kidney Detox, Sluggish Bile Flow – Take 1-2 drops with juniper berry and lemon 2x's daily.

Acne, Oily Skin, Wounds, Scars – Combine with skin care products and apply to areas of concern.

Skin & Breast Cancer – Take 1-2 drops 2x's daily with copaiba. Apply to areas of concern.

Emotional Balance –
Use aromatically & topically to get from
Distressed ⟶ Carefree.

TOP PROPERTIES – Uplifting, Refreshing, Digestive Stimulant, Cleanser, Expectorant, Calming *(for more, see pg 260).*

SAFETY –

HELICHRYSUM

Helichrysum italicum

healing · fusing · regenerating

TOP USES

Wrinkles & Stretch Marks – Apply with myrrh as needed.

Nosebleeds, Bleeding & Hemorrhaging – Apply over bridge of nose or area of concern.

Scars, Wounds & Bruising – Apply to scars and wounds to support skin renewal.

Shock, Pain Relief & Nerve Damage – Apply to back of neck or area of discomfort.

Alcohol Addiction – Apply to abdomen to clear.

Psoriasis & Skin Conditions – Apply with geranium on area of concern.

Varicose Veins – Massage diluted with cypress into affected areas.

Tinnitis & Earache – Massage behind the ears to calm spasms, pain, and inflammation.

Sinus Congestion – Combine with sandalwood and lemon, apply to forehead, swab nostrils. Diffuse.

Emotional Balance –
Use aromatically & topically to get from
Wounded ⟶ Reassured.

TOP PROPERTIES – Antispasmodic, Anticatarrhal, Neuroprotective, Neurotonic, Vasoconstrictor, Haemostatic, Nervine, Analgesic *(for more, see pg 260).*

SAFETY – N

JASMINE

Jasminum grandiflorum

euphoria · splendor · joy

TOP USES

Depression & Anxiety – Inhale from cupped hands or apply diluted under nose and back of neck.

Uterine Health, Labor & Delivery – Apply diluted over abdomen and to reflex points or diffuse.

Fine Lines & Wrinkles – Add two drops to bottle of moisturizer and apply to skin nightly.

Pinkeye – Apply diluted around *(not in)* eye.

Exhaustion – Apply diluted to back of neck and bottoms of feet.

Irritated & Dry Skin – Apply diluted to affected area.

PMS & Low Libido – Apply diluted to back of neck and over abdomen.

Ovulation & Fertility – Apply diluted over abdomen to regulate hormones.

Perfume – Combine with sandalwood or fortifying blend and apply as desired.

Emotional Balance – Use aromatically & topically to get from Hampered ⟶ Liberated.

TOP PROPERTIES – Antidepressant, Aphrodisiac, Antispasmodic, Calming, Regenerative, Carminative *(for more, see pg 260).*

SAFETY – N

JUNIPER BERRY

Juniperus communis

detoxing · revitalizing · toning

TOP USES

Jaundice, Liver Issues & Detox – Take in a capsule to support cleansing.

Kidney Stones & Infection – Take in a capsule or apply over abdomen.

Acne & Psoriasis – Apply to area of concern, diluting as needed.

Urinary Health & Water Retention – Combine with lemon and apply over abdomen or take in a capsule.

Sore Joints & Muscles – Apply to area of concern, diluting as needed.

Bacteria & Viruses – Apply down spine, bottoms of feet or take in a capsule.

High Cholesterol & Blood Sugar Levels – Take in a capsule.

TENSION, STRESS & DEPRESSION – Inhale deeply from cupped hands, diffuse, and / or apply under nose or to bottoms of feet.

Emotional Balance – Use aromatically & topically to get from Denying ⟶ Insightful.

TOP PROPERTIES – Detoxifier, Diuretic, Antiseptic, Antispasmodic, Astringent, Antirheumatic, Carminative, Anti-parasitic *(for more, see pg 260).*

SAFETY – N

KUMQUAT

Lavandula angustifolia

self-affirming · sweet · fulfilling

TOP USES

Winter Blahs, Inauthenticity & Pretense, Lack of Perspective – Diffuse or inhale from cupped hands. Apply to face, diluted.

Brain Fog, Lack of Concentration & Fatigue – Combine with green mandarin and vetiver. Diffuse, inhale, or apply under nose and to forehead.

Diabetes, Imbalanced Insulin & Glucose Levels – Take 1-2 drops in a capsule or under tongue 2x's daily along with coriander or fennel.

Bronchitis & Asthma, Flu – Diffuse. Apply to chest, back, and bottoms of feet with rosemary or Siberian fir.

Constipation & Intestinal Cramping, Ulcers – Take 1-2 drops in a capsule 2x's daily. Apply diluted to abdomen with fennel.

Bacterial, Fungal & Viral Infections, Parasites – Apply to area(s) of concern. Take 1-2 drops in a capsule 2x's or more daily.

Emotional Balance – Use aromatically & topically to get from Divided ⟶ Integrous.

TOP PROPERTIES – Antiseptic, Antimicrobial, Immunostimulant, Digestive Stimulant, Refreshing, *(for more, see pg 260).*

SAFETY –

LAVENDER

Lavandula angustifolia

calming · regenerating · healing

TOP USES

Sleep Issues – Apply under nose, to bottoms of feet or diffuse to promote better sleep.

Stress, Anxiety & Teeth Grinding – Apply over heart, on back of neck or inhale from cupped hands.

Sunburns, Burns & Scars – Apply to area of concern to soothe, heal, and reduce scarring.

Allergies & Hay Fever – Take in a capsule or under tongue with lemon and peppermint or rub in palms and inhale from cupped hands.

Colic & Upset Baby – Massage diluted along spine, abdomen or bottoms of feet to calm.

Cuts, Wounds, & Blisters – Apply on site to cleanse, heal, and limit or avoid scarring.

Bug Bites & Hives – Apply on site to soothe as a natural antihistamine.

Nosebleeds & Pink Eye – Apply across bridge of nose or around eye.

High Blood Pressure – Use on pulse points and over heart or take in a capsule.

Emotional Balance – Use aromatically & topically to get from Unheard ⟶ Expressed.

TOP PROPERTIES – Sedative, Anti-histamine, Cytophylactic, Antispasmodic, Hypotensive, Nervine, Relaxing, Soothing, Antibacterial, *(for more, see pg 260).*

SAFETY – N

SINGLE OILS

uplifting · invigorating · refreshing

★ **TOP USES**

Kidney & Gallstones – Apply diluted over area of discomfort; add a heat pack to intensify action. Ingest a few drops in water or in a capsule to break up stones.

Ph Issues & Lymphatic Cleansing – Take in a glass of water or apply to ears and ankles to cleanse and balance pH.

Edema & Water Retention – Take in a capsule, glass of water, or massage into legs and bottoms of feet.

Heartburn & Reflux – Take with ginger essential oil in a capsule or glass of water.

Congestion & Mucus – Rub over chest or diffuse.

Runny Nose & Allergies – Inhale or apply over bridge of nose to relieve runny nose. Take 2-4 drops with lavender and peppermint in glass of water or in capsule for allergy relief.

Gout, Rheumatism & Arthritis – Take in a glass of water.

★ **Emotional Balance** –
Use aromatically & topically to get from Mindless ⟶ Energized.

★ **TOP PROPERTIES** – Antiseptic, Diuretic, Antioxidant, Antibacterial, Detoxification, Disinfectant, Mucolytic, Astringent, Degreaser *(for more, see pg 260).*

⚠ **SAFETY** –

electrifying · regenerating · purifying

★ **TOP USES**

Cancer & Tumors – Take in a capsule.

Blood Pressure & Cholesterol – Take in a capsule.

Hypothyroid or Hyperthyroid – Take in a capsule.

Bladder & Kidney Infection / Stones – Use in a capsule or dilute and apply diluted over abdomen.

Constipation & Water Retention – Combine with peppermint and apply diluted over abdomen or bottoms of feet and / or take in a capsule.

Connective Tissue Injury – Apply to affected area to soothe and repair.

Joint, Tendon & Ligament Pain – Apply diluted to affected area.

Lymphatic Congestion – Take in a capsule or apply to bottoms of feet.

Cooking – Add a drop for more flavorful dishes.

★ **Emotional Balance** –
Use aromatically & topically to get from Obstructed ⟶ Flowing.

★ **TOP PROPERTIES** – Anti-inflammatory, Antimicrobial, Analgesic, Anti-carcinoma, Antimutagenic, Decongestant, Regenerative, Anti-rheumatic *(for more, see pg 260).*

⚠ **SAFETY** –

LIME

Citrus aurantifolia

renewing · energizing · purifying

TOP USES

Sore Throat – Gargle a drop with water.

Respiratory, Lymph & Liver Congestion – Take in a capsule or apply topically over area of concern.

Urinary & Digestive Issues – Drink a few drops in a glass of water.

Memory & Clarity – Inhale or diffuse.

Exhaustion & Depression – Apply to ears or back of neck or diffuse to energize and uplift.

Herpes & Cold Sores – Take in a capsule or apply to outbreaks.

Chicken Pox – Use in a capsule or apply diluted to pox.

Head Lice – Add 20 drops with 15 drops melaleuca to bottle of shampoo and apply according to directions.

Pain & Inflammation – Massage over area of discomfort or take in a capsule to and increase antioxidants and decrease inflammation.

Emotional Balance – Use aromatically & topically to get from Faint ⟶ Enlivened.

TOP PROPERTIES – Anti-inflammatory, Antiseptic, Antioxidant, Antibacterial, Tonic, Uplifting, Detoxifier, Disinfectant, Diuretic *(for more, see pg 260)*.

SAFETY –

LITSEA

Litsea cubeba

cleansing · refreshing · uplifting

TOP USES

Asthma Attack, Spastic Coughs, Bronchitis – Apply to chest or inhale from cupped hands.

Acute & Chronic Back Pain – Apply to affected area. Dilute as needed.

Eczema, Acne & Oily Skin – Apply to affected area(s) or add to cleanser or lotion.

High Blood Pressure, Irregular Heartbeat, Anxiety – Apply to chest, back of neck and / or under nose.

Cough, Cold, Chills & Infections – Apply to chest, back of neck or along spine.

Seasonal Blues, Negative Thinking Or Speaking – Diffuse or inhale from cupped hands.

Nervous Tension, Headaches, Stressed Mind – Apply across forehead, on temples, diffuse, and / or inhale from cupped hands.

Nausea, Motion Sickness, Indigestion, Poor Appetite – Massage in circular motion into abdomen. Dilute as needed.

Emotional Balance – Use aromatically & topically to get from Encumbered ⟶ Purified.

TOP PROPERTIES – Refreshing, Detoxifier, Uplifting, Antibacterial, Antifungal, Antispasmodic, Disinfectant, Digestive Stimulant *(for more, see pg 260)*.

SAFETY –

CREDIT: *Litsea photography by Neux-Neux*

MAGNOLIA

Michelia X Alba

opening · resplendent · heavenly

TOP USES

Anxiety, Depression & Lack of Energy – Apply to back of neck, forehead, under nose, or over heart. Inhale from cupped hands.

PMS & Menstrual Cramps, Hormone Imbalances – Apply in clockwise circulatory motion over lower abdomen, and to wrists and ankles.

Irritability, Anger & Rage, Hysteria, Panic, Grief & Shock – Apply to back of neck, forehead, under nose, over heart, or bottoms of feet. Inhale from cupped hands.

Respiratory, Sinus & Lymphatic Congestion – Apply to chest and back and/or to bottom of feet. Combine with cardamom or eucalyptus.

Libido & Sex Drive, Breast & Prostate Issues – Apply to wrists, chest, back of neck, or reproductive organ reflex points.

Stressed, Worried, Uptight & Tense – Apply to back of neck, forehead, under nose, or bottoms of feet. Inhale from cupped hands.

Emotional Balance –
Use aromatically & topically to get from Disturbed ⟶ Confident.

TOP PROPERTIES – Sedative, Relaxant, Antidepressant, Aphrodisiac, Decongestant, Stomachic *(for more, see pg 260)*.

SAFETY – Avoid keeping in hot places.

MANUKA

Leptospermum scoparium

supporting · transforming · harmonizing

TOP USES

Achy Joints & Muscle Pain – Massage diluted into affected area(s).

Dandruff, Scalp Issues – Apply to scalp or add 2-3 drops to shampoo or conditioner.

Athlete's Foot, Toe Fungus Or Fingernail Issues – Apply to bottoms of feet and / or drop into warm soak.

Irritated & Chaffed Skin, Acne, Rashes – Apply to affected area(s). Dilute as needed.

Cold, Fever, Cough, Sinus Congestion, Asthma – Diffuse, inhale from cupped hands, apply to chest.

Muscles Spasms & Contractions – Apply diluted with eucalyptus over affected area followed by hot compress.

Indigestion, Spicy Food Issues, & Toxicity – Apply to abdomen.

Seasonal Allergies & Sensitivity To Dust, Pets & Dander – Diffuse, inhale from cupped hands, or apply to bottoms of feet.

Emotional Balance –
Use aromatically & topically to get from Bothered ⟶ Revived.

TOP PROPERTIES – Anti-allergenic, Antibacterial, Anti-inflammatory, Antiviral, Relaxant *(for more, see pg 260)*.

SAFETY –

MARJORAM

Origanum marjorana

relaxing · connecting · pleasing

TOP USES

Carpal Tunnel, Tendinitis & Arthritis – Use on area of discomfort to soothe and calm.

Muscle Cramps & Sprains – Massage diluted to relieve cramping or sprain.

High Blood Pressure & Heart Issues – Apply over heart and to pulse points or take with 2 drops lemongrass in a capsule.

Croup & Bronchitis – Apply to neck, chest, and upper back.

Pancreatitis – Apply a drop or two over pancreas area.

Overactive Sex Drive – Apply to abdomen.

Boils, Cold Sores & Ringworm – Take in a capsule or apply to affected area.

Migraines & Headaches – Massage onto back of neck, along hairline, and temples.

Colic & Constipation – Take in a capsule or massage diluted over abdomen and on lower back.

Emotional Balance – Use aromatically & topically to get from Doubtful ⟶ Trusting.

TOP PROPERTIES – Vasodilator, Anti-spasmodic, Digestive Stimulant, Antibacterial, Antifungal, Hypotensive, Sedative *(for more, see pg 260)*.

SAFETY –

MELALEUCA

Melaleuca alternifolia

powerful · cleansing · resolving

TOP USES

Cuts & Wounds – Use to clean and disinfect wounds.

Bacteria, Viruses & Diarrhea – Take in a capsule or apply to abdomen.

Cankers & Cold Sores – Use on site to prevent and treat.

Athlete's Foot & Candida Issues – Take in a capsule or dilute and apply on affected area.

Sore Throat & Tonsillitis – Take in a capsule or gargle with warm water.

Dandruff, Scabies, Lice – Apply to affected area or add to your shampoo, lather and soak.

Ear Infections – Apply behind and around ear.

Shock – Apply under nose or along spine.

Acne, Pinkeye, Staph Infection & MRSA – Take in a capsule or apply on or around affected area.

Bronchitis, Cold & Flu – Use in a capsule, rub on throat or diffuse.

Emotional Balance – Use aromatically & topically to get from Unsure ⟶ Collected.

TOP PROPERTIES – Antiseptic, Antibacterial, Antifungal, Anti-parasitic, Antiviral, Analgesic, Decongestant *(for more, see pg 260)*.

SAFETY – N

MELISSA

Melissa officinalis

awakening · authentic · restorative

TOP USES

Fevers, Colds & Viral Infections – Apply diluted along spine, bottoms of feet, or take in a capsule to boost anti-viral strength.

Cold Sores, Herpes & Fever Blisters – Apply directly to sores or take in a gel capsule.

Depression, Anxiety & Shock – Apply to back of neck and ears, diffuse, or apply to roof of mouth and hold for 5-10 seconds.

Bites, Stings & Warts – Apply directly to area of concern or to bottoms of feet.

Allergies – Breathe in from cupped hands, or apply over bridge of nose and to bottoms of feet. Take in a capsule.

Hypertension, Palpitations & High Blood Pressure – Diffuse, take in a capsule, or apply to back of neck or over heart.

Vertigo – Use or apply behind ears and back of neck.

Eczema – Take in a capsule or apply behind ears and back of neck.

Emotional Balance –
Use aromatically & topically to get from Depressed ⟶ Light-filled.

TOP PROPERTIES – Antioxidant, Antibacterial, Antidepressant, Antispasmodic, Antihistamine, Antiviral, Hypotensive, Nervine, Sedative *(for more, see pg 260).*

SAFETY – N

MYRRH

Commiphora myrrha

drying · healing · nurturing

TOP USES

Gum Disease & Bleeding – Apply directly to gums to soothe and repair.

Fine Lines & Dry Skin – Apply to areas of concern.

Thyroid & Immune Health – Apply to base of neck and bottoms of feet.

Digestive Upset & Cramping – Apply to abdomen or take in capsule.

Eczema & Wounds – Apply to affected area, especially to weeping areas.

Infection & Virus – Take in a capsule or apply to bottoms of feet.

Congestion & Mucus – Apply to chest and diffuse to clear airways and dry up congestion.

Meditation – Diffuse to create a sense of calm.

Depression & Anxiety – Apply to flex points or diffuse.

Emotional Balance –
Use aromatically & topically to get from Disconnected ⟶ Nurtured.

TOP PROPERTIES – Anti-inflammatory, Antiviral, Antimicrobial, Expectorant, Anti-infectious, Carminative, Antifungal *(for more, see pg 260).*

SAFETY – N

NEROLI

Citrus aurantium

arousing · rejuvenating · tranquilizing

TOP USES

Loss of Sexual Arousal, Impotence, Erectile Dysfunction & Frigidity – Apply diluted to area of concern, diffuse, and / or inhale from cupped hands.

Chronic & Stress-Related Or Nervous Depression, Elevated Cortisol Levels & Tension Headaches – Diffuse, inhale from cupped hands, apply diluted to chest, solar plexus, back of neck, temples, and/or under nose.

Damaged, Dry, Wrinkled, Sagging & Scarred Skin – Apply diluted to area of concern.

Childbirth & Pregnancy – Apply under nose and / or to abdomen to soothe mother. Apply diluted to lower back to ease anxiety during labor.

Heart Palpitations, High Blood Pressure, & Seizures – Apply to heart area, area of concern, and / or back of neck.

Emotional Balance – Use aromatically & topically to get from Afflicted ⟶ Released.

TOP PROPERTIES – Antidepressant, Anti-inflammatory, Antimutagenic, Aphrodisiac, Cytophylactic, Neurotonic, Regenerative, Sedative, Warming *(for more, see pg 260)*.

SAFETY –

OREGANO

Origanum vulgare

strong · resolving · powerful

TOP USES

Viruses & Bacterial Infection – Take in a capsule.

Strep Throat & Tonsillitis – Gargle a drop as needed.

Staph Infection & MRSA – Apply diluted to affected area or take I in a capsule.

Intestinal Worms & Parasites – Take in a capsule.

Warts, Calluses & Canker Sores – Apply diluted with fractionated coconut oil and frankincense directly to affected areas.

Pneumonia & Tuberculosis – Apply diluted or neat to bottoms of feet.

Boost Progesterone – Take in a capsule.

Urinary Infection – Take with lemongrass in a capsule.

Athlete's Foot, Ringworm & Candida – Apply diluted to area of concern and / or take in a capsule.

Emotional Balance – Use aromatically & topically to get from Obstinate ⟶ Unattached.

TOP PROPERTIES – Antibacterial, Antifungal, Anti-parasitic, Antiviral, Immunostimulant *(for more, see pg 260)*.

SAFETY –

calming · recovering · stabilizing

★ TOP USES

Anxiety & Dopamine Issues – Diffuse or apply under nose and back of neck to calm emotions.

Shingles & Herpes – Apply to area of concern and bottoms of feet, and / or take in a capsule.

Dry Skin & Dandruff – Apply to area of concern.

Oily Hair & Impetigo – Apply to area of concern.

Nerve Issues – Apply to soothe and heal nerves.

Body Odor – Apply as a deodorant and take in a capsule.

Fluid Retention – Take with grapefruit in a capsule.

Insect & Mosquito Repellent – Diffuse or apply to repel pests.

Insect Bites, Snake Bites & Stings – Apply with lavender to soothe bites or stings.

★ **Emotional Balance** – Use aromatically & topically to get from Degraded ⟶ Enhanced.

★ **TOP PROPERTIES** – Aphrodisiac, Sedative, Diuretic, Antifungal, Antispasmodic, Insecticide, Antidepressant *(for more, see pg 260).*

⚠ **SAFETY** – N

adaptive · invigorating · cooling

★ TOP USES

Headaches & Migraines – Apply to temples, above ears, and back of neck.

Bad Breath & Hangover – Gargle a drop with water.

Asthma & Sinusitis – Apply to chest and back or bottoms of feet.

Decrease Milk Supply – Apply diluted to breasts, take in a capsule or in water.

Loss Of Sense Of Smell – Inhale or apply diluted over bridge of nose.

Gastritis & Digestive Discomfort – Take in a capsule, in water, or apply over abdomen.

Alertness & Energy – Inhale or apply under nose or back of neck.

Fevers & Hot Flashes – Apply on back of neck, spine, or bottoms of feet for cooling effect.

Burns & Sunburn – Apply neat or diluted to burned skin.

★ **Emotional Balance** – Use aromatically & topically to get from Hindered ⟶ Invigorated.

★ **TOP PROPERTIES** – Anti-inflammatory, Analgesic, Antispasmodic, Warming, Invigorating, Cooling, Expectorant, Vasoconstrictor, Stimulating *(for more, see pg 260).*

⚠ **SAFETY** –

SINGLE OILS

PETITGRAIN

Citrus aurantium

uplifting · invigorating · refreshing

TOP USES

Bacterial Infections & Wounds – Apply to affected area or take in a capsule.

Spastic Cough & Congestion – Apply to chest, diffuse, or take in a capsule.

Abdominal & Muscular Cramps / Spasms – Apply diluted to affected area.

Convulsions & Seizures – Apply to back of neck, and / or bottoms of feet.

Fearful & Anxious Thinking – Diffuse or inhale from cupped hands.

Sudden Anger, Shock & Hysteria – Diffuse or inhale from cupped hands.

Weakened Nerves & Insomnia – Diffuse before going to bed or add a few drops with lavender or bergamot to pillows and bedding.

Body Odor – Blend with other oils and apply as perfume, cologne, body spray, or body lotion.

Dandruff & Oily Hair – Add 2 drops to shampoo and apply, lather, soak, and rinse.

Emotional Balance – Use aromatically & topically to get from Conflicted ⟶ Harmonized.

TOP PROPERTIES – Antidepressant, Antiseptic, Antispasmodic, Cardiotonic, Detoxifier, Immunostimulant, Nervine, Sedative, Tonic, Uplifting *(for more, see pg 260).*

SAFETY –

PINK PEPPER

Schinus molle

eliminating · clarifying · enlivening

TOP USES

Lymphatic & Candida Cleansing, Cancer – Combine with frankincense and take 1-2 drops 2x's daily in water or capsule.

Crohn's Disease, Nausea & Vomiting, Gas & Bloating, Poor Appetite – Use with cardamom and apply to area(s) of concern. Take 1-2 drops multiple times per day.

Pain Med Addiction – Combine with copaiba & black pepper and take 1-2 drops 2x's daily.

Gout, Rheumatism & Arthritis – Combine with frankincense & copaiba and apply to area(s) of concern and/or take.

PMS, Cramps, Menstrual Pain, Breast Health – Apply to area(s) of concern or related reflexology points with marjoram and geranium.

Respiratory Issues & Bronchitis – Apply to chest and back over lung area or take 1-2 drops. Diffuse with melaleuca.

Poor Circulation – Take or apply diluted with clove.

Emotional Balance – Use aromatically & topically to get from Impeded ⟶ Aroused.

TOP PROPERTIES – Invigorating, Purifier, Anti-inflammatory, Antioxidant, Refreshing, Antimicrobial, Digestive Stimulant *(for more, see pg 260).*

SAFETY – Avoid use at bedtime.

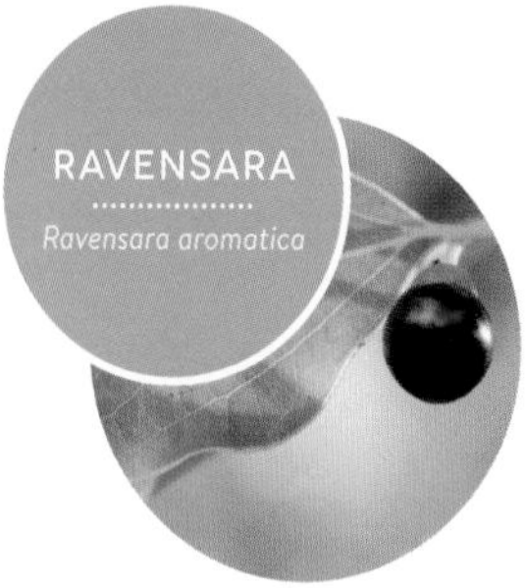

RAVENSARA

Ravensara aromatica

reviving · clearing · relaxing

TOP USES

Chills & Flu – Apply to affected area & bottoms of feet.

Whooping Cough & Bronchitis – Apply to chest, upper back, and bottoms of feet, or diffuse.

Nervous & Mental Fatigue – Apply to back of neck and adrenal pulse points.

Germs & Bugs – Diffuse to cleanse air.

Muscle & Joint Pain – Apply to affected area.

Emotional Balance – Use aromatically & topically to get from Uncommitted ⟶ Resolute.

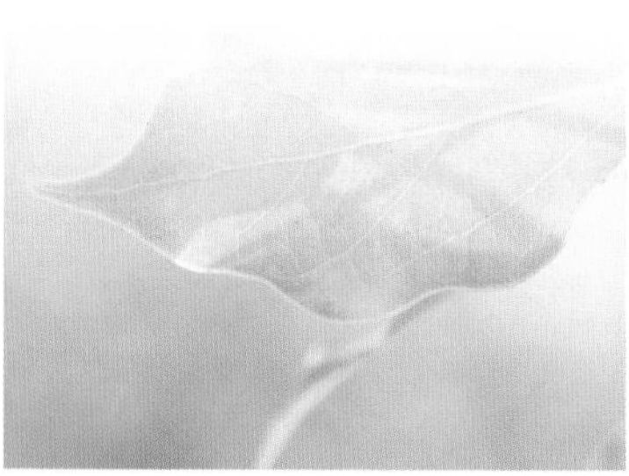

TOP PROPERTIES – Antiviral, Antibacterial, Immunostimulant, Expectorant, Analgesic, Muscle Relaxant, Stimulant *(for more, see pg 260)*.

SAFETY – N

RED MANDARIN

Citrus reticulata

cleansing · guided · supported

TOP USES

Acne & Oily Skin, Wounds – Apply to areas of concern to clarify and prevent wound infection.

Bloating, Gas, Hiccups & Indigestion, IBS, Colic, Leaky Gut – Apply to chest, back, or forehead. Take 1-2 drops under tongue or in a capsule.

Congestion, Severe & Spastic Coughs – Apply to chest , back, or forehead. Take 1-2 drops under tongue as often as needed.

Wrinkles, Age Spots, Scars, Stretch Marks – Add to daily skin care products and apply to area(s) of concern.

Bacterial, Fungal & Viral Infections – Apply to areas of concern. Take 1-2 drops in a capsule every few hours as needed.

Nervous Afflictions, Tension, Hyperactivity in Children – Apply under nose and to bottoms of feet. Diffuse. Take 1-2 drops under tongue.

Emotional Balance – Use aromatically & topically to get from Troubled ⟶ Resilient.

TOP PROPERTIES – Antimicrobial, Antiseptic, Detoxifying, Digestive Stimulant, Cyptophylactic, Immunostimulant, Antispasmodic, Uplifting *(for more, see pg 260)*.

SAFETY – Avoid keeping in hot places / sun.

ROMAN CHAMOMILE

Anthemis nobilis

bright · calming · sweet

TOP USES

Stress & Stock – Diffuse or apply to back of neck and inhale from cupped hands.

Dry, Irritated & Aging Skin – Apply to area of concern.

Lower Blood Pressure – Apply over heart, back of neck, or take in a capsule.

Sciatica & Lower Back Pain – Apply to area of concern.

Insomnia & Overexcitement – Diffuse or apply to back of neck and forehead.

PMS & Cramps – Apply to abdomen or areas of discomfort. Reapply frequently.

Fevers & Earaches – Apply to bottoms of feet and ears as needed.

Anger, Irritability & Agitation – Diffuse or apply under nose or back of neck.

Parasites & Worms – Apply to abdomen or take in a capsule to promote expulsion.

Anorexia – Apply to back of neck or take in a capsule.

Emotional Balance – Use aromatically & topically to get from Frustrated ⟶ Purposeful.

TOP PROPERTIES – Antihistamine, Antibacterial, Antifungal, Sedative, Immunostimulant, Hypnotic *(for more, see pg 260)*.

SAFETY – N

ROSE

Rosa damascena

intimate · connecting · radiant

TOP USES

Low Libido – Diffuse or inhale from cupped hands, or apply diluted to abdomen or bottoms of feet.

Scars, Wounds – Apply a drop to area of concern.

Grief & Depression – Diffuse and apply to back of neck and over heart.

Irregular Ovulation – Apply diluted over abdomen.

Seizures – Apply diluted to back of neck.

Wrinkles, Facial Capillaries & Redness – Apply diluted to area of concern.

Semen Production & Impotency – Apply a drop to navel and diluted to bottoms of feet.

Emotional Balance – Use aromatically & topically to get from Isolated ⟶ Loved.

TOP PROPERTIES – Antidepressant, Aphrodisiac, Antispasmodic, Emmenagogue, Sedative, Tonic *(for more, see pg 260)*.

SAFETY – N

SINGLE OILS

ROSEMARY

Rosmarinus officinalis

refreshing · cooling · clearing

TOP USES

Respiratory Infections & Conditions – Apply to chest and diffuse.

Prostate Issues & Nighttime Urination – Apply to bottoms of feet and in a capsule.

Cancer – Take in a capsule.

Hair Loss & Dandruff – Apply to scalp.

Memory & Focus – Apply under nose and across forehead or diffuse.

Bell's Palsy & Multiple Sclerosis – Apply to bottoms of feet or in a capsule.

Mental, Adrenal & Chronic Fatigue – Diffuse or apply under nose with basil or peppermint.

Jaundice, Liver & Kidney Issues – Apply to bottoms of feet or in a capsule.

Nervousness, Depression, Addiction & Dopamine Issues – Apply under nose or diffuse.

Muscle & Bone Pain – Apply to area of concern.

Emotional Balance – Use aromatically & topically to get from Confused ⟶ Open-minded.

TOP PROPERTIES – Analgesic, Thins mucus, Improves brain function, Stimulant *(for more, see pg 260).*

SAFETY –

SANDALWOOD

Santalum album

calming · sweet · woody

TOP USES

Dry Skin & Scalp – Use topically or in shampoo.

Calming & Relaxing – Inhale or diffuse and apply under nose.

Scars & Blemishes – Apply directly to affected area.

Wound Care & Skin Infections – Apply to heal skin.

Spasms & Cramps – Apply over area of concern.

Low Testosterone & Impotence – Apply to area of desired results.

Sinus Infection – Apply over bridge of nose, inhale from cupped hands, or take in a capsule.

Cancer & Tumors – Take in a capsule to protect against tumors.

Alzheimer's Disease – Take in a capsule or on bottoms of feet and back of neck.

Emotional Balance – Use aromatically & topically to get from Uninspired ⟶ Devoted.

TOP PROPERTIES – Anti-inflammatory, Anti-carcinoma, Astringent, Antidepressant, Calming, Sedative *(for more, see pg 260).*

SAFETY – N

CREDIT: *Siberian fir Photography by Krzysztof Ziarnek, Kenraiz*

SIBERIAN FIR

Abies sibirica

affirming · vitalizing · connecting

TOP USES

Pain & Inflammation, Rheumatism, Arthritis & Gout, Tired & Achy Muscles – Take in a capsule or massage into area of concern.

Constricted Breathing, Congestion, Cold, Flu, Fever & Sore Throat – Apply to chest, bottoms of feet, along spine, diffuse, and / or inhale from cupped hands.

Broken Bones & Osteoporosis – Apply diluted with helichrysum and cypress or take in a capsule.

Candida & Urinary Infections – Take in a capsule, and/or apply to abdomen.

Poor Circulation, Hemorrhoids & Low Blood Pressure – Apply to area of concern and / or bottoms of feet.

Sluggish Digestion, Metabolism & Liver Function – Massage into abdomen, or take in a capsule.

Emotional Balance –
Use aromatically & topically to get from Excluded ⟶ Empowered.

TOP PROPERTIES – Analgesic, Anti-fungal, Anti-inflammatory, Detoxifier, Energizing, Expectorant, Refreshing *(for more, see pg 260).*

SAFETY –

SPEARMINT

Mentha spicata

relieving · uplifting · promoting

TOP USES

Indigestion, Nausea & Colic – Apply over abdomen or take in a capsule.

Bad Breath – Swish and swallow a drop in water.

Bronchitis & Respiratory Issues – Apply to chest and back or diffuse .

Acne, Sores & Scars – Apply to area of concern.

Cooling – Apply to back of neck.

Focus Issues – Apply to back of neck and under nose.

Depression & Fatigue – Diffuse and apply to back of neck.

Stress & Nervous Issues – Diffuse and apply to back of neck.

Slow Or Heavy Menstruation – Diffuse and apply over abdomen or back of neck.

Headaches & Migraines – Diffuse and apply to temples and back of neck.

Emotional Balance –
Use aromatically & topically to get from Weary ⟶ Refreshed.

TOP PROPERTIES – Anti-inflammatory, Digestive, Stimulant, Carminative, Antiseptic *(for more, see pg 260).*

SAFETY – N

SPIKENARD

Nardostachys jatamansi

healing · rejuvenating · uplifting

TOP USES

Aging & Irritated Skin – Add a drop to facial cleanser or moisturizer.

Insomnia, Stress & Tension – Diffuse and apply to bottoms of feet.

PMS & Menstrual Issues – Apply to abdomen, back of neck, and pulse points.

Candida & Vaginal Thrush – Apply to affected area; dilute as needed.

Convulsions, Seizures & Muscle Spasms – Apply to back of neck and affected area.

Detoxing, Diuretic & Cellulite – Apply to affected area or bottoms of feet.

Terminally Ill & Hospice – Apply to bottoms of feet and diffuse.

Ulcers, Gas & Indigestion – Apply to abdomen.

Pinkeye & Rashes – Apply diluted to affected area or around eye.

Emotional Balance – Use aromatically & topically to get from Agitated ⟶ Tranquil.

TOP PROPERTIES – Anti-inflammatory, Antispasmodic, Sedative, Antibacterial, Antifungal, Deodorant, Laxative, Tonic *(for more, see pg 260).*

SAFETY – N

TANGERINE

Citrus reticulata

calming · clearing · uplifting

TOP USES

Antioxidant, Immune Boost & Cell Protection – Take in water or in a capsule.

Sadness & Irritability, Impulsiveness – Diffuse or inhale from cupped hands. Apply under nose or take in water.

Sleep Issues & Anxiety, Nervousness – Diffuse or inhale from cupped hands. Apply under nose, or take in water.

Digestive & Eliminative Disturbances, Parasites – Take in water or in a capsule and apply to abdomen.

Overthinking & Feeling Stuck – Diffuse or inhale from cupped hands or apply under nose and across forehead.

Edema, Cellulite, Pocket Fat – Massage into area of concern or take in water or in a capsule.

Skin Irritations, Rashes & Burns – Apply diluted to area of concern.

Dry, Cracked Skin & Dandruff – Apply diluted to area of concern.

Emotional Balance – Use aromatically & topically to get from Oppressed ⟶ Restored.

TOP PROPERTIES – Energizing, Sedative, Uplifting, Antioxidant, Cytophylactic, Detoxifier, Mucolytic, Sedative, Stomachic, *(for more, see pg 260).*

SAFETY –

resolving · powerful · expelling

TOP USES

Cold, Flu & Viruses – Take in a capsule or inhale.

Asthma, Croup & Pneumonia – Dilute and massage into chest and inhale from cupped hands. Take in a capsule.

Candida & Parasites – Take in a capsule or inhale.

Infertility, Progesterone, Breast, Ovary & Prostate Issues – Apply to reflex points on feet and take internally.

Memory, Concentration & Dementia – Inhale and apply to back of neck to increase alertness, memory, and brain health.

Low Blood Pressure – Apply to bottoms of feet and pulse points.

Incontinence & Bladder Infection – Combine with geranium and take in a capsule or apply over abdomen.

Fibroids & Cancer – Take in a capsule or inhale.

Emotional Balance – Use aromatically & topically to get from Unyielding ⟶ Yielding.

TOP PROPERTIES – Analgesic, Mucolytic, Stimulant, Antioxidant, Anti-rheumatic, Antiviral, Expectorant *(for more, see pg 260).*

SAFETY –

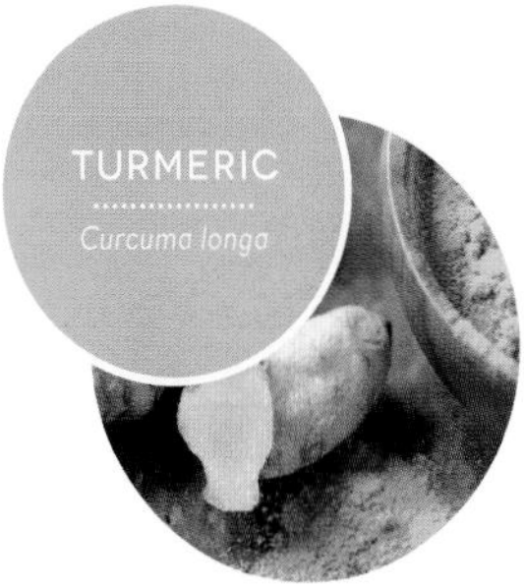

compelling · certain · dynamic

TOP USES

Cancer & Tumors, Autoimmune Disorders – Take 1-2 drops multiple times daily as part of a protocol.

Joint Pain & Swelling, Arthritis, Gout, Rheumatism – Apply to areas of concern. Take 1-2 drops multiple times daily.

Fungal, Bacterial or Viral infections – Take 1-2 drops multiple times daily and apply where needed until relief.

Alzheimer, Stroke, Poor Blood Supply – Take 1-2 drops multiple times daily. Inhale from palms. Apply to forehead, bottoms of feet, and along spine.

Intestinal Worms & Parasites – Take 1-2 drops 2x's daily or more as needed.

Depression & Discouragement, Tension & Anxiety – Diffuse. Apply to back of head and along spine.

Cavities & Oral Health – Add to toothpaste or mouthwash. Gargle, swish, and spit.

Emotional Balance – Use aromatically & topically to get from Compromised ⟶ Assured.

TOP PROPERTIES – Anti-inflammatory, Anti-carcinogenic, Detoxifier, Antibacterial, Antioxidant, Antimutagenic, Anticancer, Anti-tumoral, Decongestant, Antiviral *(for more, see pg 260).*

SAFETY – Toxic if administered to plants.

VETIVER

Vetiveria zizanioides

regenerating · reassuring · enduring

TOP USES

ADD, ADHD, Focus & Concentration – Apply to back of neck, along spine, and / or under nose.

Learning Difficulties & Poor Retention – Apply to back of neck, and / or under nose.

PTSD, Depression & Anxiety – Combine with melissa and apply to back of neck, forehead, and pulse points.

Insomnia & Irritability – Apply to bottoms of feet or back of neck.

Anorexia – Apply to back of neck or across forehead.

Vitiligo – Apply to affected areas of the skin.

Tuberculosis – Apply to feet, spine, and chest.

Breast Enlargement – Apply diluted to breasts.

Postpartum Depression– Apply to back of neck, under nose, and pulse points.

Stretch Marks, Discoloration & Scars– Apply to affected areas to ease skin variations.

Emotional Balance – Use aromatically & topically to get from Ungrounded ⟶ Rooted.

TOP PROPERTIES – Stimulant, Tonic, Sedative, Antiseptic, Immunostimulant, Vermifuge, Antispasmodic, Rubefacient *(for more, see pg 260).*

SAFETY – N

WHITE FIR

Abies alba

stimulating · clearing · calming

TOP USES

Sinusitis & Asthma – Apply to bridge of nose and chest or diffuse to ease breathing.

Muscles & Joint Pain – Massage diluted on affected area for soothing relief.

Muscle Fatigue & Regeneration – Apply diluted to area of concern.

Bursitis & Rheumatism – Apply to affected areas.

Airborne Pathogens – Diffuse to fight germs.

Circulation Issues & Bruising – Massage into affected areas to increase circulation and healing.

Stress & Foggy Mind – Diffuse with frankincense for better focus and clarity.

Bronchitis & Congestion – Apply to chest or bridge of nose.

Colds & Flu – Apply to chest and diffuse.

Urinary Infection & Edema – Apply over lower abdomen.

Furniture Polish – Apply to surface using a cloth.

Emotional Balance – Use aromatically & topically to get from Blocked ⟶ Receiving.

TOP PROPERTIES – Analgesic, Antiarthritic, Antiseptic, Stimulant, Antioxidant *(for more, see pg 260).*

SAFETY – N

WILD ORANGE

Citrus sinensis

uplifting · invigorating · renewing

TOP USES

Insomnia & Stress – Diffuse or inhale from cupped hands or take a few drops under tongue at bedtime.

Heartburn & Sluggish Bowels – Take in a capsule with ginger.

Scurvy & Colds – Diffuse or apply on bottoms of feet.

Menopause – Apply to abdomen, pulse points, and diffuse.

Depression, Fear, Anxiety & Irritability – Apply under nose, across forehead, or pulse points. Diffuse or inhale from cupped hands.

Lack Of Energy, Creativity & Productivity – Take in a capsule, apply under nose, or diffuse.

Concentration – Combine with peppermint and diffuse or inhale from cupped hands.

Detox & Regeneration – Take in a glass of water or capsule.

Emotional Balance – Use aromatically & topically to get from Drained ⟶ Productive.

TOP PROPERTIES – Energizing, Sedative, Anti-carcinoma, Carminative, Antiseptic, Anti-depressant, Immunostimulant *(for more, see pg 260).*

SAFETY –

WINTERGREEN

Gaultheria fragrantissima

warming · relieving · repairing

TOP USES

Gout & Rheumatism – Dilute and apply to affected area to soothe discomfort.

Teeth Whitening – Apply to affected area.

Warming & Circulation to Extremities – Dilute and apply to affected areas.

Arthritis & Cramps – Dilute and apply to ease pain.

Neuralgia & Cramps – Dilute and apply to relieve cramps.

Bone Spurs & Pain – Dilute and apply to affected area.

Cartilage Injury & Bruising – Dilute and apply.

Rotator Cuff Issues & Frozen Shoulder – Dilute and apply to affected area to ease pain and inflammation.

Dandruff – Mix a few drops with shampoo and apply to scalp.

Dermatitis – Dilute and apply to affected areas to reduce irritation.

Emotional Balance – Use aromatically & topically to get from Stubborn ⟶ Accepting.

TOP PROPERTIES – Anti-inflammatory, Analgesic, Anti-rheumatic *(for more, see pg 260).*

SAFETY –

YARROW

Achillea millefolium

purging · relieving · mending

TOP USES

Bleeding, Hemorrhaging, Internal Wounds & Scarring – Take I in a capsule or in water.

Varicose Veins & Hemorrhoids, Sagging & Aging Skin – Apply with carrier oil to affected area. Add a hot compress to take deeper.

Irregular or Absent Menstruation & Early Menopause – Apply to abdomen, drop in a sitz bath, and / or take in a capsule.

Pain & Inflammation, Arthritis, Rheumatism – Apply to area of concern, or take in a capsule.

Fever, Viral Infection & Allergies – Apply to abdomen, drop in a sitz bath, and / or take in a capsule.

Low Perspiration & Poor Circulation – Apply to bottoms of feet or area of concern. Use in a steam bath to promote sweating and release toxins.

Cancer & Free Radical Damage – Take in a capsule or in water for antioxidant qualities.

Emotional Balance – Use aromatically & topically to get from Invaded ⟶ Shielded.

TOP PROPERTIES – Antihemorrhagic, Anti-rheumatic, Antiviral, Emmenagogue, Regenerative *(for more, see pg 260).*

SAFETY –

YLANG YLANG

Cananga odorata

calming · floral · soothing

TOP USES

Low Libido, Impotence, Infertility & Hormone Imbalance – Apply to abdomen, pulse points, or take under tongue, or in a capsule.

Equilibrium & High Blood Pressure – Apply to back of neck, across forehead, and behind ears. Inhale from cupped hands. Take I under tongue or in a capsule.

Irregular Heartbeat & Palpitations – Apply to bottoms of feet and over the heart. Inhale from cupped hands.

Adrenal, Mental, Or Heart Fatigue / Loss Of Will Or Apathy – Apply on affected area or take in a capsule.

Anxiety, Frustration, Stress & Fear – Diffuse or inhale from cupped hands and apply under nose or to bottoms of feet.

Hair Loss – Massage into scalp to stimulate hair growth.

Colic & Stomach Ache – Apply diluted to abdomen or take in a capsule.

Emotional Balance – Use aromatically & topically to get from Burdened ⟶ Exuberant.

TOP PROPERTIES – Hypotensive, Aphrodisiac, Antispasmodic, Sedative *(for more, see pg 260).*

SAFETY – N

Oil Blends

While many companies provide blends of essential oils, the proprietary blends found in this book have been carefully and artistically crafted to offer superior efficacy and therapeutic benefits. Because natural chemistry is a crucial point of attention in the art of blending essential oils, it is important to turn to blends that possess qualities of highest purity, potency, and complementary relationships between the individual oils that comprise the blend.

Please note the symbols = aromatic = topical = internal that specify recommended usage. While all oils are meant to be used aromatically, and most topically, only verified pure therapeutic essential oils are intended for internal use. *(See "Why Quality Matters," page 18 and "How to Use Essential Oils" page 23 for further detail.)*

Following symbols for safety:

N = NEAT application = avoid sunlight for 12 hours

= dilute as needed = if pregnant or nursing, consult your physician

= avoid contact with eyes, inner ears, and sensitive areas

regenerating · youthful · replenishing

TOP USES

Wrinkles & Fine Lines – Apply to face, neck, and hands.

Sun Damage & Skin Cancer – Apply to affected area to promote renewal and healing.

Scars & Stretch Marks – Apply to affected areas.

Blemishes – Apply to affected areas.

Meditation – Apply under nose or to pulse points.

MAIN INGREDIENTS – Frankincense, Hawaiian sandalwood, Lavender, Myrrh, Helichrysum, Rose

SAFETY – N

alluring · exquisite · lovely

TOP USES

Energizing, Uplifting Mood & Environment – Diffuse. Apply to pulse points, back of neck, along spine, and/or bottoms of feet.

Calm, Supported & Relaxed – Diffuse. Apply to pulse points, back of neck, along spine, and/or bottoms of feet.

Focused Heart, Mind & Body – Diffuse. Apply to pulse points, back of neck, along spine, and/or bottoms of feet.

Empowered, Meditation & Tranquility – Diffuse. Apply to pulse points, back of neck, along spine, and/or bottoms of feet.

Be True to Self – Diffuse. Apply to pulse points, back of neck, along spine, and/or bottoms of feet.

Magnify your Radiance in Feminine Energy – Diffuse. Apply to pulse points, back of neck, along spine, and/or bottoms of feet.

Perfume – Apply to pulse points, chest, back of neck, and behind ears.

MAIN INGREDIENTS – Lime, Osmanthus, Bergamot, Frankincense

SAFETY – N

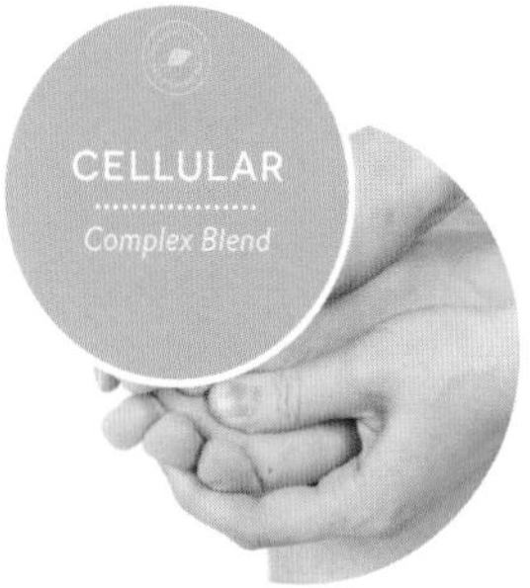

regenerating · corrective · repairing

★ **TOP USES**

Cancer & Tumors – Apply diluted to back of neck, along spine, or bottoms of feet. Take in a capsule.

Estrogen, Progesterone, & Thyroid Issues – Apply diluted to back of neck, along spine, or bottoms of feet. Take in a capsule.

Candida & Fungal Conditions – Apply to bottoms of feet or take in a capsule.

Nerve Damage – Apply diluted to back of neck, along spine, or bottoms of feet. Take in a capsule.

Autoimmune Disorders – Apply diluted to back of neck, along spine, or bottoms of feet. Take in a capsule.

Seizures & Aging Brain – Apply diluted to back of neck, along spine, or bottoms of feet. Take in a capsule for antioxidant power.

Breast Issues – Apply diluted to breasts bottoms of feet, or take in a capsule.

Hot Flashes & Night Sweats – Apply to bottoms of feet or take in a capsule.

Detox & Viruses – Apply to bottoms of feet or take in a capsule.

MAIN INGREDIENTS – Frankincense, Wild orange, Lemongrass, Thyme, Summer savory, Clove, Niaouli

⚠ **SAFETY** –

trusting · fluid · accepting

★ **TOP USES**

Complimentary Yoga Poses – Seated Meditation, Warrior II, Triangle, and Gate Pose.

SCATTERED & OVERWHELMED – Apply under nose and across forehead. Inhale deeply from cupped hands.

Aligned, Singleminded, Tranquil & Focused – Diffuse. Apply to crown, neck area, and forehead.

Accepted & Worthy – Diffuse. Apply under nose, over heart, spleen, and solar plexus.

Meditation & Prayer – Diffuse. Apply over heart, to forehead, and inhale deeply.

Apathetic & Low Energy – Diffuse. Apply to pulse points, over heart and bottoms of feet.

Anger, Rage & Imbalanced Mood – Diffuse. Apply 1-2 drops in palm of hands, rub together, inhale deeply.

Perfume – Apply to pulse points, chest, behind ears, and on ankles.

MAIN INGREDIENTS – Bergamot, Coriander, Marjoram, Peppermint, Geranium, Basil, Jasmine, Rose

⚠ **SAFETY** – N

OIL BLENDS

CHILDREN'S COURAGE

Blend

empowering · assuring · invigorating

TOP USES

Discouraged & Unenthused – Apply under nose, to back of neck, over heart, and/or bottoms of feet.

Tired & Weary – Apply under nose, to back of neck, forehead, and/or bottoms of feet.

Lack of Determination & Conviction – Apply under nose, along spine, over heart, and/or bottoms of feet.

Afraid & Scared – Apply under nose, to back of neck, along spine, and/or bottoms of feet.

Lack of Confidence & Motivation – Apply under nose, to chest, back, and/or bottoms of feet.

Confused & Overwhelmed – Apply under nose, to back of neck, and forehead.

Digestive Upset, Nervous & Agitated – Apply to abdomen, forehead, and/or bottoms of feet.

Aches & Pain – Apply to area(s) of concern.

MAIN INGREDIENTS – Wild orange, Amyris, Osmanthus, Cinnamon

SAFETY – N

CHILDREN'S FOCUS

Blend

anchoring · enlivening · signaling

TOP USES

ADD / ADHD, HYPERACTIVITY – Apply under nose, to forehead, along spine, back of neck, and/or bottoms of feet.

Over & Underactive Brain – Apply under nose, to forehead, along spine, back of neck, and/or bottoms of feet.

Lack of Mental Clarity, Focus & Concentration – Apply under nose, to forehead, along spine, back of neck, and/or bottoms of feet.

Overwhelmed & Overthinking – Apply under nose, to forehead, along spine, back of neck, and/or bottoms of feet.

Stressed Out & Ungrounded – Apply under nose, to forehead, along spine, back of neck, and/or bottoms of feet.

Nervous, Anxious & Moody – Apply under nose, to chest, along spine, back of neck, and/or bottoms of feet.

Afternoon Slump & Disconnected – Apply under nose, to chest, along spine, and/or bottoms of feet.

Seizures – Apply under nose, to forehead, along spine, back of neck, and/or bottoms of feet.

MAIN INGREDIENTS – Vetiver, Clementine, Peppermint, Rosemary

SAFETY – N

CHILDREN'S GROUNDING Blend

balancing · steadying · quieting

★ TOP USES

Uncooperative & Obstinate, Out of Control – Apply to chest, forehead, and/or bottoms of feet.

Overstimulated & Overwhelmed – Apply under nose, to back of neck, and forehead.

Disconnected from the Earth & Reality – Apply under nose, and/or to bottoms of feet.

Focus Issues & Mood Swings – Apply under nose, over heart, and/or to forehead.

Restless & Out of Control – Apply under nose, to back of neck, along spine, and/or bottoms of feet.

Anger & Frustration, Tantrums – Apply under nose, to back of neck, up spine, over heart, and/or bottoms of feet.

Grief & Sad, Disappointment – Apply under nose, to chest, forehead, and/or bottoms of feet.

Bath & Bedtime Routine – Apply to bottoms of feet. Relax in warm bath.

MAIN INGREDIENTS – Amyris, Balsam fir, Coriander, Magnolia

SAFETY – N

CHILDREN'S PROTECTIVE Blend

fortifying · shielding · boosting

★ TOP USES

Bacteria & Viruses, Airborne Pathogens – Apply to area(s) of concern and bottoms of feet.

Flu, Weak Immunity, Poor Recovery – Apply under nose, over heart, along spine, and/or bottoms of feet.

Emotional Distress & Poor Boundaries – Inhale deeply from cupped hands. Apply to bottoms of feet.

Staph, Strep Throat & Cough – Apply to throat/neck, chest, along spine, and/or bottoms of feet.

Cold Sores, Warts & Infected Wounds – Apply to areas of concern.

Cuts & Scrapes – Apply to areas of concern.

Fungus & Parasites – Apply to areas of concern, over abdomen, along spine, and/or bottoms of feet.

Chronic Fatigue & Autoimmune Disease – Apply to chest, back, and/or bottoms of feet.

MAIN INGREDIENTS – Cedarwood, Litsea, Frankincense, Rose

SAFETY – N

CHILDREN'S RESTFUL

Blend

pacifying · relaxing · unwinding

TOP USES

Unsettled & Restless, Sleep Issues – Apply under nose and to bottoms of feet.

Stressed & Anxious – Apply under nose, to back of neck and forehead.

Fussy, Easily Upset & Startled – Apply to chest, and/or bottoms of feet.

Uptight & Wound Up, Moody – Apply under nose and across forehead or inhale deeply from cupped hands.

Muscles Aches & Growing Pains – Apply to areas of concern.

Angry, Agitated & Irritable – Apply to bottoms of feet and spine.

Bath & Bedtime Routine – Apply under nose, to forehead, and bottoms of feet. Relax in warm bath.

MAIN INGREDIENTS – Lavender, Cananga, Buddha wood, Roman chamomile

SAFETY – N

CHILDREN'S SOOTHING

Blend

alleviating · calming · comforting

TOP USES

Shock, Distress & Fear – Apply under nose, back of neck, forehead, and/or bottoms of feet.

Muscle Aches & Tension – Apply to areas of concern.

Growing Pains – Apply to areas of concern.

Headache, Migraines & Neck Pain – Apply to back of neck, forehead/temples, and shoulders.

Bruises & Injuries – Apply to areas of concern.

Bath & Bedtime Routine – Apply to areas of concern and bottoms of feet. Relax in warm bath.

MAIN INGREDIENTS – Lavender, Spearmint, Copaiba, Zanthoxylum

SAFETY – N

regenerating · corrective · repairing

★ **TOP USES**

Kill Germs & Microbes – Diffuse and spray *(diluted with water)* on surfaces.

Air & Odor Cleansing – Diffuse to eliminate odors.

Discouragement – Diffuse to uplift mood and clear mind.

Addictions – Diffuse or apply under nose, across forehead, or bottoms of feet.

Allergies – Apply to chest, bottoms of feet or diffuse.

Acne – Apply topically to area of concern.

Surface Cleaning – Add 6-8 drops and one tablespoon vinegar to glass spray bottle filled with water.

Insect Repellent – Diffuse to keep bugs and insects away.

Bug Bites & Stings – Apply with lavender to soothe bites and stings.

Laundry – Add 2-4 drops to a load of laundry.

Deodorant – Apply diluted under arms.

Lymphatic Detox – Apply diluted to skin or neat to bottoms of feet.

MAIN INGREDIENTS – Lemon, Lime, Siberian fir, Austrian fir, Pine, Citronella, Melaleuca, Cilantro

⚠ **SAFETY** –

sustaining · reconciling · alleviating

★ **TOP USES**

Grief & Sadness – Diffuse or apply under nose and to chest.

Emotional Release & Reassurance – Diffuse and apply under nose and over heart.

Fear & Emotional Pain Relief – Diffuse or apply under nose and to chest.

Brain Impairment – Apply to forehead, back of neck, and toes.

Spiritual Connectivity & Meditation – Apply to forehead and chest and inhale from cupped hands.

Low Libido – Diffuse or apply to abdomen.

Skin Repair & Anti-aging – Apply to affected area with carrier oil.

Lung & Bronchial Infection – Apply to chest, bottoms of feet, and / or diffuse.

Urinary Infection, Edema & Constipation – Apply over abdomen or to bottoms of feet.

Irregular & Racing Heartbeat – Apply under nose and to chest.

Fear & Emotional Pain Relief – Diffuse or apply under nose and to chest.

MAIN INGREDIENTS – Frankincense, Patchouli, Ylang ylang, Laudanum, Sandalwood, Rose

⚠ **SAFETY** –

DETOXIFICATION

Blend

refreshing · detoxing · clearing

TOP USES

Kidney, Gallbladder & Liver Cleansing – Take in a capsule or apply diluted to lower abdomen.

Heavy Metal Detoxification – Take in a capsule.

Constipation & Urinary Tract Infection – Take or apply diluted over abdomen.

Weight Loss & Detoxification – Take in a capsule.

Colitis & Jaundice – Take in a capsule or apply to abdomen or bottoms of feet.

Endocrine & Hormone Imbalance – Take in a capsule or apply to abdomen or bottoms of feet.

Adrenal Fatigue & Exhaustion – Take in a capsule or apply diluted to abdomen, back of neck, or bottoms of feet.

Hangover – Take in a capsule or apply to bottoms of feet.

MAIN INGREDIENTS – Tangerine, Rosemary, Geranium, Juniper berry, Cilantro

SAFETY –

DIGESTION

Blend

supportive · soothing · settling

TOP USES

Bloating, Gas, Heartburn, Nausea & Indigestion – Apply over abdomen and take in a capsule.

Reflux & Colic – Take in water or in a capsule with lemon.

Dry Or Sore Throat – Drop directly onto back of throat.

Morning Sickness & Heartburn – Apply to chest, pulse points, abdomen, and / or take in a glass of water.

Motion & Travel Sickness – Inhale, apply under nose or drink in water.

Colitis & Irritable Bowel – Take in a capsule, in water, and / or massage into abdomen daily.

Diarrhea & Constipation – Take in a capsule or in water until symptoms subside.

Crohn's Disease & Chronic Fatigue – Take in a capsule or rub on abdomen.

Food Poisoning – Take in a capsule or in water frequently.

Cough & Sinus Congestion – Apply diluted to navel and over bridge of nose or drink in water.

MAIN INGREDIENTS – Ginger, Peppermint, Caraway, Coriander, Anise, Tarragon, Fennel

SAFETY – N

motivating · energizing · believing

TOP USES

Lack of Confidence, Courage or Motivation – Diffuse and apply under nose, on forehead, back of neck, or chest.

Confusion & Overwhelm – Inhale or apply under nose, on forehead, back of neck, or chest.

Mental Fatigue & Exhaustion – Diffuse or apply to temples and back of neck.

Depletion & Stagnation – Inhale from cupped hands and apply to pulse points.

Depression – Diffuse or apply to chest, forehead, and back of neck.

Physical Exhaustion – Inhale from cupped hands, apply under nose, over adrenals, or to bottoms of feet to enhance endurance.

Digestive Issues – Apply over abdomen, on pulse points, or on bottoms of feet.

Bronchitis & Asthma – Diffuse or apply to neck and chest.

Aches & Pains – Apply to affected area.

MAIN INGREDIENTS – Peppermint, Basil Clementine, Coriander, Melissa, Rosemary

SAFETY –

rising · connecting · aligning

TOP USES

Complimentary Yoga Poses – Volcano, Standing Side Stretch, and Half Moon.

Connectedness with Self and Higher Power – Diffuse. Apply to crown, over heart, and along spine.

Intentional, Action-Oriented & Manifesting – Diffuse. Apply to ankles, along spine, and bottoms of feet.

Uplifted, Courageous & Empowered – Diffuse. Apply to forehead, over heart, and bottoms of feet.

Overwhelmed, Mental Chatter, Lack of Clarity – Diffuse. Apply to forehead, heels, and behind ears.

Feeling Challenged, Depression & Mood Swings – Diffuse. Apply to crown, over heart, behind ears, bottoms of feet, and pulse points.

Perfume – Apply to pulse points, chest, behind ears, and on ankles.

MAIN INGREDIENTS – Lemon, Grapefruit, Siberian fir, Osmanthus

SAFETY – N

grounding · earthly · clarifying

TOP USES

ADD / ADHD – Apply to back of neck, spine, or bottoms of feet.

Over- & Under-active Brain Activity – Apply to back of neck or spine to balance activity.

Mental Clarity, Focus & Concentration – Apply under nose and back of neck.

Calming & Grounding – Apply under nose, back of neck or to pulse points.

Nervousness, Anxiety & Depression – Apply under nose to bottoms of feet and back of neck.

Stress & Hyperactivity – Apply to back of neck and pulse points.

Mid-Afternoon Slump – Diffuse, apply under nose and / or back of neck.

Seizures – Apply to back of neck, spine, or bottoms of feet.

MAIN INGREDIENTS – Amyris, Patchouli, Frankincense, Lime, Sandalwood, Ylang ylang, Roman chamomile

SAFETY –

stabilizing · centering · sweet

TOP USES

Stress & Anxiety – Apply to bottoms of feet and diffuse or inhale from cupped hands.

Jet Lag & Travel Anxiety – Inhale from cupped hands or apply under nose.

Mood Swings & Stress – Diffuse or apply under nose or back of neck.

Neurological Conditions – Apply to back of neck, pulse points, or bottoms of feet.

Convulsions, Epilepsy & Parkinson's – Apply to back of neck, along spine, or bottoms of feet.

Tranquility & Meditation – Apply under nose, across forehead or inhale from cupped hands.

Anger & Rage – Diffuse, apply under nose, or back of neck.

Fear, Grief & Trauma – Diffuse, apply under nose or back of neck.

MAIN INGREDIENTS – Spruce, Ho wood, Frankincense, Blue tansy, Blue chamomile

SAFETY – N

festive · warming · spicy

★ TOP USES

Refreshing & Joyful – Diffuse or inhale from cupped hands.

Immune Boost – Diffuse or inhale from cupped hands.

Seasonal Protection from Cold & Flu – Diffuse or inhale from cupped hands.

Headache & Migraine – Apply to temples and back of neck.

Tension & Stress – Apply to pulse points and diffuse.

Neck & Shoulder Discomfort – Apply to area of discomfort.

Arthritis – Apply to area of discomfort.

Protecting & Warming – Apply to back of neck and / or pulse points.

MAIN INGREDIENTS – Wild orange, Pine, Cassia, Cinnamon bark, Vanilla

SAFETY –

spontaneous · enlivening · daring

★ TOP USES

Apathy, Depression & Energy Issues – Diffuse or inhale from cupped hands to energize and uplift.

Low Libido & Sexual Performance – Diffuse or inhale in from cupped hands and apply to bottoms of feet and abdomen.

Mental Fog & Memory Issues – Apply to toes or diffuse.

Stimulating – Apply to bottoms of feet.

Sluggish Digestion & Elimination – Apply diluted to lower abdomen.

Lung & Sinus Congestion – Diffuse or inhale from hands.

Frigidity & Poor Circulation – Apply to bottoms of feet to warm and stimulate blood flow.

Menstruation & Menopause Issues – Apply diluted to lower abdomen or pressure points below inside and outside of ankles.

Infections – Apply to bottoms of feet.

Perfume – Apply diluted to wrists or neck.

MAIN INGREDIENTS – Cardamom, Cinnamon, Ginger, Clove, Sandalwood, Jasmine

SAFETY –

INVIGORATING Blend

citrus · sweet · uplifting

TOP USES

Low Energy & Exhaustion – Diffuse or apply under nose and back of neck to energize and uplift.

Stress, Anxiety & Depression – Diffuse or apply under nose and back of neck.

Air Refreshener – Diffuse to clear air of odors and uplift.

Antiseptic Cleaner – Mix with water in a glass bottle and apply to surfaces.

Eating Disorders – Diffuse or inhale from cupped hands or apply to abdomen.

Perfume – Apply to pulse points as desired.

Laundry – Add 2-4 drops to rinse cycle to freshen and kill germs.

Lymphatic & Immune Boost – Diffuse, apply under nose, and / or back of neck.

MAIN INGREDIENTS – Bergamot, Clementine, Grapefruit, Lemon, Mandarin, Tangerine, Vanilla, Wild orange

SAFETY –

JOYFUL Blend

happy · citrus · sweet

TOP USES

Elevate Mood & Mind – Diffuse and apply under nose or to pulse points.

Energize & Refresh – Diffuse and apply under nose or to pulse points.

Stress & Anxiety – Apply under nose, ears, or back of neck and inhale from cupped hands.

Depression & Mood Disorders – Apply to back of neck and inhale.

Grief & Sorrow – Diffuse and apply to chest and pulse points.

Stimulating & Uplifting – Apply under nose, back of neck, and / or inhale from cupped hands.

Immunity – Apply to bottoms of feet.

MAIN INGREDIENTS – Lavandin, Lavender, Sandalwood, Tangerine, Melissa, Ylang ylang, Elemi

SAFETY –

relieving · renewing · circulating

TOP USES

Muscle Aches & Arthritis – Apply to area of concern.

Headache, Neck & Back Pain – Apply to neck, shoulders, and along spine.

Neuropathy & Restless Leg Syndrome – Apply to area of concern to stimulate nerves and circulation.

Connective Tissue & Ligament Support – Apply to area of concern.

Lymphatic Support – Apply to bottoms of feet.

High Blood Pressure – Apply to bottoms of feet.

Poor Circulation & Cold Extremities – Apply to area of concern.

Muscle Tension, Soreness & Cramps – Apply to area of concern.

MAIN INGREDIENTS – Basil, Grapefruit, Cypress, Marjoram, Lavender, Peppermint

SAFETY –

strengthening · woody · fearless

TOP USES

Discouraged, Enraged, Agitated & Irritated – Diffuse. Apply to heart, to back of neck, spine, and/or bottoms of feet.

Calm, Grounded & Relaxed – Diffuse. Apply to pulse points and/or bottoms of feet.

Focused Heart, Mind & Body – Diffuse. Apply over heart, to forehead, and/or bottoms of feet.

Mental Clarity, Meditation & Tranquility – Diffuse. Apply to forehead, over heart, and bottoms of feet.

Cologne – Apply to pulse points, neck, and behind ears.

Women's Perfume – Blend with jasmine or captivating blend. Apply to pulse points, back of neck, or behind ears.

MAIN INGREDIENTS – Buddha Wood, Balsam fir, Black pepper, Hinoki, Patchouli, Cocoa extract

SAFETY – N

METABOLIC

Blend

cleansing · spicy · refreshing

TOP USES

Weight Loss, Obesity, & Stimulate Metabolism – Take 5 drops up to 5 times daily in capsule or water.

Cellulite – Apply to area of concern.

Over-fatigue & Eating Disorders – Take in a capsule or with water or apply to bottoms of feet or diffuse.

Appetite & Cravings – Take a drop under tongue and inhale from bottle or apply under nose to balance appetite.

Lymphatic Stimulant & Support – Diffuse or apply to bottoms of feet.

Congestion & Colds – Take in a capsule or in water.

Urinary Tract Support – Take in a capsule or in water.

Blood Sugar Balance – Take in a capsule or in water.

Detoxification & Cleansing – Take in a capsule or in water.

Digestive Stimulant & Calming – Take in a capsule or in water.

High Cholesterol – Take in a capsule or in water.

MAIN INGREDIENTS – Grapefruit, Lemon, Peppermint, Ginger, Cinnamon

SAFETY –

PROTECTIVE

or Immunity Blend

spicy · supportive · warming

TOP USES

Killing Germs & Airborne Pathogens – Take in a capsule or apply to bottoms of feet. Diffuse.

Seasonal Immune Boost – Diffuse and take in water or in a capsule.

Colds & Flu – Take in a capsule or apply to bottoms of feet.

Staph, Strep Throat & Cough – Gargle a drop in water and swallow. Apply to chest and throat or take in a capsule or with water.

Cold Sores, Warts & Infected Wounds – Apply diluted to affected area.

Oral Health – Gargle a drop in water.

Fungal & Parasite Issues – Apply to affected area or take in a capsule.

Urinary Tract Issues – Take in a capsule or apply to lower abdomen.

Antiseptic & Laundry Cleaner – Diffuse or dilute with water and apply to surfaces.

Chronic Fatigue & Autoimmune Disease – Take in a capsule or apply to bottoms of feet.

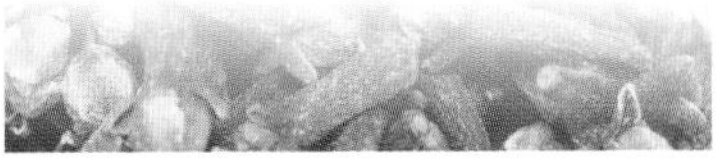

MAIN INGREDIENTS – Wild orange, Clove, Cinnamon, Eucalyptus, Rosemary

SAFETY –

REASSURING Blend

brave · composed · flowing

TOP USES

Insecurity & Worry – Apply under nose, back of neck, and inhale.

Nervousness & Irritability – Apply to bottoms of feet, back of neck, and inhale.

ADD, ADHD & Focus Issues – Inhale and apply to forehead or back of neck.

Stress, Mental Strain & Hyperactivity – Apply to under nose, back of neck, and forehead. Diffuse and inhale from cupped hands.

Addictions & Anorexia – Apply to pulse points and inhale from cupped hands.

Childbirth & Recovery – Apply to abdomen, massage into feet, or diffuse.

Allergies & Overreaction – Apply to affected area, bottoms of feet, or diffuse.

Colic & Calming – Apply to bottoms of feet and abdomen.

Infertility & Frigidity – Apply under nose, over abdomen, and to pulse points, or diffuse.

Meditation – Diffuse and apply under nose.

MAIN INGREDIENTS – Vetiver, Lavender, Ylang ylang, Frankincense, Clary sage, Marjoram, Spearmint

SAFETY – N

RENEWING Blend

relieve · release · liberate

TOP USES

Forgiveness, Attachment & Holding On – Apply to temples and back of neck or diffuse.

Anxiety – Apply under nose, across forehead, and / or back of neck, to soothe and ground.

Ulcers & Liver Issues – Apply over abdomen and affected areas.

Skin Infection & Damage – Apply to affected areas.

Addictions & Irritability – Diffuse and apply to wrist pulse points.

Circulation – Apply to chest or diffuse.

Fungus & Parasites – Apply to bottoms of feet.

Spiritual & Emotional Toxicity – Diffuse and apply under nose and / or to chest.

Hair Loss, Prostate Issues & Libido – Apply to affected areas, abdomen, or bottoms of feet.

Incontinence – Apply over abdomen or bottoms of feet.

MAIN INGREDIENTS – Spruce, Bergamot, Juniper berry, Myrrh, Arborvitae, Thyme

SAFETY –

REPELLENT
Blend

guarding · repellent · sweet

TOP USES

Repellent – Diffuse, spray on surfaces, or apply to exposed areas to repel bugs and insects.

Cellular Health – Apply to pulse points and bottoms of feet to promote healthy cell function.

Sunscreen – Apply to exposed skin with helichrysum or lavender to protect against sun exposure.

Skin Complaints – Apply with lavender to troubled skin.

Healthy Boundaries – Diffuse or apply to strengthen resolve and boundaries.

Wood Polish– Mix 4 drops with fractionated coconut oil to polish and preserve wood.

MAIN INGREDIENTS – Skimmia laureola, Catnip, Amyris, African sandalwood, Cabrueva balsam, Wild orange, White fir, Cedarwood, etc.

SAFETY – N

RESPIRATION
Blend

airy · expanding · supportive

TOP USES

Pneumonia & Asthma – Diffuse or apply under nose and on chest.

Allergies – Inhale from cupped hands or apply under nose.

Cough & Congestion – Diffuse or apply under or over bridge of nose, and to chest.

Bronchitis & Influenza – Diffuse and apply topically to chest.

Sinusitis & Nasal Polyps – Apply across or under nose.

Sleep Issues – Diffuse with lavender and / or apply to bottoms of feet.

Constricted Breathing – Diffuse and apply to chest.

Exercise-Induced Asthma – Diffuse and apply to chest.

MAIN INGREDIENTS – Laurel, Peppermint, Eucalyptus, Melaleuca, Lemon, Ravensara, Cardamom

SAFETY –

RESTFUL Blend

sweet · warm · calming

TOP USES

Insomnia & Sleep Issues – Diffuse or apply under nose or to bottoms of feet.

Stress & Anxiety – Apply under nose and to back of neck or diffuse.

Fussy Baby & Restless Child – Diffuse or apply diluted to bottoms of feet or down spine to calm.

Tension & Mood Swings – Inhale from cupped hands directly from hands or diffuse throughout the day. Rub on back of neck or over chest.

Skincare – Apply to area of concern.

Muscle Tension – Apply to area of concern.

Perfume – Apply to pulse points.

Calm Fears & Nervousness – Apply to back of neck, diffuse, or inhale from cupped hands.

Bath & Bedtime Routine – Use in baths or apply to bottoms of feet to relax and unwind.

Anger, Agitation & Irritability – Diffuse, apply under nose, and / or to bottoms of feet to calm.

MAIN INGREDIENTS – Lavender, Cedarwood, Ho wood, Ylang ylang, Marjoram, Roman chamomile, Vetiver root, Vanilla, Hawaiian Sandalwood

SAFETY – N

SKIN CLEARING Blend

cleansing · clear · sweet

TOP USES

Acne & Pimples – Apply to area of concern.

Oily Skin & Overactive Sebaceous Glands – Apply to area of concern.

Skin Blemishes & Irritations – Apply to area of concern.

Dermatitis & Eczema – Apply to area of concern.

Fungal & Bacterial Issues – Apply to area of concern.

MAIN INGREDIENTS – Black cumin, Ho wood, Melaleuca, Litsea, Eucalyptus, Geranium

SAFETY –

minty · athletic · cooling

★ TOP USES

Muscle, Back & Joint Pain – Apply to area of discomfort.

Arthritis & Aches – Apply to area of discomfort.

Neuropathy & Carpal Tunnel – Apply to area of discomfort.

Fibromyalgia & Lupus – Apply to area of discomfort.

Whiplash & Muscle Tension – Apply to area of discomfort.

Pre- & Post-Workout – Apply to area of discomfort.

Growing Pains – Apply to affected area.

Headache & Neck Pain – Apply to back of neck, shoulders, and temples.

Bruises & Injuries – Apply to affected area to reduce inflammation and scar tissue.

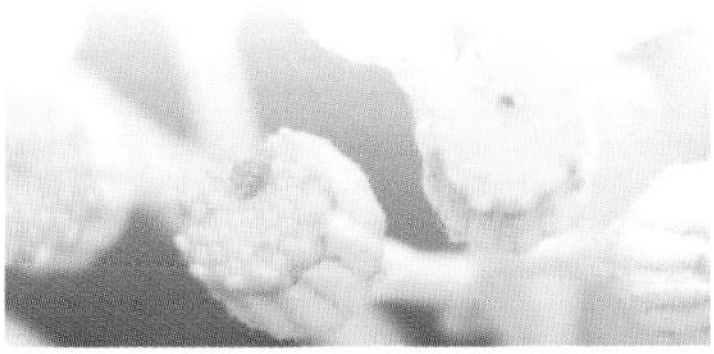

MAIN INGREDIENTS – Wintergreen, Camphor, Peppermint, Blue tansy, Blue chamomile, Helichrysum

SAFETY –

stabilizing · harmonizing · centering

TOP USES

Complimentary Yoga Poses – Seated Meditation, Seated Twist, and Bhu Mudra.

Meditation, Prayer & Focus – Diffuse. Apply to forehead, behind ears, along spine, and/or bottoms of feet.

Anchored, Courageous & Authentic – Diffuse. Apply to ankles, along spine and/or bottoms of feet.

Composed, Calm & Rested – Diffuse. Apply to back of neck, along spine and/or bottoms of feet.

Rooted to the Earth, Speaking Truth – Diffuse. Apply to throat area, along spine, and/or bottoms of feet.

Fearful & Disconnected – Diffuse. Apply 1-2 drops in palm of hands, rub together, inhale deeply.

Perfume – Apply to pulse points, chest, and behind ears.

MAIN INGREDIENTS – Lavender, Cedarwood, Frankincense, Cinnamon, Sandalwood, Black pepper, Patchouli

SAFETY – N

relieving · renewing · awakening

TOP USES

Headaches & Migraines – Apply to temples, forehead, and back of neck.

Muscles Aches, Swelling & Cramping – Apply to area of concern.

Hangover – Apply under nose and to back of neck.

Hot Flashes & Cooling – Apply to abdomen and back of neck to cool and calm.

Bruises & Burns – Apply to area of concern.

Joint Pain – Apply to area of concern.

Tension & Stress – Apply to pulse points and inhale from cupped hands.

Neck & Shoulder Pain – Apply to area of discomfort.

Arthritis – Apply to area of discomfort.

Restful Sleep – Apply to back of neck.

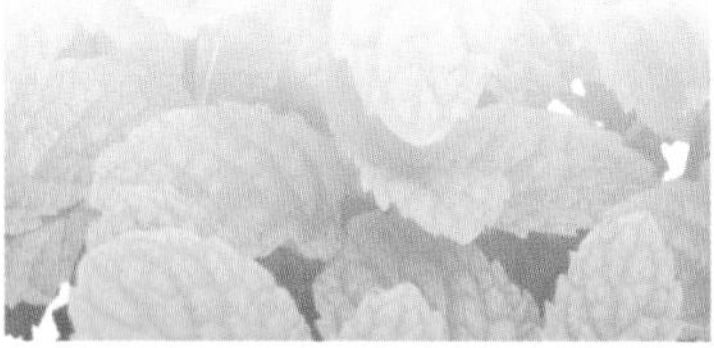

MAIN INGREDIENTS – Wintergreen, Lavender, Peppermint, Frankincense, Cilantro, Marjoram, Roman chamomile, Basil, Rosemary

SAFETY –

gladdening · illuminating · resilient

TOP USES

Depression & Discouragement – Diffuse or inhale from cupped hands or apply to pulse points or under nose and across forehead.

Hysteria & Anxiety – Diffuse or inhale from cupped hands or apply under nose and across forehead.

Disconnection – Diffuse or inhale from cupped hands or apply under nose and across forehead.

PMS – Diffuse or inhale from cupped hands or apply under nose and across forehead.

Cellular Health – Apply to bottoms of feet.

Inflammation & Stiffness – Apply diluted to affected area.

Indigestion & Irritable Bowels – Apply diluted to abdomen and bottoms of feet.

Blood Sugar & Cholesterol – Apply diluted to bottoms of feet, back of neck, or chest.

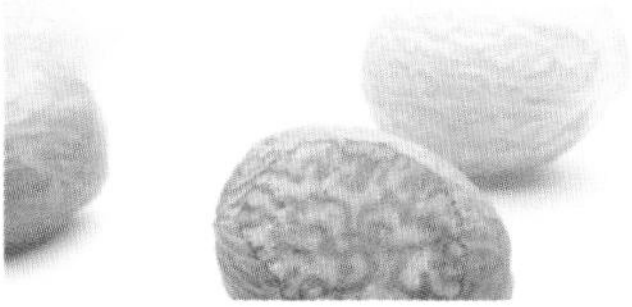

MAIN INGREDIENTS – Wild orange, Clove, Star anise, Lemon myrtle, Nutmeg

SAFETY –

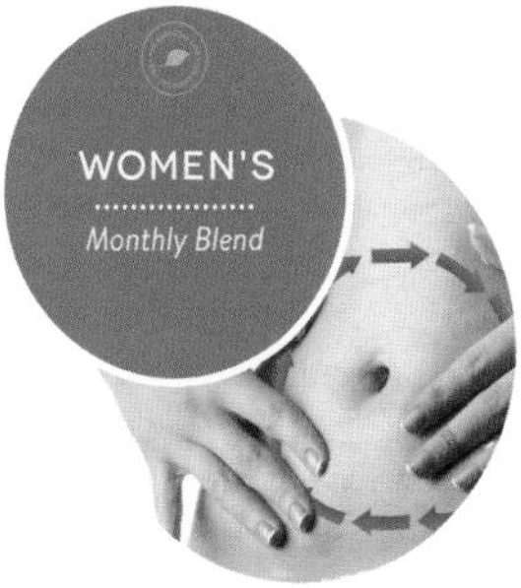

floral · warm · calming

TOP USES

Hormone Balancing – Apply to back of neck, abdomen, or bottoms of feet.

Heavy Periods, PMS & Cramps – Apply to abdomen, back of neck, or bottoms of feet.

Pre & Perimenopause – Apply to abdomen, back of neck, or bottoms of feet.

Hot & Flashes – Apply to abdomen or back of neck.

Mood Swings – Apply to abdomen, back of neck, chest, or bottoms of feet.

Skin Issues & Wounds – Apply to area of concern.

Sex Drive & Low Libido – Apply to abdomen.

MAIN INGREDIENTS – Clary sage, Lavender, Bergamot, Roman chamomile, Cedarwood, Ylang ylang, Geranium, Fennel, Carrot, Palmarosa, Vitex

SAFETY – N

sweet · warm · calming

TOP USES

Balance Hormones – Apply to pulse points and back of neck.

Perfume – Apply to pulse points and chest.

Hot Flashes – Apply to back of neck.

Libido & Sex Drive – Apply to pulse points or abdomen.

Anger – Diffuse, inhale from cupped hands, or apply to pulse points to release and calm.

Self-Expression & Presence – Diffuse, inhale from cupped hands, or apply under nose and / or to pulse points.

Self-Confidence & Creativity – Diffuse, inhale from cupped hands, and / or apply to pulse points.

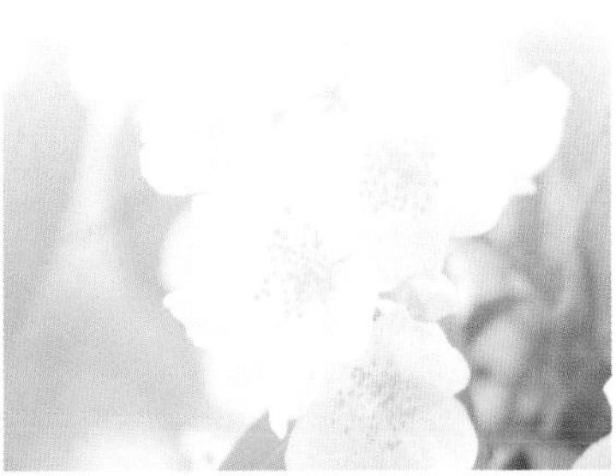

MAIN INGREDIENTS – Bergamot, Ylang ylang, Patchouli, Vanilla bean, Jasmine, Cinnamon, Labdanum, Vetiver, Sandalwood, Cocoa bean, Rose

SAFETY – N

Supplementary Products

Is your energy low? Do you experience chronic pain or discomfort in your body? Dealing with challenges in sustaining energy and concentration throughout the day, along with maintaining adequate immune and physical health, are the norm for many. However, virtually any health compromise or issue can be traced to some kind of underlying deficiency or toxicity. Numerous studies have been conducted over decades to determine the optimal nutritional state for the human body. The scientific community agrees that virtually everyone falls short in obtaining the bare minimum of recommended daily nutritional requirements in at least some areas.

These declines can be attributed to two main factors. The first is the increasing level of compromises in farming practices and the rising interest by food growers to genetically modify foods. Even those eating a wholesome, balanced diet find it challenging to consume adequate levels of certain nutrients. The second factor contributing to decline is our consumption of refined, processed, nutrient-void foods loaded with empty calories, which has been on the increase globally for decades. Similarly, adults and children alike are consuming excessive amounts of animal protein while consuming far too few fresh fruits and vegetables.

With these drastic changes in both food supply and consumption, examining one's own nutritional status is a worthy course of action. Consider asking yourself if you have any diet, health, or lifestyle habits or compromises that contribute to a lack in health and vitality and make adjustments accordingly. Whether feeling healthy or not, anyone can benefit from commitment to a daily supplemental program.

Following symbols for safety: = if pregnant or nursing, consult your physician

BONE
Nutrient Complex

This blend contains whole food created vitamins, minerals and other cofactors necessary for bone integrity, strength and overall health.

TOP USES – Weak or fragile bones, osteopenia and osteoporosis prone individuals, bone fractures, growing individuals, and anyone needing more bone density.

INGREDIENTS –

- Vitamin C
- Vitamin D2 and D3
- Biotin
- Calcium, magnesium, zinc, copper, manganese, and boron

SAFETY – Safe for women, teens and men.

CELLULAR
Complex Softgels

A blend of essential oils that have been shown in clinical studies to help protect cells against free radical damage while supporting cellular function through apoptosis of damaged and mutated cells, and proliferation of healthy cells.

TOP USES – Damaged or mutated cellular diseases, oxidative stress, autoimmune diseases and anything that requires cellular regeneration and healthy cellular function.

INGREDIENTS –

- Frankincense oil
- Wild orange oil
- Lemongrass oil
- Thyme oil
- Summer Savory oil
- Clove Bud oil

SAFETY – Not for small children.

SUPPLEMENTARY

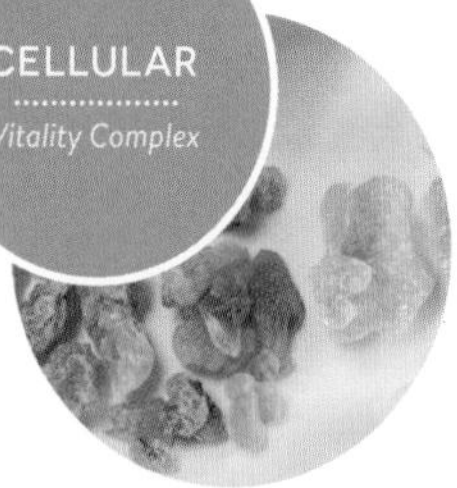

CELLULAR

Vitality Complex

Packed with nature's most potent antioxidants, natural anti-inflammatories, and energy cofactors, this blend of synergistic herbs will give life and energy to the cells and a sense of well being to the body.

TOP USES – Pain and inflammation, arthritis, osteoarthritis, fibromyalgia, foggy brain, cirrhosis, jaundice, cellular repair, fatigue, mood, and cancer prevention.

INGREDIENTS –

- Boswellia serrata gum resin
- Scutellaria Root *(baicalin)*
- Milk Thistle *(silymarin)*
- Polygonum cuspidatum *(resveratrol)*
- Green Tea Leaf *(EGCG)*
- Pomegranate Fruit extract
- Pineapple *(bromelain)*
- Turmeric extract *(curcumin)*
- Grape Seed extract
- Sesame seed extract
- Pine Bark extract *(pycnogenol)*
- Gingko Biloba Leaf
- Acetyl-L-Carnitine
- Alpha-Lipoic Acid
- Coenzyme Q10
- Quercetin

SAFETY – For men, women and teens.

CHILDREN'S

Chewable

Multivitamin, mineral and botanical chewable for children and adults that have difficulty swallowing. Blended with antioxidants and herbal compounds that increase overall health and wellness.

TOP USES – Low energy and fatigue, compromised digestion and immunity, brain fog, oxidative cell damage, poor health and malnutrition.

INGREDIENTS –

- Vitamins A, C, D3 and full B-complex
- Calcium, copper, iron, iodine, magnesium, manganese, potassium and zinc
- Superfood Blend of pineapple, pomegranate extract, lemon bioflavonoids, spirulina, sunflower oil, rice bran, beet greens, broccoli, brown rice, carrot, mango, cranberry, rose hips, acerola cherry extract
- Cellular Vitality Complex of tomato extract, turmeric extract, boswellia serrata extract, grape seed extract, marigold flower extract

SAFETY – No gluten, wheat, dairy, soy or nut products.

DEFENSIVE

Probiotic

A double-encapsulated, time-release probiotic capsule or powdered encapsulated probiotic supplement *(for children or adults who have trouble swallowing pills)* with six different strains of good bacteria and prebiotic fiber for maximum delivery and cultivation of healthy gut flora.

TOP USES – Flatulence, constipation or diarrhea, malabsorption, irritable bowel, compromised immune system, leaky gut, allergies, autoimmune diseases, malabsorption, anxiety and depression, mental disorders, and infections.

INGREDIENTS ***(capsule)*** –

- L. acidophilus, L. salivarius, L. casei
- B. lactis, B. bifidum, B. longum
- Biotin
- FOS *(fructooligosaccharides)* prebiotic

INGREDIENTS ***(powder)*** –

- L. rhamnosus. L. salivarius, L. plantarum *(LP01, LP02)*, B. breve, B. lactic strains
- FOS prebiotic

SAFETY – For all ages. NOTE: Do not mix with hot water.

DETOXIFICATION

Blend Softgels

A blend of essential oils that support natural detoxification of the body to help cleanse it of toxins and free radicals that can slow your systems down, leaving a heavy, weighted feeling.

TOP USES – Toxic liver, jaundice, cirrhosis, bloating, toxic gallbladder, pancreatitis, kidney damage, and hormonal imbalances.

INGREDIENTS –

- Tangerine Peel
- Rosemary Leaf
- Geranium Plant
- Juniper Berry
- Cilantro

SAFETY – Not for children. Keep out of reach of small children.

This complex is a proprietary blend of 14 active whole-food extracts in a patented enzyme delivery system that supports healthy cleansing and filtering functions of the liver, kidneys, colon, lungs, and skin.

TOP USES – Toxic liver, jaundice, cirrhosis, bloating, toxic gallbladder, pancreatitis, kidney damage, respiratory issues, colon issues and constipation.

INGREDIENTS –

- Barberry leaf, milk thistle seed, burdock root, clove bud, dandelion root, garlic fruit, red clover leaf
- Turkish rhubarb stem, burdock root, clove bud, dandelion root
- Psyllium seed husk, Turkish rhubarb stem, acacia gum bark, marshmallow root
- Osha root, safflower petals
- Kelp, milk thistle seed, burdock root, clove bud, garlic fruit
- Enzyme assimilation system of amylase and cellulase their natural mineral cofactor magnesium and manganese

SAFETY – Can be taken by all ages that can swallow capsules. Keep out of reach of small children.

A synergistic blend of essential oils that help ease digestion and increase digestive health.

TOP USES – Upset stomach, constipation, diarrhea, IBS, vomiting, heartburn and acid indigestion / reflux.

INGREDIENTS –

- Ginger
- Peppermint
- Tarragon
- Fennel
- Caraway
- Coriander
- Anise

SAFETY – Can be taken by all ages that can swallow capsules. Keep out of reach of small children.

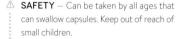

A blend of adaptogenic herbs and extracts with energy co-factors made to increase mitochondrial biogenesis and overall energy while decreasing the stress response due to physical activity and daily life.

TOP USES – Body fatigue and tiredness, adrenal fatigue, hormonal imbalance, libido, physical stress, anxiety, and poor circulation.

INGREDIENTS –

- Acetyl-L-Carnitine HCL
- Alpha-Lipoic Acid
- Coenzyme Q10
- Lychee Fruit Extract and Green Tea Leaf Polyphenol Extract
- Quercetin dihydrate
- Cordyceps Mycelium
- Ginseng *(Panax quinquefolius)* root extract
- Ashwagandha *(withania somnifera)* root extract

SAFETY – Not for children. Keep out of reach of small children.

A blend of several, active, whole-food enzymes and mineral cofactors that help the breakdown of proteins, fats, complex carbohydrates, sugars, and fiber, giving the body better digestion nutrients readily available by for absorption and utilization.

TOP USES – Poor nutrition, heartburn or indigestion, slow metabolism, upset stomach, bloating, and flatulence.

INGREDIENTS –

- Protease
- Papain
- Lipase
- Lactase
- Alpha Galactosidase
- Cellulase
- Sucrase
- Anti-Gluten Enzyme Blend
- Glucoamylase
- Betaine HCL
- ***Digestion blend of:*** peppermint leaf, ginger root, caraway seed

SAFETY – Can be taken by all ages that can swallow capsules.

A blend of whole food fruits and vegetables combined with superfruits and essential oils, provided in a powdered mix for a daily boost of convenient nutritional supplementation.

TOP USES – For people with poor nutrition, busy and stressful lifestyle habits, weight management, compromised digestion and immunity.

INGREDIENTS –

- Green Powder Blend *(kale, dandelion greens, spinach, parsley, collard greens leaf, broccoli, cabbage)*
- Grass Powder blend *(wheat grass, alfalfa juice, oat grass, barley grass, oat grass juice and barley grass juice)*
- Fruit Powder blend *(pineapple juice, guava fruit, mango juice, goji berry, mangosteen, and acerola cherry)*
- Lemon Peel and Ginger Root Essential Oils

SAFETY – For all ages. Gluten-free and non-GMO. Vegan-friendly.

A blend of essential oils that support a healthy gastrointestinal *(GI)* tract by decreasing the overgrowth of pathogens in the gut; thereby increasing gut integrity and creating a healthy environment for new, good bacteria to thrive.

TOP USES – For overgrowth of candida albicans and other negative pathogens, autoimmune diseases, compromised digestive system, brain fog, illness and infections.

INGREDIENTS –

- Oregano
- Melaleuca
- Lemon
- Lemongrass
- Peppermint
- Thyme

SAFETY – Keep out of reach of small children.

SUPPLEMENTARY

This product has both eicosapentaenoic acid *(EPA)* and docosahexaenoic acid *(DHA)* which combine to make up a balance of omega 3 essential fatty acids in fish oil form. Blended with essential oils to bring a less fishy flavor and more pleasant one.

TOP USES – Brain fog, ADD/ADHD, Cardiovascular disease, dry skin, joint pain and arthritis, anything "itis", weak muscles, and compromised immune system.

INGREDIENTS –

- EPA
- DHA
- Essential oils blend, wild orange

SAFETY – Keep out of reach of small children, keep refrigerated after opening.

A convenient and delicious weight management shake mix that provides low-fat, low-calorie, high-protein, high-fiber, nutrients as a lean alternative for individuals trying to lose fat or maintain a lean body composition through calorie reduction and exercise.

TOP USES – Weight management, poor nutrition, slow metabolism, and stressful lifestyle habits.

INGREDIENTS –

- Protein Blend *(Whey protein isolate and egg white protein)*
- Fiber Blend *(Non-GMO soluble corn fiber, xanthan gum, citrus fiber, tara gum, oligofructose)*
- Ashwagandha root / leaf extract
- Potato Protein Powder
- Vitamin and mineral blend

SAFETY – For all ages. Gluten free and non GMO.

SUPPLEMENTARY

A convenient and delicious weight management vegan shake mix that provides low-fat, low-calorie, high-protein, high-fiber, nutrients as a lean alternative for individuals trying to lose fat or maintain a lean body composition through calorie reduction and exercise.

TOP USES – Weight management, poor nutrition, slow metabolism, stressful lifestyle habits, and vegan alternative.

INGREDIENTS –

- Protein Blend *(Pea protein, quinoa, and amaranth)*
- Fiber Blend *(Non-GMO soluble corn fiber, xanthan gum, citrus fiber, tara gum, oligofructose)*
- Potato Protein Powder
- Vitamin and mineral blend

SAFETY – For all ages. Gluten-free, and non-GMO.

A blend of essential oils in convenient softgels to help manage hunger throughout the day while boosting metabolism and promoting a positive mood, cleanse the body, aide digestion, curb the appetite, provide a stimulating and positive effect on the endocrine system and to assist with weight loss.

TOP USES – Slow metabolism, overweight or obese individuals, lack of energy *(fatigue)*, diabetes, toxic liver, and compromised endocrine system.

INGREDIENTS –

- Grapefruit
- Lemon
- Peppermint
- Ginger
- Cinnamon

SAFETY – Not for children. Keep out of reach of small children.

A blend of marine base and land base omega essential fatty acids in a unique assimilation capsule with essential oils and fat-soluble vitamins.

TOP USES – Inflammation and pain, arthritis, anything "itis", compromised immune system, brain fog, concentration, ADD / ADHD, aging skin, PMS, postpartum depression, depression and anxiety, cardiovascular disease, dry skin and skin issues.

INGREDIENTS –

- Fish oil *(from Anchovy, Sardine, Mackerel, and Calamari)* concentrate
- Pomegranate and Echium plantagineum seed oil
- Vitamin A *(as Alpha and Beta carotene)*, Vitamin D3 *(as natural Cholecalciferol)*, Vitamin E
- Astaxanthin
- Lutein
- Zeaxanthin
- ***Essential oil blend of:*** caraway, clove, cumin, frankincense, German chamomile, ginger, peppermint, thyme, and wild orange

SAFETY – Can be taken by all ages that can swallow capsules.

A blend of marine base and land base omega essential fatty acids in a unique assimilation capsule with essential oils and fat-soluble vitamins.

TOP USES – Inflammation and pain, arthritis, anything "itis", compromised immune system, brain fog, concentration, ADD / ADHD, aging skin, PMS, postpartum depression, depression and anxiety, cardiovascular disease, dry skin and skin issues.

INGREDIENTS –

- ***Seed oil;*** Flax seed, Inca Inchi seed, Cranberry seed, Pomegranate seed, Pumpkin seed, Grape seed
- Algae oil *(DHA)*
- Natural vitamin D, Natural vitamin E
- Astaxanthin
- Lutein
- Zeaxanthin
- Lycopene
- Alpha and Beta carotene
- ***Essential oil blend of:*** caraway, clove, cumin, frankincense, German chamomile, ginger, peppermint, thyme, and wild orange

SAFETY – Can be taken by all ages that can swallow capsules.

Blend of standardized extracts of plant *(phyto)* estrogens and lignans to help create a balance of hormones throughout the body and eliminate unwanted metabolites.

TOP USES – Menopause, perimenopause, andropause, hormonal imbalances and mood swings (PMS).

INGREDIENTS –

- Genistein *(soy extract)*: An isoflavone antioxidant that promotes healthy breast and uterine tissue and brings balance to hormones in both men and women. Also shown to help prevent prostate cancer in men and ovarian and breast cancer in women.
- Flax seed extract *(lignans)*: Decreases estrogen metabolites for further hormone balance and protection of the sex organ tissues and cells.
- Pomegranate extract: Powerful antioxidant shown to help the reduction of free radical damage to the cells.

SAFETY – Not for children. Keep out of reach of small children.

A blend of powerful polyphenols clinically tested to help soreness and discomfort from physical activities and daily life.

TOP USES – Joint pain, inflammation, arthritis, rheumatoid arthritis and anything "itis", fibromyalgia, sore muscles, Alzheimer's Disease, and cancer prevention.

INGREDIENTS –

- Frankincense *(Boswellia serrata)* gum resin extract
- Curcumin
- Ginger root extract
- Green Tea Leaf extract *(caffeine-free)*
- Pomegranate Fruit extract
- Grape Seed extract
- Resveratrol
- Digestion blend of peppermint leaf, ginger root, caraway seed

SAFETY – Not for children. Keep out of reach of small children.

A blend of several essential oils in a convenient, organically sweetened throat lozenge that soothe the throat and protect the immune system from foreign invaders. *(pathogens)*.

TOP USES – Sore or dry throat, cough, colds and flus, illness, laryngitis, preventative care, and compromised immunity.

INGREDIENTS –

- Wild orange
- Clove
- Cinnamon
- Wild orange
- Eucalyptus
- Cinnamon
- Rosemary
- Myrrh
- Organic cane juice
- Organic brown rice syrup

SAFETY – Be aware of small children that are prone to choking.

A blend of several essential oils in a convenient softgel that protect the immune system from foreign invaders *(pathogens)*.

TOP USES – Sore or dry throat, cough, colds and flus, illness, laryngitis, preventative care, and compromised immunity.

INGREDIENTS –

- Wild Orange Peel oil
- Clove Bud oil
- Black Pepper Seed oil
- Cinnamon Bark oil
- Eucalyptus Leaf oil
- Oregano Leaf oil
- Rosemary Leaf / Flower oil
- Melissa Leaf oil

SAFETY – Not for children.

SUPPLEMENTARY

A blend of essential oils in a convenient, organically sweetened throat lozenge for the use of opening the airways a supporting the respiratory system.

★ **Top Uses** – Congestion, head cold, sore throat, bronchitis, asthma, allergies, cough, sinusitis, bad breath, and motion sickness.

Ingredients –

- Laurel Leaf
- Cardamom
- Peppermint
- Eucalyptus
- Melaleuca
- Lemon
- Ravensara

⚠ **SAFETY** – Be aware of small children that are prone to choking.

A blend of lavender essential oil and natural plant extracts to enhance a restful night's sleep by promoting relaxation without feeling groggy or sleepy the next day.

★ **TOP USES** – ***Insomnia, inability to fall asleep or wake up easily, groggy feelings upon rising in morning, lack of adequate sleep, negative impact due to lack of sleep:*** decreased ability to lose weight, learn, or control emotions; poor reaction time, increased presence of stress hormones, decreased sense of well-being negative impact on cardiovascular health and body's natural ability to recuperate and restore.

INGREDIENTS –

- Lavender oil
- L-Theanine *(non-protein amino acid found in green tea [Camellia sinensis])*
- Lemon Balm
- Passion Flower
- Chamomile

⚠ **SAFETY** – Keep out of reach of children.

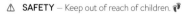

SUPPLEMENTARY

A blend of essential oils in a convenient softgel to be consumed quickly and easily when traveling, attending outdoor events, or when seasonal or environmental elements are particularly high, or on a daily basis during times of seasonal discomfort to promote clear breathing and overall respiratory health.

TOP USES – Seasonal allergies, hay fever, congestion, head colds and headaches, bronchitis, asthma, and sinusitis.

INGREDIENTS –

- Lemon
- Lavender
- Peppermint

SAFETY – Be aware of small children that are prone to choking.

Revolutionary micronutrient supplement providing naturally balanced amounts of all vitamins, minerals, trace elements, phytonutrients and antioxidants that give your body the most beneficial and safe amounts needed for long term health and vitality.

TOP USES – Low energy and fatigue, compromised digestion and immunity, oxidative cell damage, malnutrition, poor health and imbalanced nutrition.

INGREDIENTS –

- Water soluble vitamins, B-complex and C
- Fat soluble vitamins A, E and K
- Vitamin D3
- Macro-minerals *(calcium, iron, iodine, magnesium, zinc, selenium, copper, manganese and chromium)*
- Polyphenol Blend *(Grape seed extract, Quercetin, rutin, pomegranate fruit extract, citrus fruit polyphenol extract, resveratrol, Indian kino tree wood extract)*
- Whole Foods Blend *(Kale leaf extract, dandelion leaf powder, parsley leaf powder, spinach leaf powder, broccoli aerial parts powder, cabbage leaf extract, Brussels sprout immature inflorescences powder)*
- Stomach Comfort Blend of ginger root extract, peppermint extract and caraway seed extract

SAFETY – Can be taken by all ages that can swallow capsules.

Tips for Taking Supplements

- **Partner with quality.** Use supplements with optimal, not exaggerated or deficient, levels of nutrients by buying from a reputable source.
- **Dose diligence**. All products provide dose recommendations. Maximal benefits comes from the consistent use of a variety of specific and complementary supplements.
- **Start slowly.** Over the course of the first week, start with a few supplements at lower doses and then add from there. This will support awareness of how individual supplements make you feel.
- **Time it right.** Most people do better taking supplements with food while digestive processes are in action. Use on an empty stomach *(except at bedtime)* can trigger nausea. Just a few bites of food can be enough *(e.g. half a banana)*.
- **Make it a habit.** Consider targeting two set times per day to establish routine or ritual for basic daily nutrition habits.
- **Be practical.** Keep your supplements in locations that provide easy access. Most do not require refrigeration, so keeping them out on kitchen and bathroom counters creates visibility and supports routine use.
- **Stay the course.** Most people experience an increased sense of well being when beginning a supplementation program.
- **Make supplements part of your lifestyle.** Supplements to support general health can be continued indefinitely and are an excellent component of a healthy lifestyle.
- **Take them along.** When you travel, take your supplements with you. Get a pill box that contains specific, marked sections for different times of the day.
- **Store them right.** Keep supplements out of windowsills or away from other sources of bright light. Store in dark or opaque bottles away from microwaves and other electromagnetic sources.

Additional Information

- **Herxheimer reactions.** Die-off of bacteria can intensify symptoms of fatigue, muscle pain, and feeling flu-like. Generally, herxheimer reactions are more common and more intense with conventional antibiotic therapy, but they can still occur with natural supplements. If you feel that you are having herxheimer reactions, back off on dose and then increase gradually and slowly.
- **Excessive stimulation.** One of the greatest benefits of natural supplementation is an increased energy and reserves. Generally this is welcomed during the day but can be a problem at night while trying to sleep. If you notice an effect, take primary supplements in the morning and afternoon.
- **Dealing with adverse effects.** Adverse effects associated with taking natural supplements are uncommon, but possible. Fortunately, most are mild and transient, and you should be able to work around them.
- **Upset stomach.** The most common adverse effects are an upset stomach, indigestion, mild nausea, and discomfort mid-chest or on the left side under the lower rib cage *(where the stomach is located)*. First consider if consumption occurred on an empty or overly full stomach and adjust accordingly. Otherwise, if necessary, take a break from the supplements for a few days to a week. Consider adding an essential oil such as ginger, peppermint, or digestive blend to soothe upset. If chronic digestive issues already existed, additional considerations may need to be made.

Section **4**

BODY SYSTEMS & FOCUS AREAS

Take a holistic approach to wellness by learning to address wellness in terms of body systems. Think beyond the disease-symptom model, and instead focus on systems that govern the function of your entire body.

A HEALTHY BODY is like a finely tuned symphony orchestra. An orchestra is divided into sections, and sections are comprised of individual instruments. Similarly, the body is divided into sections called body systems that are comprised of individual organs. During a musical performance when out-of-tune sounds come from a single instrument, it affects not only that section, but the quality of music coming from entire orchestra. The conductor's role is to identify the underlying cause behind the affected sound, tuning and refining where necessary. So, too, is every individual the conductor of their own body's orchestrations and internal harmony in partnership with the body itself.

TAKE A HOLISTIC APPROACH

By addressing wellness in terms of body systems, each individual is taking a holistic approach to wellness. Thinking beyond a disease-symptom model and focusing on the systems that govern the function of the entire body allows one to shift away from an ambulance mentality of "if it ain't broke don't fix it" to true whole-body thinking and a prevention mindset.

A holistic approach to wellness promotes living with a prevention mindset and addressing root causes when symptoms arise by providing support to entire body systems.

Ambulance Approach

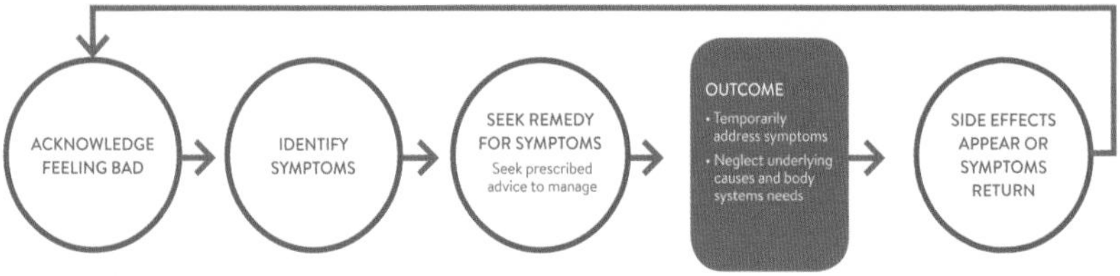

Holistic Approach

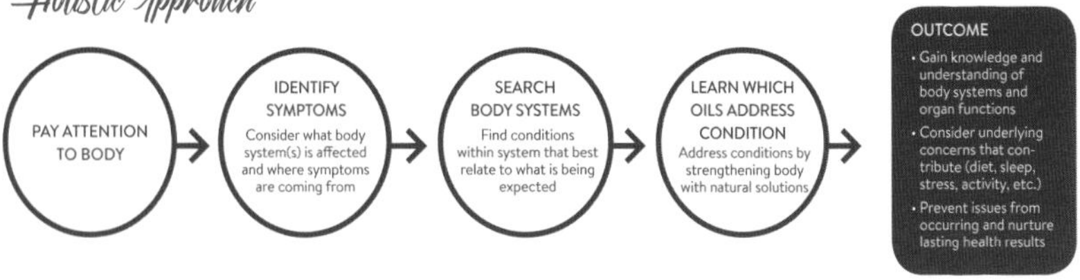

PAY ATTENTION TO BODY
IDENTIFY SYMPTOMS
Consider what body system(s) is affected and where symptoms are coming from
SEARCH BODY SYSTEMS
Find conditions within system that best relate to what is being expected
LEARN WHICH OILS ADDRESS CONDITION
Address conditions by strengthening body with natural solutions
OUTCOME
• Gain knowledge and understanding of body systems and organ functions
• Consider underlying concerns that contribute (diet, sleep, stress, activity, etc.)
• Prevent issues from occurring and nurture lasting health results

INTERCONNECTIVITY OF ALL BODY SYSTEMS

All body systems are interconnected. When one system is hindered or malfunctions other systems are impacted. Likewise, when one system is repaired and strengthened the whole body benefits and functions can be restored. For best success, think in terms of body systems to create true wellness, and learn to use natural healing tools to aid in this process.

Biological Terrain

- Quality nutrients
- Water
- Oxygen
- Waste removal
- Chemical and temperature regulation

↓

Cellular Health

- Healthy cells are at the core of wellness.
- Unhealthy cells, caused by deficiencies and toxicities, result in ailments or a diseased body.

↓

Specialized Tissues

- The needs of healthy cells are met by groups of specialized tissues. These tissues form organs and body systems. They perform functions to support cellular health, and consequently, the health of the whole body.

↓

Body System

- As body systems operate normally, they function synergistically together to create overall well being. Conditions form as specialized tissues and body systems fail to perform their normal functions. Failure to function eventually gives rise to ailments, the level where most people become conscious of their health.

USING THE BODY SYSTEMS EFFECTIVELY

The Body Systems section of this book is designed to create an opportunity to learn, first, about a body system itself and gain a basic understanding of its purpose or role, its working parts, and what can potentially go wrong. Second, each section contains common ailments that can occur (*solutions located in the Quick Reference A-Z*), key oils and supplements to be learned as go-to solutions, usage tips, additional solutions to numerous conditions, and user recommended remedies.

One additional component of each section is "By Related Properties." This section allows the user to search for solutions by related properties to certain oils. For example, if one wanted to sleep better, one would search for a properties category such as "Calming" and find an oil of choice such as lavender or roman chamomile. To take this process to a "Power Oil User" *(pg. 254)* level, discover the properties chart in the back of the book and learn numerous properties of each single oil. This is the best way to comprehend and learn the multiplicity of actions an oil is capable of.

In conclusion, the desired outcome from use of Body Systems is to become a more experienced oil user, knowing how to "think for yourself," taking attention from symptoms to root causes, solutions, and preventative actions.

ADDICTIONS

See also Limbic

SINGLE OILS

Copaiba, Helichrysum – boosts dopamine levels *(pgs. 131 & 137)*

Grapefruit – dissipates cravings; supports detoxification, renewed energy *(pg. 136)*

Basil – clears negative thought patterns that block change; restores mental energy *(pg. 125)*

Bergamot – gives sense of empowerment and self-worth *(pg. 126)*

Peppermint – supports sense of buoyancy and recovery, reprieve from painful emotions *(pg. 146)*

BLENDS

Restful blend – promotes calm, peaceful, tranquil state of being; quiets mind *(pg. 174)*

Detoxification blend –promotes elimination, detoxification of toxins *(pg. 165)*

Encouraging blend – promotes self-belief, confidence, trust *(pg. 166)*

Grounding blend – restores sense of solidity / feeling grounded in life *(pg. 167)*

Cleansing blend – cleanses and detoxifies *(pg. 164)*

SUPPLEMENTS

Cellular vitality complex, ***energy & stamina complex (pg. 183)***, essential oils cellular complex, ***omega complex (pg. 187)***, detoxification complex, food enzymes, ***liquid omega-3 (pg. 185)***, metabolic blend softgels, whole food nutrient

By Related Properties

For further information, see pages 260 and 272.

Anaphrodisiac, Analgesic, Antidepressant, Anti-parasitic, Antitoxic, Calming, Regenerative, Relaxing, Restorative, Sedative, Stimulant, Stomachic, Uplifting

Usage Tips

For best support for addiction recovery:

- **Aromatic:** Choose an oil(s) to diffuse or inhale from a bottle or hands, or whatever method seems most effective at the time. Wear an oil(s) as perfume / cologne.
- **Topical:** Apply under nose, behind ears, to base of skull *(especially in suboccipital triangles)* and forehead, and on roof of mouth *(closest location to the amygdala; place on pad of thumb, then suck on thumb)*; place oil that is best match to emotional state over heart area. Use a carrier oil as needed for sensitive skin or "hot" oils. Use to prevent and eliminate urges.
- **Internal:** For immediate impact, in addition to inhalation, place a drop or two of chosen oil under tongue, hold for 30 seconds, swallow; take oils in capsule or in glass of water. Consider detoxification products / oils or a program – see Detoxification.

SINGLE OILS

Basil, rosemary – reduces inflammatory response and supports adrenal glands *(pgs. 125 & 150)*

Blue tansy, lavender – acts as an antihistamine and calms irritation *(pgs. 127 & 139)*

Lemon – decongests and reduces mucus *(pg. 140)*

Peppermint – discharges phlegm and reduces inflammation *(pg. 146)*

BLENDS

Respiration blend – supports reduction and recovery from allergic responses *(pg. 173)*

Detoxification blend – supports permanent reduction of reactivity *(pg. 165)*

Cleansing blend – alleviates allergic responses to bites and stings *(pg. 164)*

Digestion blend – supports digestion to calm food allergy responses *(pg. 165)*

Protective blend – supports immune system *(pg. 171)*

Restful blend – acts as an antihistamine *(pg. 174)*

SUPPLEMENTS

Cellular vitality complex, detoxification complex, detoxification blend softgels, energy & stamina complex, ***food enzymes (pg. 183)***, phytoestrogen multiplex, ***respiratory lozenges (pg. 190)***, ***seasonal blend softgels (pg. 191)***, whole food nutrient

By Related Properties

For further information, see pages 260 and 272.

Anti-allergic, Antihistamine, Anti-inflammatory, Antitoxic, Calming, Cleanser, Detoxifier, Steroidal

Usage Tips

For best support for addiction recovery:

- **Aromatic:** Diffuse chosen oils; apply to chest, clothing, bedding, or other to inhale.
- **Topical:** Apply oils topically to forehead, cheeks *(avoid eyes)*, chest, bottoms of feet.
- **Internal:** Take drops of oils in water and drink, take oil(s) in a capsule, or place a drop on or under tongue.

ALLERGIES

ATHLETES

SINGLE OILS

Peppermint – pre-exercise support *(pg. 146)*

Lemongrass – connective tissue support *(pg. 140)*

Marjoram – muscle support *(pg. 143)*

BLENDS

Massage blend – post-exercise recovery *(pg. 170)*

Soothing blend, soothing blend rub – post-exercise recovery *(pg. 175)*

SUPPLEMENTS

Bone nutrient complex (pg. 179), cellular vitality complex, detoxification complex, digestion blend softgels, cellular complex softgels, omega complex, ***energy & stamina complex (pg. 183)***, food enzymes, ***polyphenol complex (pg. 188)***, whole food nutrient supplement, ***meal replacement shake (pg. 185)***, ***metabolic blend softgels (pg. 186)***

By Related Properties

For further information, see pages 260 and 272.

Analgesic, Anti-inflammatory, Energizing, Regenerative, Relaxing, Steroidal, Vasodilator, Warming

Usage Tips For best methods of use for athletes:

- **Aromatic:** Inhaling certain oils before and during workouts can invigorate, energize, and improve respiration.
- **Topical:** Use oils topically is for muscle / joint pain and injuries.

SINGLE OILS

Lemongrass – stimulates nerves and supports digestion *(pg. 140)*

Juniper berry – antioxidant and supports digestion *(pg. 138)*

Copaiba – anti-inflammatory, anti-infectious, pain reliever *(pg. 131)*

Ginger – invigorates nerves and cleanses *(pg. 136)*

Clary sage – invigorates nerves and supports endocrine system *(pg. 130)*

Turmeric – antioxidant and anti-inflammatory *(pg. 153)*

BLENDS

Cellular complex blend – supports nerves and glands *(pg. 160)*

Detoxification blend – detoxifies and supports proper digestive function *(pg. 165)*

Metabolic blend – antioxidant and improves digestion *(pg. 171)*

SUPPLEMENTS

Bone nutrient complex, ***cellular vitality complex (pg. 179)***, ***defensive probiotic (pg. 181)***, digestion blend softgels, energy & stamina complex, ***cellular complex softgels (pg. 187)***, ***omega complex (pg. 187)***, ***food enzymes (pg. 183)***, ***liquid omega-3***, ***polyphenol complex (pg. 188)***, protective blend lozenges, protective blend softgels *(use with grounding blend)*, whole food nutrient

By Related Properties

For further information, see pages 260 and 272.

Analgesic, Antiarthritic, Antidepressant, Anti-infectious, Anti-inflammatory, Antioxidant, Anti-parasitic, Regenerative, Stomachic, Tonic, Uplifting

Usage Tips *For best support for autoimmune conditions:*

- **Internal:** Place 1-5 drops in water to drink, take oil(s) in a capsule, place a drop(s) on or under tongue, or lick them off back of hand.
- **Topical:** Apply oils topically on bottoms of feet targeting reflex points for pancreas and other endocrine partners such as adrenal and thyroid locations; see Reflexology.

BLOOD SUGAR

See also Endocrine

SINGLE OILS

Coriander – promotes a healthy insulin response *(pg. 132)*

Cinnamon – balances blood sugar levels *(pg. 130)*

Cassia – balances blood sugar levels *(pg. 128)*

Turmeric – antioxidant and anti-inflammatory *(pg. 153)*

BLENDS

Metabolic blend – helps control blood sugar *(pg. 171)*

Detoxification blend – improves insulin receptivity *(pg. 165)*

Protective blend – balances blood sugar levels *(pg. 171)*

SUPPLEMENTS

Cellular vitality complex (pg. 180), digestion blend softgels, omega complex, ***metabolic blend softgels (pg. 186)***, whole food nutrient

BLOOD SUGAR

By Related Properties

For further information, see pages 260 and 272.

Antifungal, Anti-inflammatory, Antioxidant, Detoxifier, Invigorating, Stimulant, Stomachic, Vasodilator

Usage Tips

For best success at targeting blood sugar and insulin levels:

- **Internal:** Place 1-5 drops in water to drink, take oil(s) in a capsule, place a drop(s) on or under tongue, or lick them off back of hand.
- **Topical:** Apply oils topically on bottoms of feet targeting reflex points for pancreas and other endocrine partners such as adrenal and thyroid locations; see Reflexology.

BRAIN

SINGLE OILS

Sandalwood – promotes optimal brain function, repair; crosses blood-brain barrier *(pg. 150)*

Frankincense – crosses blood-brain barrier; anti-aging brain support *(pg. 135)*

Cedarwood, Arborvitae – calms, stimulates, and protects brain *(pg. 129, pg. 125)*

Rosemary – enhances brain, cognitive performance; relieves mental fatigue *(pg. 150)*

Clove and thyme – provides brain protective antioxidants *(pgs. 131 & 153)*

Petitgrain – calms and soothes the brain *(pg. 147)*

Turmeric – brain protection and antioxidant *(pg. 153)*

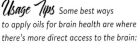

Usage Tips *Some best ways to apply oils for brain health are where there's more direct access to the brain:*

- **Aromatic:** Diffuse oils of choice to stimulate brain allowing entry through nose to olfactory system.
- **Topical:** Apply to forehead, back of skull *(especially in occipital triangles)*, under nose, roof of mouth *(place oil on pad of thumb, place on roof, "suck")* Use reflex points on foot for brain, namely big toe, underside pad.

BLENDS

Cellular complex blend – provides antioxidants and brain protection *(pg. 160)*

Detoxification blend – supports relief from mental fatigue and toxins *(pg. 165)*

Focus blend – supports oxygen and blood flow to brain, blood brain barrier *(pg. 167)*

SUPPLEMENTS

Cellular vitality complex (pg. 180), cellular complex softgels, ***omega complex (pg. 187)***, detoxification complex, ***liquid omega-3 (pg. 185)***, whole food nutrient

By Related Properties

For further information, see pages 260 and 272.

Anticonvulsant, Anti-inflammatory, Antioxidant, Anti-parasitic, Nervine, Neuroprotective, Regenerative, Stimulant

CANDIDA

See also Immune & Lymphatic

SINGLE OILS

Melaleuca – eliminates candida yeast and prevents mutation *(pg. 143)*

Oregano – eliminates and prevents candida yeast and fungus *(pg. 145)*

Pink Pepper – *(pg. 147)*

Thyme – eliminates and prevents candida yeast and fungus *(pg. 153)*

Turmeric – antioxidant and anti-inflammatory *(pg. 153)*

BLENDS

Cellular complex blend – restores health of cells *(pg. 160)*

Detoxification blend – detoxifies and eliminates free radicals *(pg. 165)*

Protective blend – helps eliminate candida / fungus *(pg. 171)*

Skin clearing blend – cleanses skin *(pg. 174)*

SUPPLEMENTS

Defensive probiotic (pg. 181), detoxification complex capsules, omega complex, ***food enzymes (pg. 183)***, whole food nutrient, ***GI cleansing softgels (pg. 184)***

By Related Properties

For further information, see pages 260 and 272.

Anti-carcinogenic, Antifungal, Antimicrobial, Antimutagenic, Antioxidant, Vermifuge

SINGLE OILS

Cypress – promotes proper circulation and blood flow throughout body *(pg. 132)*

Ylang ylang – balances heart rate and reduces high blood pressure *(pg. 156)*

Marjoram – supports the heart muscle *(pg. 143)*

Helichrysum, yarrow – repairs damaged blood vessels; stops bleeding; resolves low blood pressure *(pg. 137, pg. 156)*

Black pepper – warms and tones blood vessels; decongests circulatory / lymphatic *(pg. 127)*

Geranium – supports heart, blood, and blood vessel integrity *(pg. 135)*

BLENDS

Cleansing blend – decongests circulatory / lymphatic congestion *(pg. 164)*

Inspiring blend – promotes healthy blood flow *(pg. 168)*

Massage blend – stimulates circulation and blood flow, especially to extremities *(pg. 170)*

SUPPLEMENTS

Cellular vitality complex (pg. 180), energy & stamina complex (pg. 183), cellular complex softgels, phytoestrogen complex, polyphenol complex, defensive probiotic, whole food nutrient

By Related Properties

For further information, see pages 260 and 272.

Anticoagulant, Antihemorrhagic, Anti-inflammatory, Antitoxic, Calming, Cardiotonic, Decongestant, Detoxifier, Hypertensive, Hypotensive, Regenerative, Relaxing, Tonic, Vasoconstrictor, Vasodilator, Warming

Usage Tips

For best methods of use for cardiovascular and circulatory support consider:

- **Aromatic:** Diffuse 5-10 drops of oils of choice, inhale from product bottle or self-made blend, apply a few drops to clothing, or any other method that supports inhalation for oils especially for supporting reducing stress.
- **Topical:** Apply oils directly to chest, bottoms of feet, down spine, and / or on specific areas of concern for direct affect as needed.
- **Internal:** Place 1-5 drops in water to drink, take drops in capsule, or place drop(s) under tongue to affect internal activities that impact circulation and heart activity.

CELLULAR HEALTH

See also Immune & Lymphatic

SINGLE OILS

Turmeric – cellular health and antioxidant *(pg. 130)*

Sandalwood – promotes healthy apoptosis and cellular health *(pg. 150)*

Frankincense – promotes healthy apoptosis and cellular health *(pg. 135)*

Lemongrass – cellular detoxifier *(pg. 140)*

Tangerine, wild orange – encourages healthy DNA and optimal glutathione levels *(pg. 152, pg. 155)*

Cinnamon – promotes healthy cellular response to glucose and inflammation *(pg. 130)*

Patchouli, yarrow – supports the cell in eliminating harmful toxins *(pg. 146, pg. 156)*

Clove – powerful antioxidant; supports cellular repair *(pg. 131)*

Thyme – cellular health and DNA repair *(pg. 153)*

Arborvitae – stimulates immune support and cellular repair *(pg. 125)*

By Related Properties

For further information, see pages 260 and 272.

Anti-carcinogenic, Anti-carcinoma, Anti-inflammatory, Antimutagenic, Antioxidant, Anti-toxic, Anti-tumoral, Cleanser, Cytophylactic, Detoxifier, Purifier, Regenerative, Tonic

SUPPLEMENTS

*Cellular vitality complex **(pg. 180)***, defensive probiotic, digestion blend softgels, energy & stamina supplement, ***cellular complex softgels (pg. 187)***, omega complex, GI cleansing softgels, polyphenol complex, whole food nutrient

BLENDS

Cellular complex blend – promotes cellular health and DNA repair *(pg. 160)*

Detoxification blend – helps eliminate free radicals and heavy metals *(pg. 165)*

Uplifting blend – antioxidant; neutralizes free radicals and supports cells *(pg. 176)*

Cleansing blend – detoxifies cells and lymphatic system *(pg. 164)*

Usage Tips *For best success at supporting cellular health:*

- **Topical:** Apply oils on bottoms of feet, spine, and / or on any specific area of concern. Use Oil Touch technique regularly as desired or able.
- **Internal:** Consume oils in capsules, drop under tongue, or sip in water.

SINGLE OILS

Lavender – most used essential oil for children; all things calming *(pg. 139)*

Wild orange – gentle / powerful calming / uplifting; digestive support; boost immune / anti-infectious; promotes sense of abundance "there is enough for me!" *(pg. 155)*

Frankincense – supports brain, mood, wound healing, feeling grounded and safe / secure *(pg. 135)*

Roman chamomile – supports sense of calm / relaxation; sedative effect; diffuses agitated negative thoughts / moods; detoxifying *(pg. 149)*

Usage Tips *Children are wonderfully responsive to the use of essential oils. They love to learn about them and be involved in the process of selecting what oils are used on their behalf. They love to nurture others with the oils as well and participate in making their own personalized roller bottle blend. Allowing a child to smell an oil prior to use creates a sense of safety.*

- **Aromatic:** Use of oils at bedtime with a diffuser or smelling oils from some kind of sealed container during school can bring both peace and calming, also mental focus and concentration support. Oils supply a vast variety of emotional support.
- **Topical:** Use of oils with children is most effective when oils are combined with a carrier oil and are massaged on back, abdomen or feet.*

**NEAT - undiluted – application on feet with 1-2 drops depending on body weight is acceptable in older children; for infants and toddlers, dilute oils with a carrier oil prior to application in most cases.*

Premature babies: *Since premature babies have very thin and sensitive skin, a very conservative and highly diluted use of essential oils is recommended.*

BLENDS

Children's Restful blend – supports sense of peace and calm *(pg. 163)*

Children's Grounding blend – supports feeling grounded and stable *(pg. 162)*

Digestion blend – supports digestion and elimination *(pg. 165)*

Children's Protective blend – boosts immune system *(pg. 162)*

Children's Focus blend – supports optimal focus and concentration *(pg. 167)*

Children's Soothing blend – *(pg. 163)*

Children's Courage blend – *(pg. 161)*

SUPPLEMENTS

Children's chewable (pg. 180), defensive probiotic, *liquid omega-3 (pg. 185)*, meal replacement shake, respiratory lozenges

By Related Properties

For further information, see pages 260 and 272.

Antibacterial, Anticatarrhal, Antidepressant, Anti-inflammatory, Antiseptic, Antiviral, Calming, Decongestant, Expectorant, Immunostimulant, Invigorating, Mucolytic, Regenerative, Relaxing, Sedative, Stomachic, Uplifting

DETOXIFICATION

See also Immune & Lymphatic

SINGLE OILS

Grapefruit – antioxidant; superb detoxifier of fat, liver, gallbladder *(pg. 136)*

Lemon – antioxidant; superb "detoxifier of fat, chemicals, urinary, liver, lymph *(pg. 140)*

Lemongrass – powerhouse decongestant for any system of the body *(pg. 140)*

Clove – powerful antioxidant, blood and cellular cleanser *(pg. 131)*

BLENDS

Detoxification blend – detox liver, gallbladder, gut, kidneys, lungs, skin *(pg. 165)*

Cleansing blend – detox lymph, blood, kidneys, skin *(pg. 164)*

Cellular complex blend – detox lymph, cells, gut, brain *(pg. 160)*

Metabolic blend – detox fat, liver, gallbladder *(pg. 171)*

SUPPLEMENTS

Cellular vitality complex, ***detoxification blend softgels (pg. 181)***, ***detoxification complex (pg. 182)***, energy & stamina complex, cellular complex softgels, omega complex, food enzymes, GI cleansing softgels, whole food nutrient

By Related Properties

For further information, see pages 260 and 272.

Antitoxic, Detoxifier

Usage Tips

For detoxification, various methods will contribute to success. Here are a few to focus on:

- **Aromatic:** Consider addressing toxic emotional states during a program, as mood directly impacts health. Negative emotions and toxins are inextricably and chemically connected. Aromatic application immediately and directly impacts the amygdala, the center of emotions in the brain. See Mood & Behavior to select emotion(s) and oils that will best support a detox program.
- **Topical:** Invite tissue and organs to release fat and toxins by directly applying oils to specific areas of focus. Massage after application to ensure absorption. Applying oils to the bottoms of the feet will have a direct impact on blood and lymphatic fluids of the body, which is vital to detoxification. Additionally, use the Oil Touch technique to increase the success of a detox program.
- **Internal:** Taking essential oils and supplements internally is one of the most effective ways to deliver detox "instructions" to specific organs and tissues. Consume oils in a capsule, place under tongue, or in water to drink to accomplish these targeted efforts.

SINGLE OILS (*sorted by ailment)*

Stomach – black pepper, cardamom, fennel, ginger, wild orange

Stomach / intestinal lining – grapefruit, peppermint

Intestines – basil, cardamom, ginger, green mandarin, marjoram, peppermint

Liver – basil, cilantro, geranium, grapefruit, helichrysum, lemon, rosemary

Gallbladder – geranium, grapefruit, turmeric

Pancreas – dill, fennel, geranium, ginger, thyme

Usage Tips *For best effect on digestive and intestinal activity:*

- **Aromatic:** Apply oils topically on abdomen and / or bottoms of feet for relief.
- **Topical:** Place 1-5 drops in water and drink, take in capsule, lick off back of hand, or place drop(s) on or under tongue to allow impact directly in stomach and intestines.

BLENDS

Digestion blend – supports digestion and elimination *(pg. 165)*

Metabolic blend – supports stomach, intestines, pancreas, liver, gallbladder, fat digestion and satiation *(pg. 171)*

Massage blend – supports peristalsis and bowel tone *(pg. 170)*

Detoxification blend – supports gallbladder, liver, and pancreas *(pg. 165)*

SUPPLEMENTS

Bone nutrient complex, ***defensive probiotic (pg. 181)***, detoxification blend softgels, detoxification complex, ***digestive blend softgels (pg. 182)***, cellular complex softgels, essential oil omega complex, ***food enzymes (pg. 183)***, ***GI cleansing softgels (pg. 184)***, liquid omega-3 supplement, whole food nutrient

By Related Properties

For further information, see pages 260 and 272.

Calming, Carminative, Detoxifier, Digestive stimulant, Laxative, Stimulant, Stomachic

EATING DISORDERS

See also Limbic

SINGLE OILS

Grapefruit – helps heal relationship with body and curb emotional eating *(pg. 136)*

Patchouli – supports restoring connection to and acceptance of body *(pg. 146)*

Bergamot – balances hormones and promotes sense of self-worth *(pg. 126)*

Cinnamon – balances glucose levels and metabolism; promotes sense of safety *(pg. 130)*

BLENDS

Metabolic blend – balances metabolism and insulin *(pg. 171)*

Grounding blend – balances emotions and promotes a feeling of tranquility *(pg. 167)*

Cleansing blend – encourages release of toxic emotions *(pg. 164)*

SUPPLEMENTS

Cellular vitality complex, defensive probiotic, ***digestive blend softgels (pg. 182)***, omega complex, ***food enzymes (pg. 183)***, fruit & vegetable powder, phytoestrogen multiplex, ***whole food nutrient (pg. 191)***

By Related Properties

For further information, see pages 260 and 272.

Analgesic, Antidepressant, Antispasmodic, Calming, Energizing, Grounding, Relaxing, Stomachic

Usage Tips *Best methods of use for eating disorders:*

- **Aromatic:** Smell oils of choice, whether diffused, inhaled directly from bottle, swiped under nose, worn as a perfume / cologne, or placed on clothing, bedding, jewelry. Place oils in hands, rub together, cup over nose, inhale. Have on hand for immediate use.
- **Topical:** Apply under nose, behind ears, to base of skull *(especially in suboccipital triangles)* and forehead, on roof of mouth *(closest location to the amygdala; place on pad of thumb, then suck on thumb)*; for daily grounding, apply to bottoms of feet.
- **Internal:**
  - Drink oils to satisfy cravings or compulsions by placing a few drops in water.
  - Plan ahead for typical cravings by taking supportive oils in a capsule prior to when urges hit.
  - For more instant effects, licking a drop off back of hand to help pacify craving.
  - Apply oils to roof of mouth *(place oil on pad of thumb and then place pad on roof of mouth)*.

ENDOCRINE

SINGLE OILS

Frankincense and sandalwood – for pineal, pituitary, and hypothalamus support *(pgs. 135 & 150)*

Geranium and ylang ylang – hormone / glandular and adrenal support *(pgs. 135 & 156)*

Blue tansy, clove and lemongrass – for thyroid support *(pgs. 127, 131 & 140)*

Rosemary – stimulates glands and brain function; adrenal support *(pg. 150)*

BLENDS

Cellular complex blend – nerve repair; glandular support *(pg. 160)*

Detoxification blend – adrenal and glandular support *(pg. 165)*

Women's blend – glandular support and mood stabilizer *(pg. 177)*

SUPPLEMENTS

Cellular vitality complex, children's chewable, ***energy & stamina complex (pg. 183)***, cellular complex softgels, ***omega complex (pg. 187)***, liquid omega-3, whole food nutrient

Usage Tips

For endocrine support, a variety of methods can be successful. Suggestions:

- **Aromatic:** Diffuse 5-10 drops of oils of choice, or inhale from product bottle or self-made blend, apply a few drops to clothing, or other inhalation methods.
- **Topical:** Apply selected oils directly over location of gland or the bottoms of feet on reflex points *(see Reflexology)* twice daily. Use a carrier oil to prevent sensitivity.
- **Internal:** Consume selected oils in capsule, under tongue, or place in water to drink.

By Related Properties

For further information, see pages 260 and 272.

Anti-inflammatory, Calming, Detoxifier, Regenerative, Relaxing, Sedative, Stimulant, Uplifting, Vasodilator

ENERGY & VITALITY

See also Limbic

SINGLE OILS

Basil – stimulating and reviving *(pg. 125)*

Peppermint – invigorating and energizing *(pg. 146)*

Wild orange – uplifting and rejuvenating *(pg. 155)*

Lemon – cleansing and refreshing *(pg. 140)*

Lime – energizing and enlivening *(pg. 141)*

BLENDS

Invigorating blend – rejuvenating and energizing *(pg. 169)*

Respiration blend – invigorating and reviving *(pg. 173)*

Encouraging blend – stimulating, renewing, and strengthening *(pg. 166)*

Inspiring blend – promotes excitement, passion and joy *(pg. 168)*

Joyful blend – uplifting and energizing *(pg. 169)*

Cleansing blend – refreshing and cleansing *(pg. 164)*

SUPPLEMENTS

Cellular vitality complex (pg. 180), children's chewable, cellular complex softgels, essential oil omega complex, ***energy & stamina complex (pg. 183)***, ***whole food nutrient (pg. 191)***

By Related Properties

For further information, see pages 260 and 272.

Antidepressant, Energizing, Immunostimulant, Invigorating, Refreshing, Stimulant

Usage Tips *For best success in support optimal energy and vitality:*

- **Topical & Aromatic:** Rubbing selected and energy-producing oils on tired / sore shoulders, neck, back, legs and feet is invigorating, improves circulation, blood flow and oxygen levels in the body both by aroma and topical sensation.
- **Internal:** Consume energy-producing oils, products (e.g. *energy & vitality complex*); for oils, place a few drops of selected oils (e.g. *citrus oils*) in a capsule for systemic or on-going support. Also, drinking oils in water or dropping under the tongue is effective.

SINGLE OILS

Clove – powerful analgesic for numbing wounds *(pg. 131)*

Frankincense – universal healing properties, wound antiseptic / analgesic / healing, anti-scarring *(pg. 135)*

Helichrysum, yarrow – stop bleeding; wound repair / healing, powerful pain reliever *(pg. 137) (pg. 156)*

Lavender, blue tansy – antihistamine activity; wound, burn care, shock treatment; bite / sting recovery *(pg. 139) (pg. 127)*

Lemon – sanitize, neutralize acid; universal for immune, skin, respiratory needs *(pg. 140)*

Lemongrass – connective tissue repair, sore muscle / cramp relief *(pg. 140)*

Marjoram – muscle repair, digestive / eliminative support, sore muscle / cramp relief *(pg. 143)*

Melaleuca – gentle / powerful wound antiseptic, antimicrobial activity *(pg. 143)*

Oregano – anti-inflammatory, powerful antibacterial / antiviral *(pg. 145)*

Peppermint – cooling, burn care, pain reliever; relieve nausea, vomiting *(pg. 146)*

SUPPLEMENTS

Bone nutrient complex, ***energy & stamina complex (pg. 183), polyphenol complex (pg. 188)***

Usage Tips *For first aid success:*

- **Aromatic:** Use for emotional support for times like shock or trauma by offering immediate inhalation from a bottle or drops placed on hands.
- **Topical:** Apply oils directly to area(s) of concern such as on cuts, bruises, bites, stings, injury sites and burns.
- **Internal:** for any allergic response, place a drop of anti-histamine oil or bottoms of feet for any age; inhale as well.

BLENDS

Cellular complex blend – antitrauma, cellular, cognitive support *(pg. 160)*

Cleansing blend – antiseptic properties; sanitize, bug bite / sting recovery *(pg. 164)*

Detoxification blend – anti-allergenic, blood cleansing, anti-infectious support *(pg. 165)*

Digestion blend – excellent to resolve nausea, vomiting *(pg. 165)*

Massage blend – for injured tissue recovery; sore muscle / cramp relief *(pg. 170)*

Protective blend – immune protection, analgesic *(pg. 171)*

Repellent blend – bug repellent *(pg. 173)*

Restful blend – for shock, trauma recovery *(pg. 174)*

Skin clearing blend – antiseptic, wound care *(pg. 174)*

Soothing blend – bone / pain relief support; sore muscle / cramp relief *(pg. 175)*

By Related Properties

For further information, see pages 260 and 272.

Analgesic, Anti-allergenic, Anticonvulsant, Anti-hemorrhagic, Anti-infectious, Anti-inflammatory, Antiseptic, Antispasmodic, Calming, Hypotensive, Vasoconstrictor, Warming

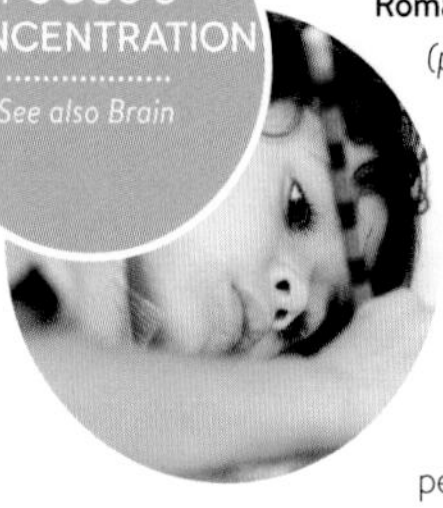

FOCUS & CONCENTRATION

See also Brain

SINGLE OILS

Roman chamomile – reduces anxiety, promotes confidence *(pg. 149)*

Vetiver – promotes focus, concentration, mental performance *(pg. 154)*

Lavender – supports mental adaptability, performance *(pg. 139)*

Clary sage – supports a calm, clear, focused mind *(pg. 130)*

Cedarwood – calms mind, supports improved mental performance *(pg. 129)*

BLENDS

Restful blend – relaxes the mind *(pg. 174)*

Focus blend – calms and stimulates the mind *(pg. 167)*

Encouraging blend – promotes motivation, mental stimulation and movement *(pg. 166)*

Grounding blend – promotes a grounded state of mind *(pg. 167)*

Children's Focus blend – calms and stimulates the mind *(pg. 161)*

SUPPLEMENTS

Bone nutrient complex, cellular vitality complex, defensive probiotic, detoxification blend softgels, detoxification complex, energy & stamina complex, cellular complex softgels, ***omega complex (pg. 187)***, food enzymes, whole food nutrient, ***liquid omega-3 (pg. 185)***

By Related Properties

For further information, see pages 260 and 272.

Antidepressant, Antifungal, Antioxidant, Calming, Energizing, Grounding, Invigorating, Neuroprotective, Refreshing, Relaxing, Sedative, Stimulant, Uplifting

Usage Tips

For best methods of use for focus and concentration consider:

- **Aromatic:** Choose to diffuse 5-10 drops of oils of choice, inhale from product bottle or self-made blend, apply a few drops to clothing, bedding, or any other method that supports inhalation for oils to enter brain via nose and olfactory system.
- **Topical:** Apply on forehead, under nose, back of neck (especially in suboccipital triangles), roof of mouth (place oil on pad of thumb, place on roof, "suck").

SINGLE OILS

Melaleuca – fights bacteria and viruses *(pg. 143)*

Cinnamon – fights bacteria and viruses *(pg. 130)*

Copaiba – fights bacteria and viruses *(pg. 131)*

Black or Pink pepper – supports digestion and boosts immunity *(pg. 127)*

Thyme – fights bacteria and viruses *(pg. 153)*

Usage Tips

For most effective use of essential oils for immune and lymphatic benefits:

- **Aromatic:** Diffuse for associated respiratory symptoms and to clear pathogens from air.
- **Topical:** Apply oils topically on bottoms of feet, especially on back side of toes, rub oils down the spine and / or on any specific area of concern. Use Oil Touch technique.
- **Internal:** Take oils in capsule, place a drop(s) under or on tongue near back of throat or sip from a glass of water.
- **Surface:** Sanitize surfaces with essential oil(s) mixed with water and emulsifier.

BLENDS

Protective blend – stimulates immune system and fights bacteria / viruses *(pg. 171)*

Detoxification blend – supports proper detoxification *(pg. 165)*

Cellular complex blend – manages abnormal cell activity and stimulates immune system *(pg. 160)*

Cleansing blend – disinfects and sanitizes *(pg. 164)*

SUPPLEMENTS

Bone nutrient complex, cellular vitality complex, children's chewable, ***defensive probiotic (pg. 181)***, detoxification complex, cellular complex softgels, omega complex, food enzymes, ***GI cleansing softgels (pg. 184)***, ***protective blend softgels (pg. 189)***, protective blend lozenges, seasonal blend softgels, whole food nutrient

By Related Properties

For further information, see pages 260 and 272.

Antibacterial, Antifungal, Anti-infectious, Anti-inflammatory, Antimicrobial, Antioxidant, Antiseptic, Antiviral, Immunostimulant, Stimulant, Warming

INTEGUMENTARY

Hair, Nails & Skin

SINGLE OILS

Lavender – supports healing and maintaining healthy tissue *(pg. 139)*

Sandalwood – promotes regeneration and toning *(pg. 150)*

Geranium – regenerates tissue and tones skin *(pg. 135)*

Frankincense – invigorates skin, reduces inflammation *(pg. 135)*

Helichrysum – regenerates tissue and reduces scarring *(pg. 137)*

BLENDS

Anti-aging blend – restores and tones skin *(pg. 159)*

Skin clearing blend – cleanses skin and reduces inflammation *(pg. 174)*

SUPPLEMENTS

Bone nutrient complex, cellular vitality complex, defensive probiotic, ***omega complex (pg. 187)***, detoxification complex, food enzymes, GI cleansing softgels, ***liquid omega-3 (pg. 185)***, whole food nutrient

By Related Properties

For further information, see pages 260 and 272.

Analgesic, Antifungal, Anti-infectious, Anti-inflammatory, Antimicrobial, Antimutagenic, Antiseptic, Antiviral, Astringent, Cytophylactic, Deodorant, Insect repellent, Regenerative, Revitalizer, Tonic

Usage Tips *For best support of hair, skin and nails:*

- **Topical:** Apply oils directly to hair, scalp, nails, and skin. Use a carrier oil to dilute and reduce sensitivity to skin when necessary, especially with infants, elderly, and compromised skin.
- **Internal:** Consume specified oils by either capsule or under tongue. Gut health is a major component of integumentary health. See Digestive & Intestinal, Candida.

SINGLE OILS

Jasmine, Neroli, and Magnolia – enhances mood and libido, euphoric *(pgs. 138, 145 & 142)*

Ylang ylang – supports a healthy libido and endocrine function *(pg. 156)*

Patchouli – improves circulation, raises body temperature, enhances mood *(pg. 146)*

Clary sage – supports the endocrine system, enhances libido *(pg. 130)*

Bergamot and Pink Pepper – balances hormones, enhances libido *(pgs. 126 & 147)*

BLENDS

Women's blend – support healthy libido *(pg. 177)*

Inspiring blend – promotes passion, excitement and joy *(pg. 168)*

Joyful blend – uplifts mood, energizes *(pg. 169)*

Massage blend– supports circulation, relieves tension *(pg. 170)*

SUPPLEMENTS

Cellular vitality complex, detoxification blend softgels, detoxification complex, ***energy & stamina complex (pg. 183)***, cellular complex softgels, omega complex, GI cleansing softgels, ***polyphenol complex (pg. 188)***, whole food nutrient

By Related Properties

For further information, see pages 260 and 272.

Anaphrodisiac, Antidepressant, Aphrodisiac, Calming, Energizing, Grounding, Invigorating, Relaxing, Rubefacient, Sedative, Stimulant, Uplifting, Vasodilator, Warming

Usage Tips

For best results to support optimal intimacy:

- **Aromatic:** Set the mood by diffusing oils of choice that are calming, warming and arousing to both parties.
- **Topical:** Enjoy using specified oils to obtain desired results. When in sensitive areas be sure to use a carrier oil.

LIMBIC

See also Immune & Lymphatic

SINGLE OILS

Melissa — reduces depression and supports trauma recovery *(pg. 144)*

Juniper berry — helps release fears, trauma, and nightmares *(pg. 138)*

Frankincense — balances brain activity; supports a sense of protection, safety and releases traumatic memories *(pg. 135)*

Patchouli — sedates, grounds, stabilizes; supports central nervous system *(pg. 146)*

Turmeric — antioxidant and anti-inflammatory *(pg. 153)*

BLENDS

Restful blend — calms feelings of fear, anger, jealousy, and rage *(pg. 174)*

Uplifting blend — brings feelings of cheerfulness, optimism and positivity *(pg. 176)*

Encouraging blend — stimulates self-belief, courage and confidence *(pg. 166)*

Joyful blend — stabilizes mood and promotes courage and cheerfulness *(pg. 169)*

Grounding blend — calms an overactive mind; promotes sense of connectivity *(pg. 167)*

By Related Properties

For further information, see pages 260 and 272.

Antidepressant, Calming, Grounding, Relaxing, Sedative

Usage Tips *The best way to affect the limbic system with essential oils is to inhale them, giving the oils the most direct access to through the olfactory bulb.*

- **Aromatic:** Diffuse oils of choice, inhale from bottle, apply a few drops to clothing, or any other method that supports inhalation for oils to enter brain via nose.
- **Topical:** Apply oils as close to brain as possible such as on forehead, under nose, back of neck *(especially in suboccipital triangles)*, *roof of mouth (place oil on pad of thumb, place thumb on roof of mouth and suck)*. Applying oils on chest allows breathing in vapors.

MEN'S HEALTH

SINGLE OILS

Frankincense – promotes longevity, supports brain and prostate health *(pg. 135)*

Melaleuca – fights bacteria and fungus with antiseptic action *(pg. 143)*

Juniper berry – supports urinary and prostate health, wound healing *(pg. 138)*

Cardamom – supports digestive, muscular, and respiratory health *(pg. 128)*

Lemon – detoxifies and has an alkalizing effect *(pg. 140)*

Usage Tips

Best results for men's health:

- **Get oils in, on and around you.** Start with a couple drops per day and go from there.
- **Use common sense.** Whether its taking oils in a capsule, glass of water, or under tongue for internal use; using as an aftershave, applying them to bottoms of feet or on an area of concern for topical use; smelling or diffusing them for aromatic purposes, enjoy the benefits to all aspect of men's health.

BLENDS

Grounding blend – makes great cologne, aftershave; brain support *(pg. 167)*

Protective blend – supports cardiovascular and immune health *(pg. 171)*

Detoxification blend – supports urinary, prostate; prevents hair loss *(pg. 165)*

Cellular complex blend – assists with cellular repair and longevity *(pg. 160)*

SUPPLEMENTS

Cellular vitality complex (pg. 180), energy & stamina complex (pg. 183), cellular complex softgels (pg. 187), omega complex (pg. 187), polyphenol complex (pg. 188), whole food nutrient (pg. 191)

By Related Properties

For further information, see pages 260 and 272.

Anti-inflammatory, Cardiotonic, Restorative, Steroidal

MOOD & BEHAVIOR

See also Limbic

SINGLE OILS

Lavender – calms and relaxes, increases the ability to express feelings *(pg. 139)*

Wild orange and tangerine – melts away anxiousness and energizes *(pg. 155) (pg. 152)*

Cedarwood – grounds, promotes a sense of belonging and being connected socially *(pg. 129)*

Bergamot – helps increase self-confidence *(pg. 126)*

Neroli or Magnolia – calms and sedates *(pgs. 145 & 142)*

BLENDS

Invigorating blend – stimulates the mind and mood; encourages creativity *(pg. 169)*

Joyful blend – energizes, balances hormones; restores a sense of buoyancy *(pg. 169)*

Uplifting blend – promotes a cheerful, positive attitude *(pg. 176)*

Restful blend – encourages a restful state for mind and body *(pg. 174)*

Encouraging blend – stimulates belief, courage and confidence *(pg. 166)*

Grounding blend – promotes a state of balance and calm *(pg. 167)*

SUPPLEMENTS

energy & stamina complex (pg. 183), cellular complex, ***omega complex (pg. 187)***, food enzymes, ***liquid omega-3 (pg. 185)***, ***phytoestrogen multiplex (pg. 188)***, whole food nutrient

By Related Properties

For further information, see pages 260 and 272.

Antidepressant, Calming, Energizing, Grounding, Invigorating, Relaxing, Sedative, Stimulant, Uplifting

Usage Tips *For best effect for mood and behavior:*

- **Aromatic:** Diffuse oils of choice, inhale from bottle, apply a few drops to clothing, or any other method that supports inhalation for oils to enter brain via nose.
- **Topical:** Apply oils as close to brain as possible such as on forehead, under nose, back of neck *(especially in suboccipital triangles)*, roof of mouth *(place oil on pad of thumb, place thumb on roof of mouth and suck)*. Applying oils on chest allows breathing in vapors.
- **Internal:** Place one to five drops of chosen oil in water to drink or take in a capsule, drop under tongue, lick a drop off back of hand, apply to roof of mouth *(place oil on pad of thumb and then place pad on roof of mouth)*.

SINGLE OILS

Lemongrass – soothes muscle aches, supports connective tissue repair *(pg. 140)*

Cypress – promotes blood flow to muscle and connective tissue, reduces pain and spasms *(pg. 132)*

Marjoram – relaxes muscles and decreases spasms *(pg. 143)*

Ginger and Turrmeric – reduces spasms and muscle aches and pain *(pgs. 136 & 153)*

BLENDS

Massage blend – promotes circulation and relieves pain *(pg. 170)*

Soothing blend – soothes muscle and joint pain and inflammation *(pg. 175)*

Tension blend – soothes sore muscles and tissue; releases tension *(pg. 176)*

Cellular complex blend – helps with connective tissue repair and soothes pain *(pg. 160)*

SUPPLEMENTS

Bone nutrient complex (pg. 179), cellular vitality complex, detoxification complex, detoxification blend softgels, ***energy & stamina complex (pg. 183)***, cellular complex softgels, ***omega complex (pg. 187)***, ***polyphenol complex (pg. 188)***, whole food nutrient

By Related Properties

For further information, see pages 260 and 272.

Analgesic, Anticonvulsant, Anti-inflammatory, Antispasmodic, Energizing, Regenerative, Steroidal, Tonic

Usage Tips

For best results with muscles and connective tissue:

- **Aromatic:** Apply oils directly to area of concern, massage in thoroughly whenever possible. Drive oils in with heat, cold, or moisture. Use carrier oil as needed or desired. Layering multiple oils over affected area, placing them on tissue one at a time, is very effective. Any kind of cream or carrier barrier will slow absorption if placed on first and improve it if placed on last.
  - › *Acute:* Apply often, every 20-30 minutes, until symptoms subside, then reduce to every two to six hours.
  - › *Chronic:* Apply two to three times daily.
- **Internal:** Consume oils to support resolving inflammation in a capsule or under tongue.

NERVOUS SYSTEM

SINGLE OILS

Helichrysum – invigorates nerves and relieves pain *(pg. 137)*

Peppermint – stimulates nerves and supports repair *(pg. 146)*

Lemongrass – stimulates nerves and electrical system of body *(pg. 140)*

Patchouli – provides nerve protection and supports regeneration; removes toxins *(pg. 146)*

Basil – stimulates, energizes and restores nerves; relaxes tension *(pg. 125)*

Frankincense – provides nerve protection and supports regeneration *(pg. 135)*

Neroli or Magnolia – calms and sedates *(pgs. 145 & 142)*

BLENDS

Focus blend – helps with mental focus and reduces inflammation *(pg. 167)*

Massage blend – increases circulation *(pg. 170)*

Soothing blend – invigorates and stimulates nerves *(pg. 175)*

Cellular complex blend – regenerates and protects nerves *(pg. 160)*

Anti-aging blend – regenerates nerves and increases clarity *(pg. 159)*

SUPPLEMENTS

Bone nutrient complex, cellular vitality complex, energy & stamina complex, ***cellular complex softgels (pg. 187)***, ***omega complex (pg. 187)***, food enzymes, ***liquid omega-3 (pg. 185)***, polyphenol complex, whole food nutrient

By Related Properties

For further information, see pages 260 and 272.

Analgesic, Antifungal, Anti-inflammatory, Calming, Grounding, Nervine, Neuroprotective, Neurotonic, Regenerative, Relaxing, Steroidal, Stimulant

Usage Tips

For best success in support the nerves and nervous system:

- **Aromatic:** Inhaling from a preparation or diffusing selected oils can have direct impact on brain and nervous system via olfactory pathways.
- **Topical:** Apply selected oil(s) directly to any area of concern remembering to use a carrier oil if necessary to prevent sensitivity.
- **Topical:** Consume oils in a capsule or under tongue to address nervous issues and bring a particular chemical message to affected areas.

SINGLE OILS

Myrrh – fights gum disease, infections and sores; soothes gums *(pg. 144)*

Clove – protects nerves, soothes pain; prevents tooth decay *(pg. 131)*

Peppermint – freshens breath; reduces swelling, inflammation, and tenderness *(pg. 146)*

Wintergreen – protect nerves, soothes pain; prevents tooth decay *(pg. 155)*

Turmeric – relieves pain and inflammation *(pg. 153)*

BLENDS

Protective blend – helps fight infection and bacteria; prevents tooth decay *(pg. 171)*

Cellular complex blend – protects nerves, soothes pain; prevents tooth decay *(pg. 160)*

Tension blend – reduces tension, inflammation, swelling, and pain in jaw *(pg. 176)*

SUPPLEMENTS

Bone nutrient complex (pg. 179), cellular vitality complex, detoxification softgels, omega complex, food enzymes, fruit & vegetable powder, protective blend softgels, whole food nutrient

By Related Properties

For further information, see pages 260 and 272.

Analgesic, Antibacterial, Anti-infectious, Anti-inflammatory, Detoxifier, Immunostimulant

Usage Tips For oral health support

- **Topical:** Apply oils directly to area of concern in mouth such as gums, teeth, tongue, sores, etc. To relieve pain, also apply pain-relieving oils to outside cheek / jaw area *(can use a carrier oil as needed)*; apply frequently as needed for acute situations.
- **Internal:** Place oils on toothbrush and brush teeth with selected oils to affect surface of teeth. Ingest oils *(e.g. lemon)* to change pH *(alkalize)* in body / mouth which affects tooth and oral health.

PAIN & INFLAMMATION

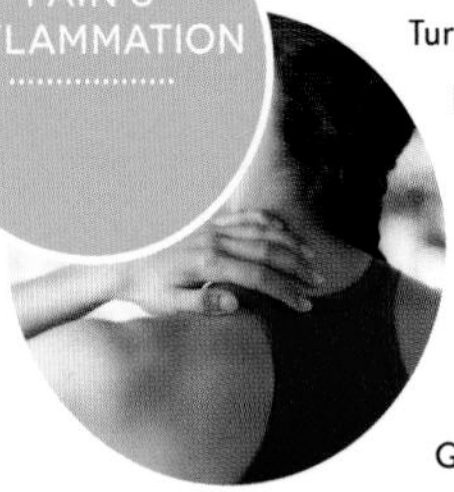

SINGLE OILS

Copaiba – relieves pain and inflammation *(pg. 131)*

Turmeric – relieves pain and inflammation *(pg. 153)*

Helichrysum – reduces pain; accelerates healing; chelates toxins *(pg. 137)*

Wintergreen, Birch – soothes aches and pain, warms; has a cortisone-like effect; supports bone healing *(pg. 155) (pg. 126)*

Peppermint – reduces inflammation and pain, cools, invigorates, and stimulates *(pg. 146)*

Ginger – invigorates nerves, promotes circulation and healing to bones and muscles *(pg. 136)*

Black and Pink pepper – reduces inflammation, relieves pain, increases circulation *(pg. 127)*

Basil, Rosemary – calms nerves, improves circulation and healing; steroidal action *(pg. 125) (pg. 150)*

BLENDS

Soothing blend – invigorates nerves and reduces inflammation *(pg. 175)*

Cellular complex blend – protects cells against free-radical damage while supporting healthy cellular function and renewal *(pg. 160)*

Tension blend – soothes joints and tissues *(pg. 176)*

Massage blend – stimulates circulation and blood flow *(pg. 170)*

SUPPLEMENTS

Cellular vitality complex (pg. 180), defensive probiotic, ***cellular complex softgels (pg. 187)***, ***omega complex (pg. 187)***, ***polyphenol complex (pg. 188)***, whole food nutrient

By Related Properties

For further information, see pages 260 and 272.

Analgesic, Anti-inflammatory, Calming, Neurotonic, Purifier, Relaxing, Sedative, Steroidal

Usage Tips

Best practices for essential oil use for relief from pain and inflammation:

- **Topical:** Very effective for many situations especially when it is more structural; most importantly, apply oils directly to any area of concern remembering to use a carrier oil if necessary to prevent sensitivity. Apply often, every 20-30 minutes, until symptoms subside, then reduce to every two to six hours for acute pain. For chronic pain, apply two to three times daily. Layering is also very effective for using multiple oils at the same time; apply one at a time.
- **Internal:** Highly effective for more chronic or internal pain; place oils in a capsule or drop under tongue *(hold for 30 seconds; swallow)*.

PARASITES

SINGLE OILS

Blue tansy — *(pg. 127)*
Cinnamon — *(pg. 130)*
Clove — *(pg. 131)*
Thyme *(pg. 153)*
Lemongrass — *(pg. 140)*
Oregano — *(pg. 145)*
Roman chamomile — *(pg. 149)*
Turmeric *(pg. 153)*
— to establish an unfriendly environment for parasites and encourage elimination

BLENDS

Cellular complex blend — *(pg. 160)*
Cleansing blend — *(pg. 164)*
Detoxification blend — *(pg. 165)*
Digestion blend — *(pg. 165)*
Protective blend — *(pg. 171)*
Skin clearing blend *(pg. 174)* — to establish an unfriendly environment for parasites and encourage elimination

SUPPLEMENTS

cellular complex softgels, defensive probiotic, ***detoxification complex (pg. 182)***, digestion blend softgels, food enzymes, ***GI cleansing softgels (pg. 184)*** *(When conducting an intestinal parasite cleanse, it is essential to keep the intestinal tract moving so toxins do not remain in the body.)*

Usage Tips *For parasite elimination:*

- **The goal is to get oils to location(s)** where parasite(s) lives *(e.g. on skin or in gut)*. Consume or apply topically accordingly. Use a carrier oil to prevent sensitivity wherever needed.

PREGNANCY LABOR & NURSING

SUPPLEMENTS

Bone nutrient complex (pg. 179), *defensive probiotic (pg. 181)*, digestion blend softgels, cellular complex softgels, *essential oil omega complex (pg. 187)*, *food enzymes (pg. 183)*, whole food nutrient

By Related Properties

For further information, see pages 260 and 272.

Analgesic, Antidepressant, Anticoagulant, Antiemetic, Antihemorrhagic, Antispasmodic, Calming, Carminative, Digestive stimulant, Energizing, Galactagogue, Immunostimulant, Invigorating, Regenerative, Relaxing, Sedative, Stomachic, Uplifting, Warming

pregnancy

SINGLE OILS

Wild orange – energizes and lifts mood *(pg. 155)*

Ginger – relieves nausea and morning sickness *(pg. 136)*

Peppermint – relieves digestive upsets and supports memory *(pg. 146)*

BLENDS

Soothing blend – soothes aches and pains *(pg. 175)*

Tension blend – relieves tension *(pg. 176)*

Metabolic blend – balances glucose levels and metabolism *(pg. 171)*

Digestion blend – supports digestion and relieves morning sickness *(pg. 165)*

Women's blend – balances hormones *(pg. 177)*

NOTE: *The use of clary sage by women who have a history of preterm labor or miscarriage or are experiencing such should be avoided.*

Usage Tips

Here are a few safety guidelines to use when selecting oils for use during pregnancy:

- **Use truly therapeutic, superior grade essential oils** that are certified as pure, potent, genuine and authentic and subjected to rigorous testing to ensure no harmful ingredients are present.
- **Be aware.** When using pure and potent oils, be aware of what they might do before using them.
- **Be a wise steward.** The first three months are the time baby develops rapidly. Simply be more cautious during the first trimester.

labor

SINGLE OILS

Clary sage – broad-spectrum support to labor process *(pg. 130)*

Jasmine – assists with labor and afterbirth *(pg. 138)*

Geranium – supports perineum, labor performance, mood and healing *(pg. 135)*

Lavender – calms and soothes mood and tissues *(pg. 139)*

Frankincense – lessens stress and trauma; promotes healing *(pg. 135)*

Basil – relieves pain; enhances labor performance *(pg. 125)*

Helichrysum – slows / stops bleeding and promotes healing *(pg. 137)*

BLENDS

Grounding blend – improves coping capacity *(pg. 167)*

Tension blend – relieves tension *(pg. 176)*

Women's monthly blend – enhances labor performance *(pg. 177)*

Soothing blend – soothes aches and pains *(pg. 175)*

nursing

SINGLE OILS

Fennel – promotes milk production; prevents clogged ducts, infection, and thrush *(pg. 134)*

Ylang ylang – alleviates tender breasts and depression *(pg. 156)*

Clary sage – promotes milk supply and hormone balancing; boosts mood *(pg. 130)*

Lavender – promotes milk production; prevents / heals tender sore breasts, nipples, and clogged milk ducts *(pg. 139)*

BLENDS

Women's blend – balances hormones and increases libido *(pg. 177)*

Joyful blend – supports mood and alleviates depression *(pg. 169)*

NOTE: *The use of peppermint oil while nursing can limit milk production for some women and therefore it is recommended for them to reduce or stop usage while breastfeeding. Fennel, clary sage, or basil can counteract effects of peppermint on lactation as they increase milk supply.*

- **Pay attention to how the body** responds to dosages.
- **Use oils aromatically** as a safe method during pregnancy. They are excellent for boosting mood and energy and creating an uplifting environment.
- **Consider the source.** When it comes to trying to decipher facts regarding essential oil use during pregnancy and nursing, human studies are not conducted.
- **Err on the side of safety.** In conclusion, use prudence, dilute, and avoid anything that simply doesn't feel right.

RESPIRATORY

SINGLE OILS

Black or Pink pepper — reduces inflammation and mucus *(pgs. 127 & 147)*

Eucalyptus — opens airways, supports proper respiratory function *(pg. 134)*

Peppermint — opens airways, expels mucus *(pg. 146)*

Rosemary — helps with many different respiratory issues *(pg. 150)*

BLENDS

Cleansing blend — decongests *(pg. 164)*

Protective blend — fights respiratory infections, helps resolve respiratory issues *(pg. 171)*

Respiration blend — addresses a broad spectrum of respiratory issues *(pg. 173)*

SUPPLEMENTS

cellular complex softgels, omega complex, food enzymes, ***protective blend lozenges (pg. 189)***, ***defensive probiotic (pg. 181)***, ***respiratory lozenges (pg. 190)***, whole food nutrient

By Related Properties

For further information, see pages 260 and 272.

Anticatarrhal. Anti-inflammatory, Antispasmodic, Decongestant, Expectorant, Immunostimulant, Mucolytic, Steroidal

Usage Tips *Whether for preventative measures (to clear airborne pathogens and sterilize air) or to* ***resolve respiratory conditions,*** *essential oils are excellent for "clearing the air" in both the environment and the body's own respiratory system as well as addressing contributing factors such as poor digestion.*

- **Aromatic:** Diffuse *(using a diffuser)* or inhale selected oils. For a quick treatment, drop oil(s) in hands, rub together, cup around nose and mouth area *(can avoid touching face)* and repeatedly, deeply inhale through mouth and nose. Additionally, use oils can be applied under the nose, on clothing or bedding, or on jewelry made for diffusing purposes or such to create long-lasting inhalation exposure.
- **Topical:** Rub oils on chest *(for aromatic benefit as well)*, back, forehead *(sinuses)*, and on back side of toes and ball of foot *(reflex points for head and chest)*.
- **Internal:** Place drops of oils in a capsule or in water for systemic or chronic support.
- **Internal:** Make a spray mixing essential oils in water with witch hazel for surfaces such as countertops and door knobs for cleaning purposes will also support eradicating bacteria, viruses, fungi, or other harmful germs.

SINGLE OILS

Turmeric – relieves pain and inflammation *(pg. 153)*

Copaiba – relieves pains and inflammations *(pg. 131)*

Lemongrass – enhances connective tissue repair *(pg. 140)*

Wintergreen – reduces aches, pains, and inflammation; stimulates bone repair *(pg. 155)*

Birch – reduces inflammation and stimulates bone repair *(pg. 126)*

Helichrysum – relieves pain and inflammation; accelerates bone repair *(pg. 137)*

Siberian fir – eases bone and joint pain; reduces inflammation *(pg. 151)*

BLENDS

Soothing blend – soothes, relaxes, and relieves aches and pains; helps with after injuries / surgery healing *(pg. 175)*

Tension blend – helps relieve and resolve tension, soreness, and stiffness *(pg. 176)*

Cellular complex blend – reduces / resolves inflammation and regenerates tissue *(pg. 160)*

SUPPLEMENTS

Bone nutrient complex (pg. 179), cellular vitality complex, defensive probiotic, digestion blend softgels, cellular complex softgels, ***omega complex (pg. 187)***, food enzymes, ***polyphenol complex (pg. 188)***, whole food nutrient

By Related Properties

For further information, see pages 260 and 272.

Analgesic, Antiarthritic, Anti-inflammatory, Anti-rheumatic, Regenerative, Steroidal

Usage Tips *For best results with skeletal and connective tissue issues:*

- **Topical:** Apply oils directly to area of concern for structural issues and in the case of injury, massage in thoroughly whenever possible. Drive oils in with heat, cold, or moisture. Use carrier oil as needed or desired. Layering multiple oils over affected area, placing them on tissue one at a time, is very effective. Any kind of cream or carrier oil will slow absorption if placed on first and improve it if placed on last.
  - › Acute: Apply often, every 20-30 minutes, until symptoms subside, then reduce to every two to six hours. › Chronic: Apply two to three times daily.
- **Internal:** Consume oils *(to support resolving inflammation and bone repair)* in a capsule or under tongue. Place oils in a capsule or drop under tongue *(hold for 30 seconds; swallow)*.

SINGLE OILS

Lavender – calms, relaxes, and sedates; supports parasympathetic system *(pg. 139)*

Vetiver – grounds and promotes tranquility *(pg. 154)*

Roman chamomile – balances hormones; sedates, calms, and relaxes *(pg. 149)*

BLENDS

Restful blend – calms mind / emotions; promotes relaxation and restful sleep *(pg. 174)*

Grounding blend – promotes sense of well being and supports autonomic nervous system *(pg. 167)*

Focus blend – balances brain activity and calms overstimulation *(pg. 167)*

SUPPLEMENTS

Bone nutrient complex (pg. 179), cellular vitality complex, defensive probiotic, ***detoxification blend softgels (pg. 181)***, detoxification complex, energy & stamina, ***omega complex (pg. 187)***, liquid omega-3, phytoestrogen multiplex, ***whole food nutrient (pg. 191)***

By Related Properties

For further information, see pages 260 and 272.

Analgesic, Antidepressant, Calming, Detoxifier, Grounding, Relaxing, Restorative, Sedative

Usage Tips ***To support optimal and restful sleep, inhalation and topical use of essential oils gives direct access to the brain through smell, relaxes tense muscles, and calms active minds.***

- **Aromatic:** Diffuse selected oil(s) of choice, apply a few drops to clothing, bedding *(e.g. pillow)*, or any other method that supports inhalation. Start exposure just before bedtime.
- **Topical:** Combine oils with soothing and relaxing massage techniques; apply oils on forehead, back, shoulders, under nose, and especially bottoms of feet from a pre-made or prepared roller bottle blend for ease. Applying oils on chest allows breathing in vapors. For chronic issues, use Oil Touch technique regularly.

SINGLE OILS

Lavender – calms and relieves stress *(pg. 139)*

Roman chamomile – calms reduces stress *(pg. 149)*

Tangerine, wild orange – energizes while reducing anxiety and depression *(pg. 152) (pg. 155)*

Frankincense – reduces depression, trauma, and tension *(pg. 135)*

Vetiver – improves focus and sedates *(pg. 154)*

Usage Tips *Managing and eliminating stress. Essential oils are extremely effective for stress reduction. Any method of application can be successful. Here are some primary methods:*

- **Aromatic:** Get / create exposure to an aroma as a first step to success for an immediate invitation to relax, calm down, get focused or whatever is needed at the time. Diffuse favorite oils, inhale from bottle or hands, apply a few drops to clothing, or apply under nose.
- **Topical:** Apply to tense or tired muscles on back, shoulders, neck, legs, or anywhere the stress is affecting the body. This topical use also allows for an aromatic experience. Consider use on the chest, gland locations, base of skull *(especially in suboccipital triangles)*, behind ears, or across forehead, and perfume points.
- **Internal:** Stress often affects internal activity such as digestion; choose and use oils according to needs.

BLENDS

Invigorating blend – energizes while reducing anxiety and depression *(pg. 169)*

Grounding blend – balances mood while reducing stress and trauma *(pg. 167)*

Restful blend – reduces anxiety and stress *(pg. 174)*

Tension blend – relieves tension and stress *(pg. 176)*

Women's blend – balances hormones and calms anxiety *(pg. 177)*

SUPPLEMENTS

Bone nutrient complex (pg. 179), cellular vitality complex, digestion blend softgels, ***energy & stamina complex (pg. 183)***, ***omega complex (pg. 187)***, liquid omega-3, phytoestrogen multiplex, ***whole food nutrient (pg. 191)***

By Related Properties

For further information, see pages 260 and 272.

Calming, Energizing, Grounding, Refreshing, Relaxing, Uplifting

STRESS

URINARY

SINGLE OILS

Lemon – helps dissolve stones and acts as diuretic *(pg. 140)*

Juniper berry – acts as diuretic; tonifies bladder and supports urinary system *(pg. 138)*

Lemongrass – decongests urinary tract and fights urinary infections *(pg. 140)*

Cypress – resolves incontinence and excessive water / fluid retention *(pg. 132)*

Thyme – supports healthy prostate and circulation; fights urinary infections *(pg. 153)*

Eucalyptus – relieves infection, stones *(pg. 134)*

Cardamom – antioxidant and combats infection *(pg. 128)*

BLENDS

Cellular complex blend – antioxidant; cleanses and disinfects urinary tract *(pg. 160)*

Detoxification blend – supports proper liver and kidney function *(pg. 165)*

Metabolic blend – acts as diuretic and detoxifies *(pg. 171)*

Protective blend – promotes blood flow and elimination of waste *(pg. 171)*

SUPPLEMENTS

Cellular vitality complex, ***detoxification blend softgels (pg. 181)***, ***detoxification complex (pg. 182)***, ***cellular complex softgels (pg. 187)***, metabolic blend softgels, ***protective blend softgels (pg. 189)***, whole food nutrient

By Related Properties

For further information, see pages 260 and 272.

Anti-infectious, Anti-inflammatory, Cleanser, Detoxifier, Diuretic, Purifier

Usage Tips

For best success in supporting urinary conditions:

- **Aromatic:** Diffuse oils through night for nighttime concerns such as bed-wetting.
- **Topical:** Place over urinary areas of bladder/kidneys. Use carrier oil as needed to prevent sensitivity; spine, bottoms of feet also excellent locations.
- **Internal:** Use softgels or place drops of oil(s) in a capsule and consume every few hours for acute situations; or under tongue or in water.

SINGLE OILS

Grapefruit – curbs cravings, reduces appetite, and induces fat burning *(pg. 136)*

Cinnamon – inhibits formation of new fat cells; balances blood sugar *(pg. 130)*

Peppermint – enhances sense of fullness; reduces cravings and appetite *(pg. 146)*

Ginger – encourages fat burning and promotes satiation *(pg. 136)*

Usage Tips *For weight management, the focus is primarily on what and how much food is consumed (appetite) and how well it is utilized as fuel by the body (metabolism). Additionally, balancing other processes such as elimination, blood sugar, and hormones is often necessary for long-lasting results. See suggested programs in "Remedies" below. With that in mind:*

- **Aromatic:** Excellent for supporting appetite control. Inhale as needed.
- **Topical:** Use to assist the body to detox and target specific zones. Consider applying blends of oils to areas like the abdomen, thighs, and arms as a treatment. Use a carrier oil if necessary to prevent sensitivity especially with oils like cinnamon.
- **Internal:** Ingesting oils for support with appetite, cravings and metabolism, including the ability to burn fat and release it along with toxins is very effective. Place drops of oils in a capsule for systemic or on-going support. Drink oils in water; drop on tongue. Be generous with usage for this purpose.

BLENDS

Metabolic blend – balances metabolism, eliminates cravings, and lifts mood; acts as diuretic *(pg. 171)*

Detoxification blend – support body's ability to remove toxins and waste effectively *(pg. 165)*

Cellular complex blend – improves function of the endocrine system and thyroid *(pg. 160)*

SUPPLEMENTS

Cellular vitality complex, defensive probiotic, ***detoxification complex (pg. 182)***, digestion blend softgels, omega complex, fruit & vegetable powder, ***meal replacement shake (pg. 185)***, ***metabolic blend softgels (pg. 186)***, phytoestrogen multiplex, whole food nutrient

By Related Properties

For further information, see pages 260 and 272.

Analgesic, Antidepressant, Calming, Detoxifier, Energizing, Steroidal, Stimulant, Stomachic, Uplifting

WOMEN'S HEALTH

SINGLE OILS

Rose – helps overcome frigidity and infertility; promotes healthy menstruation *(pg. 149)*

Geranium – supports hormone, emotional balance, and fertility *(pg. 135)*

Neroli and ylang ylang – promotes healthy libido; relaxes *(pg. 145) (pg. 156)*

Clary sage – enhances endocrine system function and balances hormones *(pg. 130)*

Grapefruit – supports healthy progesterone levels and breast health *(pg. 136)*

Jasmine – promotes a healthy uterus, libido *(pg. 138)*

Ginger – promotes healthy menstruation and libido; relieves cramps *(pg. 136)*

Fennel – supports healthy estrogen levels and supports healthy ovaries *(pg. 134)*

Thyme and oregano – supports healthy progesterone levels *(pg. 153) (pg. 145)*

BLENDS

Women's blend – stabilizes mood and supports proper endocrine function *(pg. 177)*

Women's monthly blend – supports monthly cycle *(pg. 177)*

Encouraging blend – supports healthy reproductive function *(pg. 166)*

SUPPLEMENTS

Bone nutrient complex (pg. 179), cellular vitality complex, cellular complex softgels, ***omega complex (pg. 187)***, liquid omega-3, ***phytoestrogen multiplex (pg. 188)***, ***whole food nutrient (pg. 191)***

By Related Properties

For further information, see pages 260 and 272.

Analgesic, Antidepressant, Antihemorrhagic, Aphrodisiac, Detoxifier, Emmenagogue, Galactagogue

Usage Tips For best results for women's health:

- **Aromatic:** Women are very sensitive and emotionally responsive to aromas. Consider regular use for promoting emotional stability. Diffuse selected oils that derive desired results. Additionally, use favorite oils to wear as perfume; apply to wrists and neck. Smell wrists throughout the day. Reapply as needed.
- **Topical:** Apply selected oils to back of neck and shoulders or other areas of need (e.g. *back, for menstrual cramps*) to reduce tension, soothe sore muscles, reduce spasms.

Emotional Well-being

There is a significant connection between emotional and physical health. The body releases various chemicals in response to emotions. For example, the body's release of serotonin, dopamine, or oxytocin results in an uplifting emotion and positive sensation in the body. An experience of stress causes the brain to instruct the release of cortisol, and the body's response will be one of urgency and perhaps even fear.

Emotional stress, whether acute or chronic, can have profound effects on the body. A range of illnesses, from headaches to digestive issues, lack of sleep, and heart disease, can be the result of emotions such as grief, anxiety, and depression taking a toll on the immune system and other cells, tissues, and organs of the entire body.

Examining activity at a cellular level can assist in the understanding of how emotions can affect body functions. Embedded in the surface of the cell membrane are protein molecules known as receptors. These receptors face outward and continuously scan for, communicate with, and solicit needed chemicals that exist outside the cell.

These solicited chemicals attach to receptors, distribute information, and produce biochemical responses within the cell to adapt to environment and stimuli. In this way the receptors play a unique and important role in cellular communication. The binding chemical, called a ligand, is classified as a "messenger molecule," because it sends information to cells that will influence the cell's development and function. A ligand can be a neurotransmitter, hormone, pharmaceutical drug, toxin, parts of a virus, or a neuropeptide used by neurons to communicate with each other.

While numerous receptors are found in most cells, each receptor will only bind with ligands of a particular structure, much like how a lock will only accept a specifically shaped key. When a ligand binds to its corresponding receptor, it activates or inhibits the receptor's associated biochemical pathway.

There are two types of ligands: endogenous and exogenous. Endogenous ligands, such as serotonin, are produced in the body and can have an impact on emotions. Exogenous ligands are substances that are introduced into the body and have a similar effect. They, too, are messenger molecules and can come from a variety of sources such as medications or essential oils.

THE MESSAGES OF EMOTIONS

The hypothalamus – the "control and command center" of the brain – converts mental thoughts and emotions into hundreds of different types of ligands, specifically neuropeptides. The emotions triggered by a perceived threat, for example, are powerful and initiate the release of specific messenger molecule chemicals which, as indicated above, attach to certain receptor sites of cells and affect cell function. What the hypothalamus "believes to be true" determines what the "factory" produces, and chemical production ensues. Neuropeptides affect our chemistry, and our chemistry affects our biology. ***Bottom line: emotions trigger cell activity!***

THE SCENT ALARM

The sense of smell is our most primal, and it exerts a powerful influence over our thoughts, emotions, moods, memories, and behaviors. A healthy human nose can distinguish over one trillion different aromas through hundreds of distinct classes of smell receptors. By way of comparison, we only have three types of photoreceptors used to recognize visual stimuli. Olfaction is far more complex than sight, and we are ten thousand times more capable of smelling than tasting.

It's accurate to say we "smell" danger. Our sense of smell is inextricably connected to our survival, and it plays a major role in remembering what is and isn't safe and what is pleasurable. Why remember danger, stress, trauma, and pleasure? To learn from experience so we can protect ourselves, survive, and procreate. If it wasn't safe this time, we can avoid it the next time; or if it was pleasurable *(e.g. food, physical intimacy)*, we want to participate again. ***People, environments, food: smelling them is part of everyday life.***

OLFACTORY SYSTEM

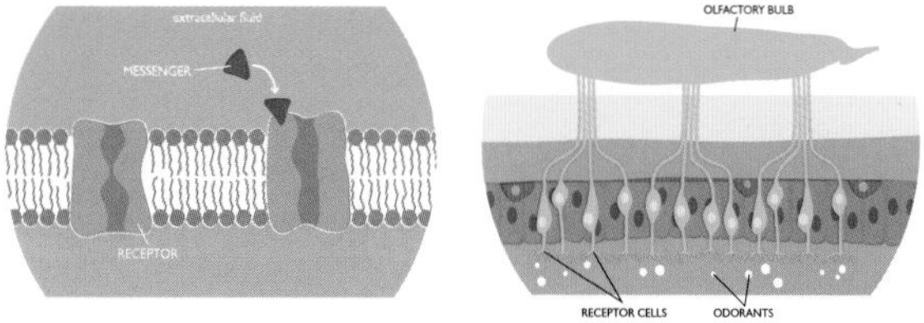

Aromas serve as exogenous ligands. They are received via olfactory receptors, which are highly concentrated in the limbic system, the primitive part of the brain and seat of emotion. In the center lies the amygdala, which instantly receives the incoming scent information before other higher brain centers. By the time the information reaches our "thinking" and decision-making cortex and we actually figure out what we smelled, the scent has already triggered emotional and body chemistry responses.

The amygdala is the storehouse of traumas and contains the densest concentration of neuropeptides, affecting cellular memory. Smell is the primary sense that unconsciously activates and affects traumatic memories stored there. Acting as the watchdog, the amygdala is constantly on the lookout for danger or threats. As it belongs to the more primitive part of our brain it doesn't have the intelligence to discern between real threats versus perceived threats *(e.g. a saber-toothed tiger versus a missed bus stop or being late to work and an angry boss)*. It passes on its concerns and notifies the hypothalamus when safety and security are at risk, which then in turn notifies the pituitary, which alerts the adrenal glands, which sets off the alarm for fight-or-flight stress response and releases cortisol and adrenaline. ***Bottom line: The emotional stress triggered the release of the stress hormones.***

Food and Mood

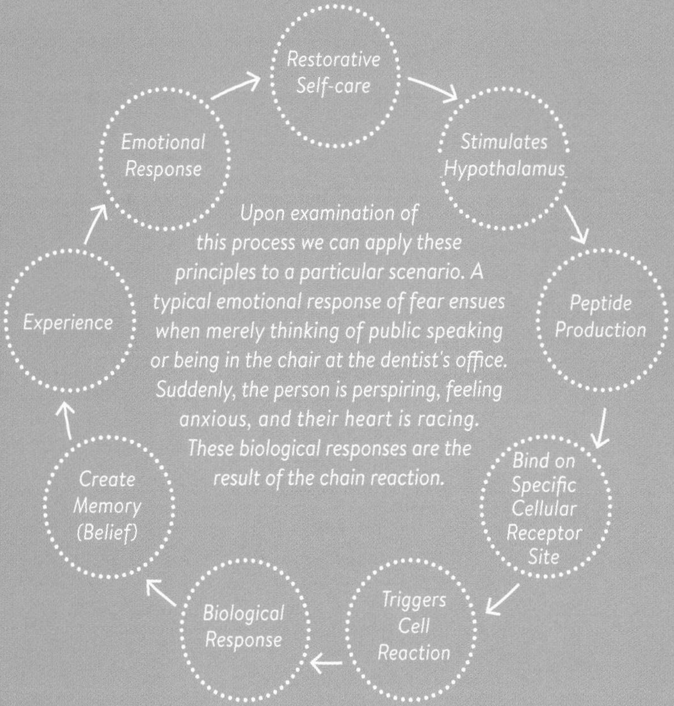

Upon examination of this process we can apply these principles to a particular scenario. A typical emotional response of fear ensues when merely thinking of public speaking or being in the chair at the dentist's office. Suddenly, the person is perspiring, feeling anxious, and their heart is racing. These biological responses are the result of the chain reaction.

What you put in your mouth has a direct impact on emotions. Nutritional deficiencies, food sensitivities, blood sugar imbalances, substance abuse, and stimulants *(like caffeine)* affect biochemistry and contribute to mood fluctuations and compromised emotional states.

Additives in processed foods generate adverse chemical reactions within the body and drastically affect mood and behavior in many children and adults. Some of these synthetic substances are labeled "excitotoxins" by nutritionists and wellness experts. These include additives such as high fructose corn syrup, trans-fats, artificial flavors, artificial colors, artificial sweeteners, MSG, and other preservatives. These chemicals deliver messages to the brain and cells of the body just like any exogenous ligand. More than one specific ligand can "fit" into a receptor. As heroin fits in the same opiate site as endorphins, so can these toxic food chemicals unlock receptor sites in our brain and transmit influences that, if we knew, we would never let in.

So once again, we have a choice on what chemical soup we want to ingest. The old adage, "we are what we eat," could not ring more true. Or perhaps it gets rewritten here: We emote or express emotionally what we eat.

Many researchers agree that physical illnesses are often the result of an emotional inflammatory response to trauma or negative experiences. What can begin as "emotional inflammation" can later become physical issues and disease. Although medical technology is not advanced enough to see them, memories, trauma, and painful emotions are stored in the body and eventually manifest as physical inflammation when the body's tissues follow suit.

THE IMPORTANCE OF THE SENSE OF SMELL

Smell can be used beneficially in healing efforts as well. Scents are experienced long before words. Whether for relieving stress, stabilizing mood, improving sleep, eliminating pain, relieving nausea, or improving memory and energy levels, scents can actually change nervous system biochemistry.

Essential oils can facilitate a rapid emotional response in the brain and the body to facilitate such a release. Essential oils are powerful biochemical agents for emotional balance, wellness, and toxic release, which can be paired or partnered with any holistic or medically-derived program to create a successful approach to mental and emotional wellness.

THE POWER OF ESSENTIAL OILS CHOOSE YOUR MOOD

Moods are often perceived as having chosen us, as if they are happening to us. Rather, the chemical impact of our emotions and other exogenous ligands is the real chooser of moods. That's why we reach for certain foods, sugar, caffeine, or a drug of choice *(see "Food & Mood" for more information)*, interact with certain people, do certain things, and act out certain behaviors because of how it makes us feel and to get a "chemical" hit.

What if we could use this knowledge to choose the mood we want to feel and then actually feel it – without harmful substances or recreational drugs? What if we could think of a desired mood and then choose to use a healthful exogenous ligand that is capable of creating it? With essential oils, we have the ability to direct our own emotional traffic!

Our Second Brain

Digestive issues and disorders are growing rampant, in part because of the refined and processed foods that are prevalent in today's diets. The gut is considered the body's "second brain" because of its impact on mood states. In recent years, scientists have discovered that there are more neurotransmitters *(a type of ligand)* in the gut than there are in the brain, and, among other things, healthy mood management depends on how well these neurotransmitters relay messages to each other.

Serotonin is a chemical responsible for maintaining mood balance, social behavior, appetite and digestion, sleep, memory, and sexual desire and function. The majority of the body's serotonin, between 80-90 percent, can be found in the gastrointestinal tract. Gut health, then, promotes emotional health and mood stabilization. How can an individual hope to experience healthy moods if their cells are depleted of nutrition and if their neurotransmitters reside in an area with blockages and inflammation? How can the over one hundred million neurons embedded in the gut influence healthy emotions when inflammation, blockages, candida, and other harmful bacteria are overpopulated and system imbalances are standard?

Detoxifying the body can improve emotional health. Toxicity symptoms in the body can directly mirror many depressive symptoms and may include insomnia, foggy thinking, low energy, digestive issues, dampened immune function, and allergies. New studies even suggest that depression may be a type of "allergic reaction" to inflammation.

Chemical compounds found in essential oils stimulate a range of gentle to more intense detoxification effects (depending on use) and promote a natural cleanse for the digestive, endocrine, immune, and lymphatic and other detoxification systems and channels of the body. This, in turn, boosts mood and restores mental and physical energy.

Blood sugar imbalances can also trigger depressive symptoms. Certain essential oils, like cinnamon, coriander, and fennel, support metabolic function and assist in moderating blood sugar levels. Omega 3-fatty acids, food enzymes, chelated minerals and B and D vitamins found in a whole food nutrient supplement, antioxidants, and polyphenol supplements also help to regulate blood sugar levels, as well as reduce inflammation, boost energy, and support the gut with the right combination of good fats and other nourishing components.

Emotional healing and rebalancing of moods is accomplished when a new stimulus is introduced to the same chain of command in the brain. As we've already discussed, an aroma *(stimulus)* enters the olfactory system, and in turn the limbic system and amygdala, hypothalamus, and other parts of the brain and body. Depending on what aroma is introduced and the information it conveys determines the brain's response. Traumatic memories stored in the amygdala can be released by utilizing the sense of smell and essential oils. If the significance an individual attaches to a past experience can be shifted, the amygdala can release the trauma of the memory. This is what makes aromatherapy a wonderful means for emotional healing and rebalancing moods. *Here is an example:*

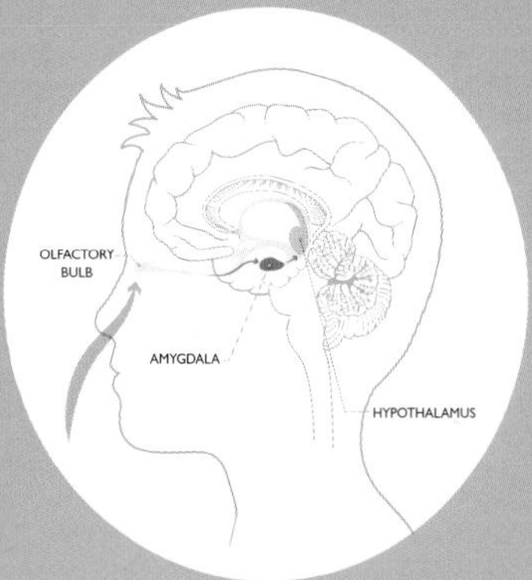

Rather than feeling victimized by our emotional states, what if we had our own apothecary of essential oils in the home? Such a collection offers a cornucopia of emotional states for ready access. Like an eager child opening a box of candy, relishing the array of colors and designs and imagining the flavors waiting to tantalize her tongue and brighten her spirit, we, too, can delight in selecting and generating moods with the use of essential oils.

As natural exogenous ligands, essential oils can powerfully influence our emotions, much like mood-altering drugs like morphine, but with healthful results. Unlike synthetic medications or drugs that are designed to alter behavior, their complex molecular structure allows them to intelligently bind to the receptor sites of cells in our body and support a desired effect to restore balance and healthy function.

If an individual is deficient in serotonin for an extended period of time, their habitual response to life's situations might be more anxious or angry, more hopeless, more sad, more phobic, more thoughts of "what-if?". If he begins using wild orange, for example, a known antidepressant oil due to its capacity to uplift, detoxify, and calm, he would find himself irresistibly more happy and with a plausible capacity to be more hopeful, trusting, less reactive, and more calm. He also, therefore, has a potential to react to experiences and respond to memories differently. Here's another example. A young child experiences a high level of trauma, such as a parent suffering with cancer who subsequently passes away. The child's body experiences tremendous chemical expenditures to support the experiences of stress, trauma, and grief. And then, if more trauma occurs, say the deceased parent is replaced and the surviving parent remarries, additional chemicals are released to cope with a new stepparent and step-siblings.

If, during, or after traumatic seasons of this child's life, her chemical reserves are not replenished, her coping capacity is literally chemically diminished. She might find herself crying more, experiencing meltdowns more easily, perhaps being teased for being a crybaby, or simply coping less effectively with everyday life. A missed homework deadline, low grade, or athletic performance failure may seem a crushing blow. The same exact events could happen to another person with full reserves who moves through it gracefully. What's the difference?

One of the most important chemicals we have to work in these kinds of situations is endorphins. The name itself reveals it to be an endogenous ligand: "endo-morphine," self-made morphine or endorphin. When endorphins are lacking, coping challenges arise. Endorphins serve us not only in our ability to experience pleasure, but also to appropriately buffer us from pain, both physical and emotional. The craving for its benefits will drive any number of behaviors when levels are low.

Typically two types of addictions may arise. One is generally met by abnormally intense levels of thrill or pleasure, as intensity is required in order to get the chemical "hit." The endogenous ligand, endorphins, is the body's "drug" of choice, received on an opiate receptor site. Activities of greater and greater intensity may be pursued to increase the production of endorphins. Bungee jumping, pornography use, playing intense video games, exaggerated sexual activity, gambling, overconsumption of comfort foods, or other behaviors known to generate endorphins become appealing in an attempt to fill a need.

The second addiction is usually focused on exogenous ligands in the form of pain-numbing opiate drugs, including opium, heroin, vicodin, oxycodone, and other prescription pain medications. Opiate drugs are received on the same opiate receptor sites. Either type of addiction is powerful as chemical needs remain unmet.

Returning to the story of the child who lost her parent, one of the main chemicals likely low, based on circumstances described, is endorphins. If those diminished reserves of endorphins were never replenished, she would potentially grow into an adult continually experiencing the inability to cope with life or fully experience pleasure, never fully recovering from the trauma, ever searching for ways to numb the pain and meet her emotional needs. Her body is simply lacking the chemical capacity to fully heal. The body needs to increase its reserves and ability to manufacture the chemicals needed.

Now to explore a potential solution, the essential oil of helichrysum. Helichrysum has powerful analgesic and pain-relieving therapeutic benefits. It is high in many chemical constituents, one known as ketones; a compound with powerful, regenerative benefits. As the child-turned-adult uses this oil and her body experiences this chemistry, she is exposed to generous amounts of healthy pain-killing / numbing chemicals. What science has yet to identify is what happens in the body from here.

Whether a chemical need is met or a pathway of reception is opened up is not known. What is happening potentially for the woman, however, is she finally feels relief from "pain." Her coping capacity is increased. She handles life better. With natural, healing chemicals on board in rich supply she finally experiences healing.

The diverse and concentrated chemical constituents in essential oils work to cleanse, ground, lift, balance, and calm the central nervous system and the emotional body. Some essential oils – like frankincense, patchouli and sandalwood - have high concentrations of sesquiterpene molecules that have been clinically demonstrated to cross the blood-brain barrier. These molecules have significant oxygen supporting effects on the brain and, when combined with aromatic stimulation, can assist the amygdala in releasing the effects of stored memories.

Here are some additional demonstrated mental and emotional benefits:

- Cleanse negative memories
- Reduce stress, anxiety, and tension
- Offset mental fatigue
- Uplift mood
- Calm the central nervous system
- Relax muscular tension
- Induce restful sleep
- Invigorate the senses
- Increase feelings of courage and determination
- Promote a cathartic effect *(facilitating the release of stuck emotions)*
- Support DNA correction and expression

In conclusion, aromatherapy offers many practical healing advantages, but perhaps one of the most fascinating is the relationship it has with emotional well being. Inhalation of essential oils with the resulting aromatic exposure is the most effective method of impacting the brain for emotional wellness. Some studies demonstrate that essential oils have the highest bio-frequency of any consumable natural substance.

Essential oils offer a fresh, effective support tool to aid in the emotional healing process and to shift out of old habits and ineffective coping patterns. Aromatherapy allows the individual to harness the olfactory power of plants for healing, or simply to enhance a state of well being using scents to create a powerful influence over how one thinks, feels, and behaves.

Move it, Move it

Studies indicate that moderate exercise of thirty minutes a day for three days a week has an antidepressant effect on a large percentage of depressed subjects. But many who are anxious or depressed lack the energy or sensory motivation to begin an exercise regime. Essential oils like peppermint, cypress, and wintergreen support the flow of blood and oxygen and the sensory "oomph" to engage in physical activity. Other oils aid in relieving muscle tension and assisting with muscle recovery. Helichrysum, for example, contains natural chemical components that have a regenerative effect both physically and emotionally.

PRACTICAL APPLICATION

As essential oils are used topically, aromatically, and internally, the body's vibration is raised and its emotional frequencies are impacted, as is the capacity for emotional well being. Each individual oil with its diverse chemistry has the ability to be a tremendous multi-tasker and work in multiple areas of interest simultaneously. Additional benefits to essential oil use comes from combining oils to create synergistic blends. See Application Methods in this book to learn more.

Application methods also impact the body's response to aromatherapy in emotional health and healing:

Aromatic use is the fastest way to access the mood center of the brain and invite the release of negative stored emotions. It is also helpful to use the oils aromatically when resetting new, healthy belief patterns.

Topical use assists the body in moving from a stress response to a repair or restore response necessary to create an environment where emotional healing can take place.

Internal use of essential oils supports healthy chemical reactions in the body, nourishment of cells, and release of toxins. This internal support fosters a healthy and balanced emotional environment. Cleansing the internal environment allows emotions to be recognized and processed more readily.

Sweet Dreams

Adequate sleep is crucial to mental health and brain function. Insomnia and restless sleep are a problem for many who experience depressed or anxious mood states. Pairing a resin or tree essential oil like vetiver, cedarwood, sandalwood, or frankincense with a citrus oil like wild orange, lime, lemon, or bergamot has been found to stabilize mood fluctuations, ground the body, and promote a relaxation response in preparation for sleep. Flower oils like lavender, roman chamomile, clary sage, geranium, and ylang ylang aid in quieting mental chatter and calming the nervous system.

Similarly, many studies have been conducted on the powerful mental, physical, and emotional benefits of meditation. Meditation is a practice that seeks to achieve a focused state of relaxation. The essential oils listed above can help to still the mind, open air pathways, and calm the mind and heart.

Emotions Index

Essential oils are some of nature's most powerful remedies for emotional health. Below are lists designed to introduce the concept of associating an oil to an emotion or vice versa as well as serve as an ongoing resource. Select specific targeted emotional states to address and then identify corresponding oils. ***If you want to research specific mood conditions, refer to Focus & Attention (pg. 214) and Mood & Behavior (pg. 220) sections of this book.***

Essential Oil	Unbalanced Emotion	Balanced Emotion
Arborvitae	Overzealous	Composed
Basil	Inundated	Relieved
Bergamot	Inadequate	Worthy
Birch	Cowardly	Courageous
Black pepper	Repressed	Honest
Blue tansy	Overwhelmed	Encouraged
Cardamom	Self-centered	Charitable
Cassia	Uncertain	Bold
Cedarwood	Alone	Connected
Cilantro	Obsessed	Easygoing
Cinnamon bark	Denied	Receptive
Clary sage	Limited	Enlightened
Clove	Dominated	Supported
Copaiba	Plagued	Directed
Coriander	Apprehensive	Participating
Cypress	Stalled	Progressing
Dill	Avoiding	Intentional
Douglas fir	Upset	Renewed
Eucalyptus	Congested	Stimulated
Fennel	Unproductive	Flourishing
Frankincense	Separated	Unified
Geranium	Neglected	Mended
Ginger	Apathetic	Activated
Grapefruit	Rejected	Validated
Green Mandarin	Distressed	Carefree
Helichrysum	Wounded	Reassured
Jasmine	Hampered	Liberated
Juniper berry	Denying	Insightful
Kumquat	Divided	Integrous

Lavender	*Unheard*	*Expressed*
Lemon	*Mindless*	*Energized*
Lemongrass	*Obstructed*	*Flowing*
Lime	*Faint*	*Enlivened*
Litsea	*Encumbered*	*Purified*
Manuka	*Bothered*	*Revived*
Magnolia	*Disturbed*	*Confident*
Marjoram	*Doubtful*	*Trusting*
Melaleuca	*Unsure*	*Collected*
Melissa	*Depressed*	*Light-filled*
Myrrh	*Disconnected*	*Nurtured*
Neroli	*Afflicted*	*Released*
Oregano	*Obstinate*	*Unattached*
Patchouli	*Degraded*	*Enhanced*
Peppermint	*Hindered*	*Invigorated*
Petitgrain	*Conflicted*	*Harmonized*
Pink Pepper	*Impeded*	*Aroused*
Ravensara	*Uncommitted*	*Resolute*
Red Mandarin	*Troubled*	*Resilient*
Roman chamomile	*Frustrated*	*Purposeful*
Rose	*Isolated*	*Loved*
Rosemary	*Confused*	*Open-minded*
Sandalwood	*Uninspired*	*Devoted*
Siberian fir	*Excluded*	*Empowered*
Spearmint	*Weary*	*Refreshed*
Spikenard	*Agitated*	*Tranquil*
Tangerine	*Oppressed*	*Restored*
Thyme	*Unyielding*	*Yielding*
Turmeric	*Compromised*	*Assured*
Vetiver	*Ungrounded*	*Rooted*
White fir	*Blocked*	*Receiving*
Wild orange	*Drained*	*Productive*
Wintergreen	*Stubborn*	*Accepting*
Yarrow	*Erratic*	*Balanced*
Ylang ylang	*Burdened*	*Exuberant*

Positive Emotions

If you want to feel the positive emotion listed, use the associated oil.

Accepting	wintergreen
Activated	ginger
Aroused	pink pepper
Assured	turmeric
Bold	cassia
Carefree	green mandarin
Charitable	cardamom
Collected	melaleuca
Composed	arborvitae
Confident	magnolia
Connected	cedarwood
Courageous	birch
Devoted	sandalwood
Directed	copaiba
Easygoing	cilantro
Empowered	Siberian fir
Encouraged	blue tansy
Energized	lemon
Enhanced	patchouli
Enlightened	clary sage
Enlivened	lime
Expressed	lavender
Exuberant	ylang ylang
Flourishing	fennel
Flowing	lemongrass
Guided	red mandarin
Harmonized	petitgrain
Honest	black pepper
Insightful	juniper berry
Integrous	kumquat
Intentional	dill
Invigorated	peppermint
Liberated	jasmine
Light-filled	melissa
Loved	rose
Mended	geranium
Nurtured	myrrh
Open-minded	rosemary
Participating	coriander
Productive	wild orange
Progressing	cypress
Purified	litsea
Purposeful	Roman chamomile
Reassured	helichrysum
Receiving	white fir
Receptive	cinnamon bark
Refreshed	spearmint
Released	neroli
Relieved	basil
Renewed	Douglas fir
Revived	manuka
Resolute	ravensara
Restored	tangerine
Rooted	vetiver
Shielded	yarrow
Stimulated	eucalyptus
Supported	clove
Tranquil	spikenard
Trusting	marjoram
Unattached	oregano
Unified	frankincense
Validated	grapefruit
Worthy	bergamot
Yielding	thyme

Negative Emotions

If you are feeling the negative emotion listed, use the associated oil.

Afflicted	neroli
Agitated	spikenard
Alone	cedarwood
Apathetic	ginger
Apprehensive	coriander
Avoiding	dill
Blocked	white fir
Bothered	manuka
Burdened	ylang ylang
Compromised	turmeric
Conflicted	petitgrain
Confused	rosemary
Congested	eucalyptus
Cowardly	birch
Degraded	patchouli
Denied	cinnamon bark
Denying	juniper berry
Depressed	melissa
Disconnected	myrrh
Distressed	green mandarin
Disturbed	magnolia
Divided	kumquat
Dominated	clove
Doubtful	marjoram
Drained	wild orange
Encumbered	litsea
Excluded	Siberian fir
Faint	lime
Frustrated	Roman chamomile
Hampered	jasmine
Hindered	peppermint
Impeded	pink pepper
Inadequate	bergamot
Inundated	basil
Invaded	yarrow
Isolated	rose
Limited	clary sage
Mindless	lemon
Neglected	geranium
Obsessed	cilantro
Obstinate	oregano
Obstructed	lemongrass
Oppressed	tangerine
Overwhelmed	blue tansy
Overzealous	arborvitae
Plagued	copaiba
Rejected	cilantro
Repressed	black pepper
Self-centered	cardamom
Separated	frankincense
Stalled	white fir
Stubborn	cypress
Troubled	red mandarin
Uncertain	cassia
Uncommitted	ravensara
Ungrounded	vetiver
Unheard	lavender
Uninspired	sandalwood
Unproductive	fennel
Unsure	melaleuca
Unyielding	thyme
Upset	Douglas fir
Weary	spearmint
Wounded	helichrysum

EMOTIONS

Section 5

SUPPLEMENTAL

Turn to these resources to explore research used, deepen understanding of ailments, and find oil properties.

Be a Power User

The Essential Life is about focusing on the core elements of amazing wellness, and YOU hold the power to create this into your reality. This section will teach you how to become a confident power user of the healing tools that will elevate your essential life.

LIVE AN ESSENTIAL LIFESTYLE

To achieve elevated wellness, first understand the components that contribute to wellness, or if neglected, lack of wellness. The natural tools in this book can assist you in each of these key areas.

Body Fuel: What you put into your body becomes your body. If you want a high-energy, vibrant, high-functioning body, then put high-energy, vibrant, high-functioning food & fuel into your body! ***Add vitality supplements and energizing oils to a great diet.***

Activity: Your body was built to move. As you enjoy some kind of active moment every day, your body systems will have good reason to stay active and healthy. ***Enhance activity with oils for muscle, joint, and respiratory support.***

Rest: Meaningful rest is necessary for your systems to reset and regenerate. Commit to giving yourself adequate time to recover through meaningful sleep and personal care each day. ***Learn the oils that your body responds to for great sleep.***

Stress Management: Emotional and physical stressors are at the root of all illness and disease. Create space and use good tools to reduce stressors in your life. ***Pause briefly throughout each day to enjoy emotional balancing with your oils.***

Toxic Reduction: Toxicity can be found in our water, air, household cleaners and chemicals, and many things we put into our bodies. Minimize toxicity to create a clean environment inside your body. ***Use oils to safely clean your home and detox your body.***

Restorative Self-care: Knowing how to use safe, effective natural remedies is empowering. It allows you to restore health, prevent unwanted issues, and be prepared for the unexpected. ***Learn the uses of the best oils for your health needs.***

SUPPLEMENTAL

GOOD HEALTH LOVES PREPARATION

Be prepared for anything by having your essential oils and other remedies handy. *Try a few of these:*

- **Around the House** — Keep frequently used oils handy by your bedside, in the bathroom, the kitchen, and main family living space. You'll use them more often and see better results, and your family will join in if they're easily accessible.
- **Purse or Keychain** — Have a small bag of oils you need for mood support, digestive support, and immune protection when you're out and about. If you don't carry a purse or bag, get a keychain that holds small vials *(5/8 dram)* of your favorite oils.
- **Car** — Keep oils for focus and stress management in your car to turn driving time into useful rejuvenation time.
- **Diaper Bag or Stroller** — Kids love to do the unexpected, which is why you'll always be glad to have oils ready for bumps and bruises, skin irritations, and temper tantrums wherever you go.

Tip

Consistency makes magic. While oils are fast-acting, consistency breeds the best long-term results.

Tip

Frequency Trumps Quantity. Use smaller amounts of oil more frequently to maximize results.

FIND BRILLIANT ANSWERS

Learning to how to fully take ownership of your personal health and wellness can be stressful. Where do you turn to find resources, which are both trustworthy and always up-to-date?

The Essential Life team is dedicated to helping you eliminate the stress of learning to take charge of your health and wellness by providing both the printed version and app of *The Essential Life* book along with additional resources at: EssentialLife.com/resources

Go to EssentialLife.com to:

- **Buy** *The Essential Life, The Essential Basics, The Essential Quick Reference* book.
- **Download** *The Essential Life* App to look up remedies on the go and stay in sync with the community as they share their remedies and insights.

EXPLORE DIFFERENT USAGE METHODS

- **Aromatic.** Keep a diffuser in high-traffic areas in the home and in sleeping areas. Diffusers are a great way to let everyone around enjoy the benefits of the oils.
- **Topical.** Have a carrier oil like fractionated coconut oil on hand for use on sensitive skin, and to use as a remedy if someone experiences sensitivity after an oil has been applied. Try recipes for skin creams and lotions with your oils.
- **Internal.** Keep veggie capsules near your oils for easy internal use. Try putting some in a small plastic baggie so you can have them ready on the go. Remember to only use oils internally if they are verified pure and therapeutic.

Tip

Layering vs. Blending: While blending oils is a valuable art, you may have success with layering. Apply one oil topically, wait several seconds, and then apply the next one, etc.

Tip

Focus your efforts. You'll achieve greater results as you concentrate your efforts on a few key wellness goals.

SUPERCHARGE YOUR OILS

While you can use oils a seemingly infinite number of ways, you'll also find methods that work best for you and your family. ***Try some of these tips to enhance the effectiveness of your oils:***

- **Add heat** – Use a hot compress to drive the oils in deeper when using topically.
- **Add frankincense** – Frankincense enhances the therapeutic effects of many protocols, and brings powerful healing properties.
- **Massage** – Massaging oils into the needed area stimulates tissues and increases person giving and the person receiving the massage.
- **Combine oils that complement each other** – Don't be afraid to try different oil combinations. You can find an ocean of essential oil recipes and protocols because nature complements itself in so many ways. Try different combinations, and enjoy the process of discovering what resonates with your body.

SUPPLEMENTAL

SUPERCHARGE YOUR OILS

Reflexology is the application of pressure to the feet and hands with specific thumb, finger, and hand techniques without the use of oil or lotion. It is based on a system of zones and reflex areas that reflect an image of the body on the feet and hands, with the premise that such work effects a physical change to the body.

Ear Reflexology is a simple and efficient way to relieve stress and pain by applying minimal pressure to the reflex points on the ear. Each ear contains a complete map of the body, rich with nerve endings and multiple connectors to the central nervous system. For example, if the reflex point for the bladder is tender, the body may be in the beginning stages of a bladder infection. One can take preventative measures to head off the bladder infection by applying an essential oil to the reflex point on the ear followed by minimal pressure.

To begin treatment, start at the top of the right ear and slowly work your thumb and forefinger along the outer edges. Hold each point for five seconds before continuing to the end of the earlobe. For best results, repeat this procedure at least five times. Next, work the inner crevices of the ear using the pointer finger and applying minimal pressure. Repeat procedure on left ear. If any areas in and around the crevices of the ear are sensitive, consult the ear reflexology chart to pinpoint the area of the body that may be out of balance.

This a great technique to use personally, on family or friends, as well as with those whose hands and feet are not accessible for hand and foot reflexology. Young children are especially receptive to having their outer ears worked on, finding it calming and soothing.

Foot Reflexology is an effective method to bring the body systems into balance by applying pressure to specific places on the feet. Hand reflexology can be utilized in a similar manner. The nerves in the feet correspond with various parts of the body; thus, the entire body is mapped on the feet, telling a story of emotional and physical well being.

One way to find imbalances in the body is to massage all the areas noted on the foot reflexology chart and feel for triggers or small knots underneath the skin. When a trigger is found, apply an essential oil to the location on the foot and continue to massage the trigger until it releases. Another way to use reflexology is to address a specific ailment. For instance, if a person has a headache, locate the brain on the foot chart and the corresponding point on the foot. Apply an essential oil of choice and massage the pad of the big toe to reduce tension. If a person has a tight chest induced by stress, locate the lungs/chest on the foot chart and the corresponding point on the foot. Apply an essential oil of choice followed by medium to light circular massage on the ball of the foot.

The autonomic nervous system is then engaged, helping to alleviate symptoms and heal the body naturally.

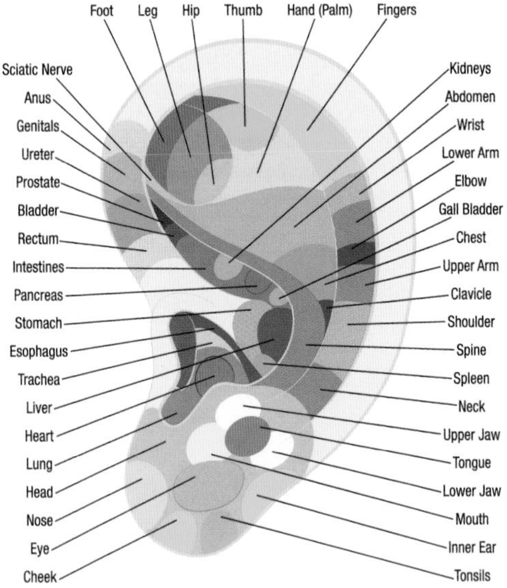

Reflexology Reference

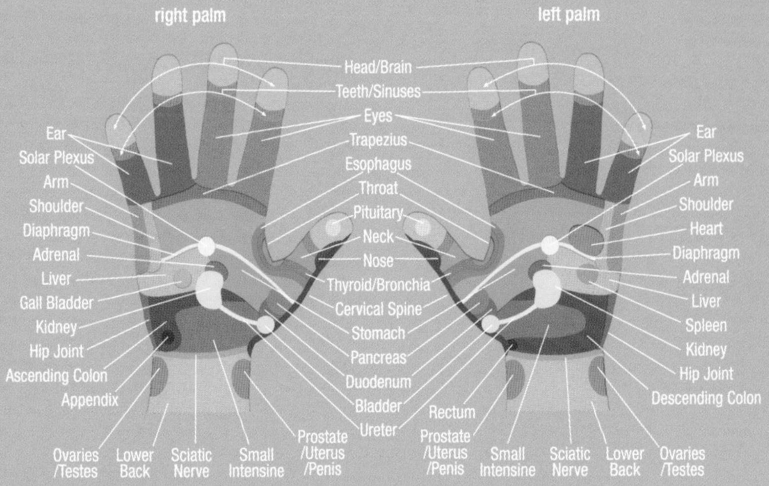

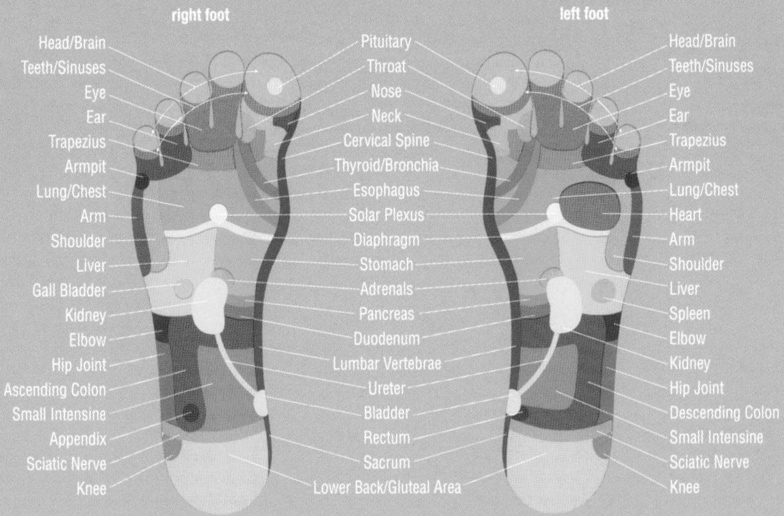

Oil Properties

ARBORVITAE *Thuja plicata*

anaphrodisiac, analgesic, antiarthritic, antibacterial, anticarcinogenic, anti-carcinoma, antifungal, antihistamine, anti-infectious, anti-inflammatory, antimicrobial, antioxidant, antiseptic, anti-tumoral, antiviral, astringent, cleanser, cytophylactic, detoxifier, disinfectant, diuretic, emmenagogue, expectorant, immunostimulant, insect repellent, neurotonic, purifier, stimulant, stomachic, tonic, vermifuge

BASIL *Ocimum basilicum*

analgesic, antibacterial, anticatarrhal, antidepressant, antiemetic, anti-infectious, anti-inflammatory, antimicrobial, antioxidant, antiseptic, antispasmodic, antiviral, calming, carminative, decongestant, digestive stimulant, disinfectant, diuretic, emmenagogue, energizing, expectorant, galactagogue, grounding, laxative, mucolytic, nervine, neurotonic, regenerative, relaxing, restorative, sedative, steroidal, stimulant, stomachic, tonic, vermifuge

BERGAMOT *Citrus bergamia*

analgesic, antibacterial, antidepressant, antifungal, anti-infectious, anti-inflammatory, anti-parasitic, antiseptic, antispasmodic, antitoxic, calming, carminative, deodorant, digestive stimulant, diuretic, energizing, laxative, neurotonic, rubefacient, sedative, steroidal, stimulant, tonic, uplifting, vermifuge

BIRCH *Betula lenta*

analgesic, antibacterial, anti-inflammatory, anti-rheumatic, antiseptic, antispasmodic, astringent, disinfectant, diuretic, insect repellent, rubefacient, steroidal, stimulant, tonic, warming

BLACK PEPPER *Piper nigrum*

analgesic, antibacterial, anticatarrhal, anti-inflammatory, antioxidant, anti-parasitic, antiseptic, antispasmodic, antitoxic, aphrodisiac, calming, digestive stimulant, expectorant, hypotensive, laxative, neurotonic, rubefacient, stimulant, warming

BLUE TANSY *Tanacetum annuum*

analgesic, anti-allergenic, antiarthritic, antibacterial, antifungal, antihistamine, anti-inflammatory, antimicrobial, anti-parasitic, anti-rheumatic, antispasmodic, antiviral, calming, carminative, grounding, hypotensive, insect repellent, insecticidal, laxative, relaxing, sedative, stimulant, stomachic, vasodilator, vermicide

CARDAMOM *Elettaria cardamomum*

analgesic, antibacterial, anticoagulant, anticonvulsant, antidepressant, antifungal, anti-inflammatory, antimicrobial, antiseptic, antispasmodic, aphrodisiac, astringent, calming, carminative, deodorant, digestive stimulant, emmenagogue, galactagogue, grounding, hypotensive, mucolytic, nervine, neurotonic, relaxing, sedative, stomachic, tonic, uplifting, vermicide

CASSIA *Cinnamon cassia*

analgesic, antibacterial, antiemetic, antifungal, antihistamine, anti-infectious, anti-inflammatory, antioxidant, anti-parasitic, anti-rheumatic, antiseptic, antispasmodic, anti-tumoral, antiviral, aphrodisiac, carminative, disinfectant, energizing, expectorant, immunostimulant, nervine, regenerative, stimulant, vermifuge, warming

CEDARWOOD *Juniperus virginiana*

antibacterial, antifungal, anti-infectious, anti-inflammatory, antiseptic, astringent, diuretic, emmenagogue, expectorant, grounding, insect repellent, insecticidal, mucolytic, regenerative, relaxing, sedative, steroidal, stimulant, tonic, uplifting, vermifuge

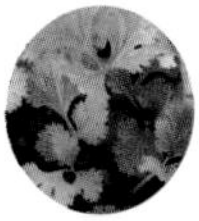

CILANTRO *Coriandrum sativum*

antibacterial, antifungal, antimicrobial, antioxidant, carminative, cleanser, detoxifier

CINNAMON *Cinnamomum zeylanicum*

analgesic, antibacterial, antidepressant, antifungal, anti-infectious, anti-inflammatory, antimicrobial, antimutagenic, antioxidant, anti-parasitic, antiseptic, antispasmodic, antitoxic, antiviral, aphrodisiac, astringent, carminative, digestive stimulant, emmenagogue, immunostimulant, insect repellent, purifier, stimulant, stomachic, vermifuge, warming

CLARY SAGE *Salvia sclarea*

analgesic, antibacterial, anticoagulant, anticonvulsant, antidepressant, antifungal, anti-inflammatory, antimicrobial, antiseptic, antispasmodic, aphrodisiac, astringent, calming, carminative, deodorant, digestive stimulant, emmenagogue, galactagogue, grounding, hypotensive, mucolytic, nervine, neurotonic, relaxing, sedative, stomachic, tonic, uplifting, vermicide

CLOVE *Eugenia caryophyllata*

analgesic, antibacterial, antiemetic, antifungal, antihistamine, anti-infectious, anti-inflammatory, antioxidant, anti-parasitic, anti-rheumatic, antiseptic, antispasmodic, anti-tumoral, antiviral, aphrodisiac, carminative, disinfectant, energizing, expectorant, immunostimulant, nervine, regenerative, stimulant, vermifuge, warming

COPAIBA *Copaiba offincinalis*

analgesic, antiarthritic, antibacterial, anti-carcinoma, antiemetic, antifungal, anti-infectious, anti-inflammatory, antimicrobial, antimutagenic, antioxidant, anti-rheumatic, antiseptic, anti-tumoral, antiviral, calming, cardiotonic, carminative, decongestant, deodorant, disinfectant, diuretic, hypotensive, immunostimulant, insecticidal, laxative, mucolytic, vasodilator

CORIANDER *Coriandrum sativum*

analgesic, antibacterial, antidepressant, antiemetic, antifungal, anti-inflammatory, antimicrobial, antioxidant, anti-rheumatic, antispasmodic, antitoxic, aphrodisiac, calming, carminative, deodorant, digestive stimulant, insecticidal, regenerative, revitalizer, sedative, stimulant, stomachic, tonic

CYPRESS *Cupressus sempervirens*

analgesic, antibacterial, antifungal, anti-infectious, anti-inflammatory, antimicrobial, anti-rheumatic, antiseptic, antispasmodic, astringent, cardiotonic, carminative, decongestant, deodorant, detoxifier, diuretic, energizing, grounding, mucolytic, neurotonic, refreshing, relaxing, stimulant, tonic, uplifting, vasoconstrictor

DILL *Anethum graveolens*

antibacterial, antidepressant, antifungal, anti-inflammatory, antimicrobial, antispasmodic, antiviral, carminative, digestive stimulant, emmenagogue, expectorant, galactagogue, grounding, hypotensive, stimulant

DOUGLAS FIR *Pseudotsuga menziesii*

analgesic, antibacterial, antioxidant, antiseptic, astringent, diuretic, energizing, expectorant, laxative, sedative, stimulant, stomachic

EUCALYPTUS *Eucalyptus radiata*

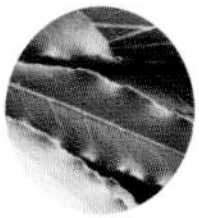

analgesic, antibacterial, anticatarrhal, antifungal, anti-infectious, anti-inflammatory, antimicrobial, antioxidant, anti-rheumatic, antispasmodic, antiviral, cleanser, decongestant, deodorant, disinfectant, diuretic, expectorant, hypotensive, immunostimulant, insect repellent, insecticidal, purifier, rubefacient, stimulant, vermifuge, warming

FENNEL *Foeniculum vulgare*

analgesic, anticonvulsant, antiemetic, antifungal, anti-inflammatory, antimicrobial, anti-parasitic, antiseptic, antispasmodic, antitoxic, calming, cardiotonic, carminative, digestive stimulant, diuretic, emmenagogue, expectorant, galactagogue, grounding, immunostimulant, laxative, mucolytic, relaxing, steroidal, stimulant, stomachic, tonic, vermifuge

FRANKINCENSE *Boswellia frereana*

analgesic, anticarcinogenic, anti-carcinoma, anticatarrhal, antidepressant, anti-infectious, anti-inflammatory, antimicrobial, antioxidant, anti-parasitic, antiseptic, anti-tumoral, astringent, calming, cytophylactic, digestive stimulant, disinfectant, diuretic, galactagogue, immunostimulant, neuroprotective, regenerative, restorative, sedative, tonic

GERANIUM *Pelargonium graveolens*

anti-allergenic, antibacterial, anticonvulsant, antidepressant, antifungal, antihemorrhagic, anti-infectious, anti-inflammatory, antiseptic, antispasmodic, antitoxic, astringent, calming, cytophylactic, deodorant, detoxifier, diuretic, insect repellent, refreshing, regenerative, relaxing, sedative, tonic, vermifuge

GINGER *Zingiber officinale*

analgesic, antiarthritic, antibacterial, antiemetic, antifungal, anti-inflammatory, antimutagenic, antioxidant, anti-rheumatic, antiseptic, antiviral, cardiotonic, carminative, decongestant, emmenagogue, expectorant, immunostimulant, laxative, neurotonic, rubefacient, stimulant, stomachic, tonic, warming

GRAPEFRUIT *Citrus X paradisi*

antibacterial, anti-carcinoma, antidepressant, antioxidant, antiseptic, antitoxic, astringent, cardiotonic, cleanser, decongestant, digestive stimulant, disinfectant, diuretic, energizing, invigorating, purifier, refreshing, stimulant, tonic, uplifting

GREEN MANDARIN *Citrus Nobilis*

antibacterial, anticarcinogenic, antiemetic, anti-inflammatory, antimicrobial, antioxidant, antiseptic, antispasmodic, astringent, calming, carminative, cleanser, detoxifier, digestive stimulant, diuretic, expectorant, nervine, regenerative, restorative, rubefacient, sedative, tonic, uplifting

HELICHRYSUM *Helichrysum italicum*

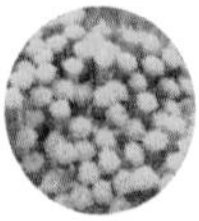

analgesic, anti-allergenic, antibacterial, anticatarrhal, anticoagulant, antifungal, antihemorrhagic, anti-inflammatory, antimicrobial, antioxidant, antiseptic, antispasmodic, antiviral, astringent, digestive stimulant, diuretic, expectorant, mucolytic, nervine, regenerative, rubefacient, vasoconstrictor

JASMINE *Jasminum grandiflorum*

analgesic, antidepressant, anti-inflammatory, antiseptic, antispasmodic, aphrodisiac, calming, cardiotonic, carminative, emmenagogue, expectorant, galactagogue, grounding, regenerative, relaxing, sedative

JUNIPER BERRY *Juniperus communis*

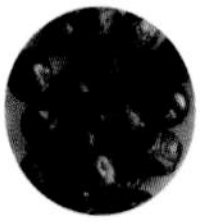

analgesic, antioxidant, anti-parasitic, anti-rheumatic, antiseptic, antispasmodic, antitoxic, aphrodisiac, astringent, calming, cardiotonic, carminative, cleanser, detoxifier, digestive stimulant, diuretic, emmenagogue, nervine, revitalizer, rubefacient, sedative, stimulant, stomachic, tonic

KUMQUAT *Fortunella Japonica*

antibacterial, anticarcinogenic, antifungal, anti-inflammatory, antimicrobial, antioxidant, antiseptic, antiviral, astringent, carminative, cleanser, cytophylactic, digestive stimulant, energizing, hypotensive, immunostimulant, invigorating, mucolytic, nervine, neuroprotective, refreshing, regenerative, restorative, revitalizer, sedative, stimulant, stomachic, tonic, uplifting, vermicide

LAVENDER *Lavandula angustifolia*

analgesic, anticoagulant, anticonvulsant, antidepressant, antiemetic, antifungal, antihistamine, anti-infectious, anti-inflammatory, antimicrobial, antimutagenic, anti-parasitic, anti-rheumatic, antiseptic, antispasmodic, antitoxic, anti-tumoral, astringent, calming, cardiotonic, carminative, cytophylactic, deodorant, diuretic, emmenagogue, hypotensive, insecticidal, nervine, neuroprotective, regenerative, relaxing, rubefacient, sedative, tonic, vermicide, vermifuge

LEMON *Citrus limon*

anti-carcinoma, antidepressant, antifungal, antimicrobial, antioxidant, anti-rheumatic, antiseptic, antispasmodic, antitoxic, antiviral, carminative, cleanser, decongestant, detoxifier, disinfectant, diuretic, energizing, hypotensive, immunostimulant, insecticidal, invigorating, mucolytic, refreshing, revitalizer, rubefacient, tonic, uplifting, vermifuge

LEMONGRASS *Cymbopogon flexuosus*

analgesic, antibacterial, anti-carcinoma, antidepressant, antifungal, anti-inflammatory, antimicrobial, antimutagenic, antioxidant, anti-rheumatic, antiseptic, antitoxic, carminative, decongestant, deodorant, digestive stimulant, energizing, expectorant, galactagogue, grounding, insecticidal, nervine, purifier, regenerative, revitalizer, sedative, tonic, vasodilator, warming

LIME *Citrus aurantifolia*

antibacterial, anti-inflammatory, antioxidant, anti-rheumatic, antiseptic, antispasmodic, antiviral, detoxifier, disinfectant, diuretic, energizing, immunostimulant, purifier, refreshing, restorative, revitalizer, stimulant, tonic, uplifting

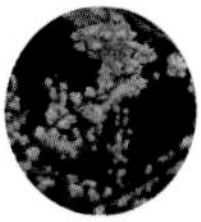

LITSEA *Litsea cubeba*

analgesic, antibacterial, anti-carcinoma, antifungal, anti-infectious, anti-inflammatory, antimicrobial, antispasmodic, antiviral, astringent, calming, cardiotonic, carminative, deodorant, detoxifier, digestive stimulant, disinfectant, hypotensive, insect repellent, invigorating, relaxing, uplifting, vasodilator

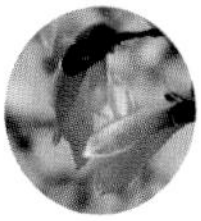

MAGNOLIA *Michelia x alba*

analgesic, anti-allergenic, antibacterial, antidepressant, antimicrobial, antiseptic, aphrodisiac, calming, decongestant, detoxifier, grounding, mucolytic, neuroprotective, purifier, relaxant, rubefacient, sedative, stomachic

MANUKA *Leptospermum scoparium*

anti-allergenic, antiarthritic, antibacterial, antifungal, antihistamine, anti-inflammatory, antimicrobial, anti-rheumatic, antiseptic, antiviral, cardiotonic, cytophylactic, deodorant, hypotensive, purifier, regenerative, relaxing, revitalizer, vasodilator

CREDIT: *Litsea photography by Neux-Neux*

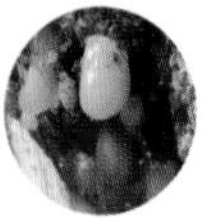

MARJORAM *Origanum marjorana*

anaphrodisiac, analgesic, antibacterial, anti-infectious, antiseptic, antispasmodic, cardiotonic, digestive stimulant, emmenagogue, expectorant, hypotensive, purifier, relaxing, sedative, stomachic, tonic, vasodilator, warming

MELALEUCA *Melaleuca alternifolia*

analgesic, antibacterial, antifungal, anti-infectious, anti-inflammatory, antioxidant, anti-parasitic, antiseptic, antiviral, decongestant, digestive stimulant, expectorant, grounding, immunostimulant, insecticidal, neurotonic, purifier, refreshing, regenerative, stimulant, vermifuge, nervine, sedative, stomachic, tonic, uplifting

MELISSA *Melissa officinalis*

antibacterial, antidepressant, antihistamine, anti-inflammatory, antimicrobial, antiseptic, antispasmodic, antiviral, astringent, calming, cardiotonic, carminative, hypertensive, immuno-stimulant, nervine, sedative, stomachic, tonic, uplifting

MYRRH *Commiphora myrrha*

antibacterial, anticarcinogenic, anti-carcinoma, anticatarrhal, antifungal, anti-infectious, anti-inflammatory, antimicrobial, antiseptic, anti-tumoral, antiviral, astringent, cardiotonic, carminative, digestive stimulant, emmenagogue, expectorant, mucolytic, regenerative, relaxing, stimulant, tonic

NEROLI *Citrus aurantium*

antiarthritic, antibacterial, anticatarrhal, anticonvulsant, antidepressant, anti-inflammatory, antimicrobial, antimutagenic, antioxidant, antiseptic, antispasmodic, aphrodisiac, carminative, cytophylactic, deodorant, disinfectant, hypotensive, neurotonic, regenerative, relaxing, restorative, sedative, tonic, vasodilator, warming

OREGANO *Origanum vulgare*

analgesic, antibacterial, antidepressant, antifungal, anti-inflammatory, antimicrobial, anti-oxidant, anti-parasitic, anti-rheumatic, antiseptic, antiviral, calming, cardiotonic, carminative, digestive stimulant, disinfectant, emmenagogue, expectorant, immunostimulant, purifier, vermicide, warming

PATCHOULI *Pogostemon cablin*

antibacterial, antidepressant, antiemetic, antifungal, anti-infectious, anti-inflammatory, antimicrobial, antiseptic, antispasmodic, antitoxic, aphrodisiac, astringent, calming, cardiotonic, carminative, decongestant, deodorant, detoxifier, digestive stimulant, diuretic, hypertensive, immunostimulant, insect repellent, insecticidal, nervine, regenerative, restorative, sedative, steroidal, stimulant, tonic

PEPPERMINT *Menta piperita*

analgesic, antibacterial, anticarcinogenic, antiemetic, anti-inflammatory, antiseptic, antispasmodic, antiviral, aphrodisiac, cardiotonic, carminative, emmenagogue, energizing, expectorant, invigorating, nervine, refreshing, stomachic, vasoconstrictor, vermifuge, warming

PETITGRAIN *Citrus aurantium*

antibacterial, antidepressant, antiemetic, anti-infectious, antiseptic, antispasmodic, calming, cardiotonic, deodorant, detoxifier, immunostimulant, relaxing, sedative, tonic, uplifting

PINK PEPPER *Jasminum grandiflorum*

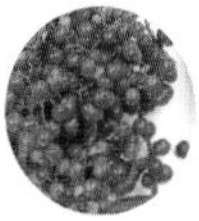

analgesic, antibacterial, anti-carcinoma, antidepressant, antiemetic, anti-inflammatory, antimicrobial, antioxidant, anti-rheumatic, antiseptic, antispasmodic, antiviral, aphrodisiac, cardiotonic, digestive stimulant, diuretic, energizing, expectorant, insect repellent, invigorating, laxative, purifier, refreshing, relaxant, rubefacient, stimulant, stomachic, tonic, uplifting, warming

RAVENSARA *Ravensara aromatica*

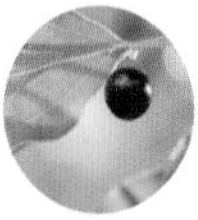

analgesic, antibacterial, antidepressant, antifungal, antimicrobial, antiseptic, antispasmodic, antiviral, aphrodisiac, disinfectant, diuretic, expectorant, immunostimulant, relaxing, tonic

RED MANDARIN *Citrus Reticulata*

antibacterial, anticarcinogenic, antiemetic, antifungal, anti-inflammatory, antimicrobial, antioxidant, antiseptic, antispasmodic, anti-tumoral, antiviral, astringent, calming, carminative, cleanser, cytophylactic, detoxifier, digestive stimulant, diuretic, expectorant, immunostimulant, nervine, refreshing, relaxant, restorative, rubefacient, sedative, stomachic, tonic, uplifting

ROMAN CHAMOMILE *Anthemis nobilis*

anti-infectious, anti-inflammatory, anti-parasitic, antispasmodic, calming, cardiotonic, carminative, emmenagogue, neuroprotective, relaxing, sedative, tonic, vermifuge

ROSE *Rosa damascena*

antidepressant, anti-infectious, antiseptic, antispasmodic, antiviral, aphrodisiac, cardiotonic, carminative, emmenagogue, laxative, nervine, sedative, stomachic, tonic

ROSEMARY *Rosmarinus officinalis*

analgesic, antibacterial, anti-carcinoma, anticatarrhal, antifungal, anti-infectious, anti-inflammatory, antimicrobial, antioxidant, anti-parasitic, anti-rheumatic, antiseptic, antispasmodic, aphrodisiac, astringent, calming, cardiotonic, carminative, cytophylactic, detoxifier, diuretic, emmenagogue, energizing, expectorant, hypertensive, immunostimulant, nervine, restorative, rubefacient, steroidal, stimulant, stomachic, tonic, vasodilator, vermifuge

SANDALWOOD *Santalum album*

antibacterial, anti-carcinoma, anticatarrhal, antidepressant, antifungal, anti-inflammatory, antiseptic, antispasmodic, anti-tumoral, aphrodisiac, astringent, calming, cardiotonic, carminative, diuretic, expectorant, hypertensive, insecticidal, refreshing, regenerative, restorative, sedative, tonic, uplifting

SIBERIAN FIR *Abies Sibirica*

analgesic, antibacterial, antifungal, anti-inflammatory, antimicrobial, antiseptic, antispasmodic, antiviral, decongestant, deodorant, energizing, expectorant, grounding, hypertensive, immunostimulant, invigorating, purifier, refreshing, rubefacient, stimulant, tonic, vasoconstrictor

SPEARMINT *Mentha spicata*

antibacterial, anticatarrhal, antifungal, anti-inflammatory, antiseptic, antispasmodic, aphrodisiac, cardiotonic, carminative, digestive stimulant, emmenagogue, energizing, immunostimulant, insecticidal, invigorating, restorative, stimulant

CREDIT: *Siberian fir Photography by Krzysztof Ziarnek, Kenraiz*

SPIKENARD *Nardostachys jatamansi*

antibacterial, antidepressant, antifungal, anti-inflammatory, anti-infectious, antioxidant, antiseptic, deodorant, immunostimulant, insecticidal, laxative, regenerative, sedative, stimulant, tonic, vasoconstrictor

TANGERINE *Citrus reticulata*

anticarcinogenic, anti-carcinoma, anticoagulant, anticonvulsant, antidepressant, anti-inflammatory, antimutagenic, antioxidant, anti-parasitic, antiseptic, antispasmodic, calming, carminative, cytophylactic, detoxifier, digestive stimulant, diuretic, energizing, laxative, mucolytic, purifier, restorative, sedative, stimulant, stomachic, tonic, uplifting

THYME *Thymus vulgaris*

antibacterial, antifungal, antimicrobial, antioxidant, anti-parasitic, anti-rheumatic, antiseptic, antispasmodic, antitoxic, antiviral, aphrodisiac, cardiotonic, carminative, cleanser, diuretic, emmenagogue, expectorant, hypertensive, immunostimulant, insect repellent, insecticidal, nervine, neuroprotective, rubefacient, steroidal, stimulant, vasodilator, vermifuge, warming

TURMERIC *Curcuma longa*

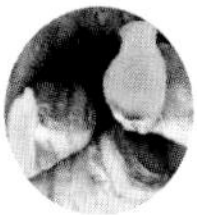

analgesic, anti-allergenic, antibacterial, anticarcinogenic, anti-carcinoma, anticonvulsant, antifungal, anti-inflammatory, antimicrobial, antimutagenic, antioxidant, anti-parasitic, antiseptic, anti-tumoral, antiviral, carminative, decongestant, detoxifier, digestive stimulant, expectorant, insect repellent, neuroprotective, relaxant, sedative, stomachic, warming

VETIVER *Vetiveria zizanioides*

antioxidant, antiseptic, antispasmodic, aphrodisiac, calming, cardiotonic, carminative, grounding, immunostimulant, insect repellant, insecticidal, neuroprotective, rubefacient, sedative, stimulant, tonic, vermifuge

WHITE FIR *Abies alba*

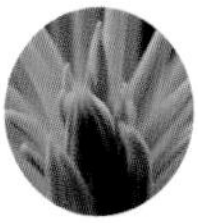

analgesic, antiarthritic, anticatarrhal, anti-rheumatic, antiseptic, antiviral, astringent, calming, decongestant, deodorant, diuretic, energizing, expectorant, hypotensive, immunostimulant, relaxing, rubefacient, stimulant, tonic, vasoconstrictor

WILD ORANGE *Citrus sinensis*

analgesic, antibacterial, anti-carcinoma, antidepressant, antifungal, anti-inflammatory, antioxidant, antiseptic, antispasmodic, aphrodisiac, cardiotonic, carminative, cleanser, detoxifier, digestive stimulant, diuretic, energizing, immunostimulant, invigorating, purifier, refreshing, regenerative, stomachic, tonic, uplifting, vermifuge

WINTERGREEN *Gaultheria procumbens*

analgesic, anti-inflammatory, anti-rheumatic, antiseptic, antispasmodic, astringent, calming, cardiotonic, carminative, disinfectant, diuretic, emmenagogue, galactagogue, grounding, invigorating, refreshing, steroidal, stimulant, vermicide, vermifuge, warming

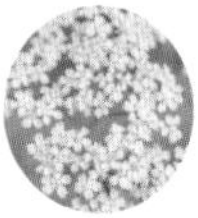

YARROW *Achillea millefolium*

analgesic, anticarcinogenic, anti-carcinoma, antihemorrhagic, antihistamine, anti-inflammatory, antioxidant, anti-rheumatic, antispasmodic, antiviral, astringent, calming, carminative, decongestant, detoxifier, digestive stimulant, emmenagogue, energizing, expectorant, hypotensive, immunostimulant, laxative, mucolytic, purifier, regenerative, sedative, stomachic, tonic

YLANG YLANG *Cananga odorata*

antibacterial, antidepressant, antiseptic, antispasmodic, aphrodisiac, grounding, hypotensive, immunostimulant, insect repellent, relaxing, sedative, stimulant, tonic, uplifting, vasoconstrictor

Oils by Property

ANAPHRODISIAC

Arborvitae, Marjoram

ANALGESIC

Arborvitae, Basil, Bergamot, Birch, Black pepper, Blue tansy, Cassia, Cinnamon, Clary sage, Clove, Copaiba, Coriander, Cypress, Douglas fir, Eucalyptus, Fennel, Frankincense, Ginger, Helichrysum, Jasmine, Juniper berry, Lavender, Lemongrass, Litsea, Marjoram, Magnolia, Melaleuca, Oregano, Peppermint, Pink pepper, Ravensara, Rosemary, Siberian fir, Turmeric, White fir, Wild orange, Wintergreen, Yarrow

ANTI-ALLERGENIC

Blue tansy, Geranium, Helichrysum, Magnolia, Manuka, Turmeric

ANTIARTHRITIC

Arborvitae, Blue tansy, Cassia, Copaiba, Ginger, Manuka, Neroli, White fir

ANTIBACTERIAL

Arborvitae, Basil, Bergamot, Birch, Black pepper, Blue tansy, Cardamom, Cassia, Cedarwood, Cilantro, Cinnamon, Clary sage, Clove, Copaiba, Coriander, Cypress, Dill, Douglas fir, Eucalyptus, Geranium, Ginger, Grapefruit, Green mandarin, Helichrysum, Kumquat, Lemongrass, Lime, Litsea, Magnolia, Manuka, Marjoram, Melaleuca, Melissa, Myrrh, Neroli, Oregano, Patchouli, Peppermint, Petitgrain, Pink pepper, Ravensara, Red mandarin, Rosemary, Sandalwood, Siberian fir, Spearmint, Spikenard, Thyme, Turmeric, Wild orange, Ylang ylang

ANTICARCINOGENIC

Arborvitae, Frankincense, Green mandarin, Kumquat, Myrrh, Peppermint, Red mandarin, Tangerine, Turmeric, Yarrow

ANTI-CARCINOMA

Arborvitae, Copaiba, Frankincense, Grapefruit, Kumquat, Lemon, Lemongrass, Litsea, Myrrh, Pink pepper, Rosemary, Sandalwood, Tangerine, Turmeric, Wild orange, Yarrow

ANTICATARRHAL

Basil, Black pepper, Eucalyptus, Frankincense, Helichrysum, Myrrh, Neroli, Rosemary, Sandalwood, Spearmint, White fir

ANTICOAGULANT

Clary sage, Helichrysum, Lavender, Tangerine

ANTICONVULSANT

Clary sage, Fennel, Geranium, Lavender, Neroli, Tangerine, Turmeric

ANTIDEPRESSANT

Basil, Bergamot, Cinnamon, Clary sage, Coriander, Dill, Frankincense, Geranium, Grapefruit, Jasmine, Lavender, Lemon, Lemongrass, Melissa, Magnolia, Neroli, Oregano, Patchouli, Petitgrain, Pink pepper, Ravensara, Rose, Sandalwood, Spikenard, Tangerine, Wild orange, Ylang ylang

ANTIEMETIC

Basil, Cardamom, Cassia, Clove, Copaiba, Coriander, Fennel, Ginger, Green mandarin, Lavender, Patchouli, Peppermint, Petitgrain, Pink, pepper, Red mandarin

ANTIFUNGAL

Arborvitae, Bergamot, Blue tansy, Cassia, Cedarwood, Cilantro, Cinnamon, Clary sage, Clove, Copaiba, Coriander, Cypress, Dill, Eucalyptus, Fennel, Geranium, Ginger, Helichrysum, Kumquat, Lavender, Lemon, Lemongrass, Litsea, Manuka, Melaleuca, Myrrh, Oregano, Patchouli, Ravensara, Red mandarin, Rosemary, Sandalwood, Siberian fir, Spearmint, Spikenard, Thyme, Turmeric, Wild orange

ANTIHEMORRHAGIC

Geranium, Helichrysum, Yarrow

ANTIHISTAMINE

Arborvitae, Blue tansy, Clove, Lavender, Manuka, Melissa, Yarrow

ANTI-INFECTIOUS

Arborvitae, Basil, Bergamot, Cardamom, Cedarwood, Cinnamon, Clove, Copaiba, Cypress, Eucalyptus, Frankincense, Geranium, Lavender, Litsea, Marjoram, Melaleuca, Myrrh, Patchouli, Petitgrain, Roman chamomile, Rose, Rosemary, Spikenard

ANTI-INFLAMMATORY

Arborvitae, Basil, Bergamot, Birch, Black pepper, Blue tansy, Cardamom, Cassia, Cedarwood, Cinnamon, Clary sage, Clove, Copaiba, Coriander, Cypress, Dill, Eucalyptus, Fennel, Frankincense, Geranium, Ginger, Green mandarin, Helichrysum, Jasmine, Kumquat, Lavender, Lemongrass, Lime, Litsea, Magnolia, Manuka, Melaleuca, Melissa, Myrrh, Neroli, Oregano, Patchouli, Peppermint, Pink pepper, Red mandarin, Roman chamomile, Rosemary, Sandalwood, Siberian fir, Spearmint, Spikenard, Tangerine, Turmeric, Wild orange, Wintergreen, Yarrow

ANTIMICROBIAL

Arborvitae, Basil, Blue tansy, Cardamom, Cassia, Cilantro, Cinnamon, Clary sage, Copaiba, Coriander, Cypress, Dill, Eucalyptus, Fennel, Frankincense, Green mandarin, Helichrysum, Kumquat, Lavender, Lemon, Lemongrass, Litsea, Magnolia, Manuka, Melissa, Myrrh, Neroli, Oregano, Patchouli, Pink pepper, Ravensara, Red mandarin, Rosemary, Siberian fir, Thyme, Turmeric

ANTIMUTAGENIC

Cinnamon, Copaiba, Ginger, Lavender, Lemongrass, Neroli, Tangerine

ANTIOXIDANT

Arborvitae, Basil, Black pepper, Cassia, Cilantro, Cinnamon, Clove, Copaiba, Coriander, Douglas fir, Eucalyptus, Frankincense, Ginger, Grapefruit, Green mandarin, Helichrysum, Juniper berry, Kumquat, Lemon, Lemongrass, Lime, Melaleuca, Neroli, Oregano, Pink pepper, Red mandarin, Rosemary, Spikenard, Tangerine, Thyme, Turmeric, Vetiver, Wild orange, Yarrow

ANTI-PARASITIC

Bergamot, Black pepper, Blue tansy, Cinnamon, Clove, Fennel, Frankincense, Juniper berry, Lavender, Melaleuca, Oregano, Roman chamomile, Rosemary, Tangerine, Thyme, Turmeric

ANTI-RHEUMATIC

Birch, Blue tansy, Cassia, Clove, Copaiba, Coriander, Cypress, Eucalyptus, Ginger, Juniper berry, Lavender, Lemon, Lemongrass, Lime, Manuka, Oregano, Pink pepper, Rosemary, Thyme, White fir, Wintergreen, Yarrow

ANTISEPTIC

Arborvitae, Basil, Bergamot, Birch, Black pepper, Cardamom, Cedarwood, Cinnamon, Clary sage, Clove, Copaiba, Cypress, Douglas fir, Fennel, Frankincense, Geranium, Ginger, Grapefruit, Green mandarin, Helichrysum, Jasmine, Juniper berry, Kumquat, Lavender, Lemon, Lemongrass, Lime, Magnolia, Manuka, Marjoram, Melaleuca, Melissa, Myrrh, Neroli, Oregano, Patchouli, Peppermint, Petitgrain, Pink pepper, Ravensara, Red mandarin, Rose, Rosemary, Sandalwood, Siberian fir, Spearmint, Spikenard, Tangerine, Thyme, Turmeric, Vetiver, White fir, Wild orange, Wintergreen, Ylang ylang

ANTISPASMODIC

Basil, Bergamot, Birch, Black pepper, Blue tansy, Cardamom, Cassia, Cinnamon, Clary sage, Clove, Coriander, Cypress, Dill, Eucalyptus, Fennel, Geranium, Green mandarin, Helichrysum, Jasmine, Juniper berry, Lavender, Lemon, Lime, Litsea, Marjoram, Melissa, Neroli, Patchouli, Peppermint, Petitgrain, Pink pepper, Ravensara, Red mandarin, Roman chamomile, Rose, Rosemary, Sandalwood, Siberian fir, Spearmint, Tangerine, Thyme, Vetiver, Wild orange, Wintergreen, Yarrow, Ylang ylang

ANTITOXIC

Bergamot, Black pepper, Cinnamon, Coriander, Fennel, Geranium, Grapefruit, Juniper berry, Lavender, Lemon, Lemongrass, Patchouli, Thyme

ANTI-TUMORAL

Arborvitae, Clove, Copaiba, Frankincense, Lavender, Myrrh, Red mandarin, Sandalwood, Turmeric

ANTIVIRAL

Arborvitae, Basil, Blue tansy, Cassia, Cinnamon, Clove, Copaiba, Dill, Eucalyptus, Ginger, Helichrysum, Kumquat, Lemon, Lime, Litsea, Manuka, Melaleuca, Melissa, Myrrh, Oregano, Peppermint, Pink pepper, Ravensara, Red mandarin, Rose, Siberian fir, Thyme, Turmeric, White fir, Yarrow

APHRODISIAC

Black pepper, Cardamom, Cinnamon, Clary sage, Clove, Coriander, Jasmine, Juniper berry, Magnolia, Neroli, Patchouli, Peppermint, Pink pepper, Ravensara, Rose, Rosemary, Sandalwood, Spearmint, Thyme, Vetiver, Wild orange, Ylang ylang

ASTRINGENT

Arborvitae, Birch, Cassia, Cedarwood, Cinnamon, Clary sage, Cypress, Douglas fir, Frankincense, Geranium, Grapefruit, Green mandarin, Helichrysum, Juniper berry, Kumquat, Lavender, Litsea, Melissa, Myrrh, Patchouli, Red mandarin, Rosemary, Sandalwood, White fir, Wintergreen, Yarrow

CALMING

Basil, Bergamot, Black pepper, Blue tansy, Cassia, Clary sage, Copaiba, Coriander, Fennel, Frankincense, Geranium, Green mandarin, Jasmine, Juniper berry, Lavender, Litsea, Magnolia, Melissa, Oregano, Patchouli, Petitgrain, Red mandarin, Roman chamomile, Rosemary, Sandalwood, Tangerine, Vetiver, White fir, Wintergreen, Yarrow

CARDIOTONIC

Cassia, Copaiba, Cypress, Fennel, Ginger, Grapefruit, Jasmine, Juniper berry, Lavender, Litsea, Manuka, Marjoram, Melissa, Myrrh, Oregano, Patchouli, Peppermint, Petitgrain, Pink pepper, Roman chamomile, Rose, Rosemary, Sandalwood, Spearmint, Thyme, Vetiver, Wild orange, Wintergreen

CARMINATIVE

Basil, Bergamot, Blue tansy, Cardamom, Cassia, Cilantro, Cinnamon, Clary sage, Clove, Copaiba, Coriander, Cypress, Dill, Fennel, Ginger, Green mandarin, Jasmine, Juniper berry, Kumquat, Lavender, Lemon, Lemongrass, Litsea, Melissa, Myrrh, Neroli, Oregano, Patchouli, Peppermint, Pink pepper, Roman chamomile, Red mandarin, Rose, Rosemary, Sandalwood, Spearmint, Tangerine, Thyme, Turmeric, Vetiver, Wild orange, Wintergreen, Yarrow

CLEANSER

Arborvitae, Cilantro, Eucalyptus, Grapefruit, Green mandarin, Kumquat, Juniper berry, Lemon, Red mandarin, Thyme, Wild orange

CYTOPHYLACTIC

Arborvitae, Frankincense, Geranium, Kumquat, Lavender, Manuka, Neroli, Red mandarin, Rosemary, Tangerine

DECONGESTANT

Basil, Cardamom, Cassia, Copaiba, Cypress, Eucalyptus, Ginger, Grapefruit, Lemon, Lemongrass, Magnolia, Melaleuca, Patchouli, Siberian fir, Turmeric, White fir, Yarrow

DEODORANT

Bergamot, Clary sage, Copaiba, Coriander, Cypress, Eucalyptus, Geranium, Lavender, Lemongrass, Litsea, Magnolia, Manuka, Neroli, Patchouli, Petitgrain, Siberian fir, Spikenard, White fir

DETOXIFIER

Arborvitae, Cassia, Cilantro, Cypress, Geranium, Juniper berry, Green mandarin, Lemon, Lime, Litsea, Magnolia, Patchouli, Petitgrain, Red mandarin, Rosemary, Tangerine, Turmeric, Wild orange, Yarrow

DIGESTIVE STIMULANT

Basil, Bergamot, Black pepper, Cardamom, Cinnamon, Clary sage, Coriander, Dill, Fennel, Frankincense, Grapefruit, Helichrysum, Juniper berry, Green mandarin, Kumquat, Lemongrass, Litsea, Marjoram, Melaleuca, Myrrh, Oregano, Patchouli, Pink pepper, Red mandarin, Spearmint, Tangerine, Turmeric, Wild orange, Yarrow

DISINFECTANT

Arborvitae, Basil, Birch, Clove, Copaiba, Eucalyptus, Frankincense, Grapefruit, Lemon, Lime, Litsea, Neroli, Oregano, Ravensara, Wintergreen

DIURETIC

Arborvitae, Basil, Bergamot, Birch, Cardamom, Cedarwood, Copaiba, Cypress, Douglas fir, Eucalyptus, Fennel, Frankincense, Geranium, Grapefruit, Green mandarin, Helichrysum, Juniper berry, Lavender, Lemon, Lime, Patchouli, Pink pepper, Ravensara, Red mandarin, Rosemary, Sandalwood, Tangerine, Thyme, White fir, Wild orange, Wintergreen

EMMENAGOGUE

Arborvitae, Basil, Cassia, Cedarwood, Cinnamon, Clary sage, Dill, Fennel, Ginger, Jasmine, Juniper berry, Lavender, Marjoram, Myrrh, Oregano, Peppermint, Roman chamomile, Rose, Rosemary, Spearmint, Thyme, Wintergreen, Yarrow

ENERGIZING

Basil, Bergamot, Clove, Cypress, Douglas fir, Grapefruit, Kumquat, Lemon, Lemongrass, Lime, Peppermint, Pink pepper, Rosemary, Siberian fir, Spearmint, Tangerine, White fir, Wild orange, Yarrow

EXPECTORANT

Arborvitae, Basil, Black pepper, Cardamom, Cedarwood, Clove, Dill, Douglas fir, Eucalyptus, Fennel, Ginger, Green mandarin, Helichrysum, Jasmine, Lemongrass, Marjoram, Melaleuca, Myrrh, Oregano, Peppermint, Pink pepper, Ravensara, Red mandarin, Rosemary, Sandalwood, Siberian fir, Thyme, Turmeric, White fir, Yarrow

GALACTAGOGUE

Basil, Clary sage, Dill, Fennel, Frankincense, Jasmine, Lemongrass, Wintergreen

GROUNDING

Basil, Blue tansy, Cedarwood, Clary sage, Cypress, Dill, Fennel, Jasmine, Lemongrass, Magnolia, Melaleuca, Siberian fir, Vetiver, Wintergreen, Ylang ylang

HYPERTENSIVE

Melissa, Patchouli, Rosemary, Sandalwood, Siberian fir, Thyme

HYPOTENSIVE

Black pepper, Blue tansy, Clary sage, Copaiba, Dill, Eucalyptus, Kumquat, Lavender, Lemon, Litsea, Manuka, Marjoram, Neroli, White fir, Yarrow, Ylang ylang

IMMUNOSTIMULANT

Arborvitae, Cassia, Cinnamon, Clove, Copaiba, Eucalyptus, Fennel, Frankincense, Ginger, Kumquat, Lemon, Lime, Melaleuca, Melissa, Oregano, Patchouli, Petitgrain, Ravensara, Red mandarin, Rosemary, Siberian fir, Spearmint, Spikenard, Thyme, Vetiver, White fir, Wild orange, Yarrow, Ylang ylang

INSECT REPELLENT

Arborvitae, Birch, Blue tansy, Cedarwood, Cinnamon, Eucalyptus, Geranium, Litsea, Patchouli, Pink pepper, Spikenard, Thyme, Turmeric, Vetiver, Ylang ylang

INSECTICIDAL

Blue tansy, Cedarwood, Copaiba, Coriander, Eucalyptus, Lavender, Lemon, Lemongrass, Melaleuca, Patchouli, Sandalwood, Spearmint, Spikenard, Thyme, Vetiver

INVIGORATING

Grapefruit, Kumquat, Lemon, Litsea, Peppermint, Pink pepper, Siberian fir, Spearmint, Wild orange, Wintergreen

LAXATIVE

Basil, Bergamot, Black pepper, Blue tansy, Copaiba, Douglas fir, Fennel, Ginger, Pink pepper, Rose, Spikenard, Tangerine, Yarrow

MUCOLYTIC

Basil, Cedarwood, Clary sage, Copaiba, Cypress, Fennel, Helichrysum, Kumquat, Lemon, Magnolia, Myrrh, Tangerine, Yarrow

NERVINE

Basil, Clary sage, Clove, Helichrysum, Juniper berry, Green mandarin, Kumquat, Lavender, Lemongrass, Melissa, Patchouli, Peppermint, Red mandarin, Rose, Rosemary, Thyme

NEUROPROTECTIVE

Frankincense, Kumquat, Lavender, Magnolia, Roman chamomile, Thyme, Turmeric, Vetiver

NEUROTONIC

Arborvitae, Basil, Bergamot, Black pepper, Clary sage, Cypress, Ginger, Melaleuca, Neroli

PURIFIER

Arborvitae, Cinnamon, Eucalyptus, Grapefruit, Lemongrass, Lime, Magnolia, Manuka, Marjoram, Melaleuca, Oregano, Pink pepper, Siberian fir, Tangerine, Wild orange, Yarrow

REFRESHING

Cypress, Geranium, Grapefruit, Kumquat, Lemon, Lime, Melaleuca, Peppermint, Pink pepper, Red mandarin, Sandalwood, Siberian fir, Wild orange, Wintergreen

REGENERATIVE

Basil, Cedarwood, Clove, Coriander, Frankincense, Geranium, Green Mandarin, Helichrysum, Jasmine, Kumquat, Lavender, Lemongrass, Manuka, Melaleuca, Myrrh, Neroli, Patchouli, Sandalwood, Spikenard, Wild orange, Yarrow

RELAXING

Basil, Blue tansy, Cassia, Cedarwood, Clary sage, Cypress, Fennel, Geranium, Jasmine, Lavender, Litsea, Magnolia, Manuka, Marjoram, Myrrh, Neroli, Petitgrain, Pink pepper, Ravensara, Red mandarin, Spikenard, Roman chamomile, Turmeric, White fir, Ylang ylang

RESTORATIVE

Basil, Frankincense, Green mandarin, Kumquat, Lime, Neroli, Patchouli, Red mandarin, Rosemary, Sandalwood, Spearmint, Tangerine

REVITALIZER

Coriander, Juniper berry, Kumquat, Lemon, Lemongrass, Lime, Manuka

RUBEFACIENT

Bergamot, Birch, Black pepper, Eucalyptus, Ginger, Green mandarin, Helichrysum, Juniper berry, Lavender, Lemon, Magnolia, Pink pepper, Red mandarin, Rosemary, Siberian fir, Thyme, Vetiver, White fir

SEDATIVE

Basil, Bergamot, Blue tansy, Cedarwood, Clary sage, Coriander, Douglas fir, Frankincense, Geranium, Green mandarin, Jasmine, Juniper berry, Kumquat, Lavender, Lemongrass, Magnolia, Marjoram, Melissa, Neroli, Patchouli, Petitgrain, Red mandarin, Roman chamomile, Rose, Sandalwood, Spikenard, Tangerine, Turmeric, Vetiver, Yarrow, Ylang ylang

STEROIDAL

Basil, Bergamot, Birch, Cedarwood, Fennel, Patchouli, Rosemary, Thyme, Turmeric, Wintergreen

STIMULANT

Arborvitae, Basil, Bergamot, Birch, Black pepper, Blue tansy, Cardamom, Cedarwood, Cinnamon, Clove, Coriander, Cypress, Dill, Douglas fir, Eucalyptus, Fennel, Ginger, Grapefruit, Juniper berry, Kumquat, Lime, Melaleuca, Myrrh, Patchouli, Pink pepper, Rosemary, Siberian fir, Spearmint, Spikenard, Tangerine, Thyme, Vetiver, White fir, Wintergreen, Ylang ylang

STOMACHIC

Arborvitae, Basil, Blue tansy, Cardamom, Cinnamon, Clary sage, Coriander, Douglas fir, Fennel, Ginger, Juniper berry, Kumquat, Magnolia, Marjoram, Melissa, Peppermint, Pink pepper, Red mandarin, Rose, Rosemary, Tangerine, Turmeric, Wild orange, Yarrow

TONIC

Arborvitae, Basil, Bergamot, Birch, Cardamom, Cedarwood, Clary sage, Coriander, Cypress, Fennel, Frankincense, Geranium, Ginger, Grapefruit, Green mandarin, Juniper berry, Kumquat, Lavender, Lemon, Lemongrass, Lime, Marjoram, Melissa, Myrrh, Neroli, Patchouli, Petitgrain, Pink pepper, Ravensara, Red mandarin, Roman chamomile, Rose, Rosemary, Sandalwood, Siberian fir, Spikenard, Tangerine, Vetiver, White fir, Wild orange, Yarrow, Ylang ylang

UPLIFTING

Bergamot, Cardamom, Cedarwood, Clary sage, Cypress, Grapefruit, Green mandarin, Kumquat, Lemon, Lime, Litsea, Melissa, Petitgrain, Pink pepper, Red mandarin, Sandalwood, Tangerine, Wild orange, Ylang ylang

VASOCONSTRICTOR

Cypress, Helichrysum, Peppermint, Siberian fir, Spikenard, White fir, Ylang ylang

VASODILATOR

Blue tansy, Copaiba, Lemongrass, Litsea, Manuka, Marjoram, Neroli, Rosemary, Thyme

VERMICIDE

Blue tansy, Clary sage, Kumquat, Lavender, Oregano, Wintergreen

WARMING

Birch, Black pepper, Cassia, Cinnamon, Clove, Eucalyptus, Ginger, Lemongrass, Marjoram, Neroli, Oregano, Peppermint, Pink pepper, Thyme, Turmeric, Wintergreen

Section 6

INDEX

INDEX

Notes

Notes

Notes